*So Worthy a Friend:*

WILLIAM
SHAKESPEARE

*Books by* CHARLES NORMAN

§ *Poetry* §

POEMS [*1929*]
THE BRIGHT WORLD
THE SAVAGE CENTURY
A SOLDIER'S DIARY

§ *Biography* §

THE MUSES' DARLING
The Life of Christopher Marlowe

SO WORTHY A FRIEND:
William Shakespeare

# So Worthy a Friend:
# WILLIAM SHAKESPEARE

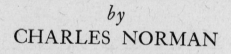

*by*
## CHARLES NORMAN

*Rinehart & Company, Incorporated*
NEW YORK : TORONTO

*To*
*Willard R. Trask*

# Contents

# Contents

## BOOK EIGHT

# Illustrations

*Collotypes printed by Paul L. Baruch*

## Foreword

I OFFER a life of William Shakespeare, begun with enthusiasm, and finished with relief, after difficulties not always confined to the complexity of my subject, but of which it is unnecessary or useless to speak here.

An author who presents a new account of a famous personage is expected to justify his act. It was Keats who said, 'Shakespeare led a life of allegory; his works are the comments on it.' I believe that the first essential for a biography of Shakespeare is a practicing knowledge of the art of poetry in the biographer. The *Sonnets* were a special problem. I have labored on these with a persistence which was at length rewarding; or so it seems to the laborer. My readers may find some enlightenment where for long I found nothing but frustration and despair.

Shakespeare is the supreme moralist and preceptor of mankind, as well as the bountiful father of all the English poets after him. This much may be said without making a virtue of idolatry. I believe idolatry is absent from this book. In the greatest of the arts, he was the greatest artist. He was also terribly human. I have not given a great man an incommensurate godhead. Shakespeare is phenomenon enough without detaching him from his own complexities, his time and the great men who were his associates, particularly Marlowe. He who would fully understand Shakespeare must first read Marlowe; and I trust I will be forgiven if I have gone over some old ground in order to make certain that my readers shall do just that.

I have put the facts of Shakespeare's life in an orderly sequence, which may be a feat in itself, since it seems not to have been done before—not in exactly the same way. Only those plays and poems which bear directly on other biographical sources have been dealt with. To show how he worked, I have quoted passages from his source material: Holinshed's *Chronicles*, Plutarch's *Lives*, and anonymous plays which were the fore-runners of his own. It may prove exciting to read what Shakespeare read before he began to write. Biographical and dramatic documents are given in full, but essential excerpts from business records have been made to suffice. Shakespeare's will, which I quote in its entirety, is a sufficient résumé of all his business dealings. He died landed and propertied beyond the usual lot of poets. Did he die a Catholic or a Protestant? I think the latter; but only nominally. Those who strive to make him an adherent of the old or the new faith must be misguided, for familiarity with his life and work reveals only an affiliation with the multitudinous sect of humanity.

As in my first venture in this field, I have worked from transcripts and facsimiles of the original documents, drawing the conclusions which appeared to me to be probable. I have felt free to disregard the judgments of others, and sometimes to adopt them.

I have deferred to the wishes of my publishers in using a standard text for the quotations from Shakespeare's work. The one I have followed is that of *The Complete Works of William Shakespeare*, edited by W. J. Craig, Oxford University Press. It is perhaps the best known, and I have had to be content with it, despite its seemingly whimsical punctuation and occasionally whimsical spelling. To be consistent, I quote Marlowe and other contemporaries in modern spelling. I have, however, as in the case of *The Muses' Darling*, retained the old spelling of the documents, and those who wish may grumble at me, but those who read will be rewarded.

My indebtedness to the research of others is great, for which this and the Selected Bibliography are only a partial acknowledgment. I follow Dr. Leslie Hotson as regards the dating of *The Merry Wives of Windsor* and the identification of Justice Shallow in a living and litigious justice of the peace. I have again had the benefit of advice from Dr. S. A. Tannenbaum, a veteran laborer in this field, who though busy with his own endeavors, never failed to accord my queries a hearing, and who has conferred a final benefit by reading the galleys. I wish also to thank, once more, Mr. John S. Lamont, of Rinehart & Company, Inc., for his patience and encouragement, and to acknowledge his erudition in a subject not often a specialty of editors. To Miss Esther Willard Bates I owe special thanks for her kindness in looking over the galleys and discussing this work with me at the MacDowell Colony, where a considerable portion of it was written and where final proofs were read. It is perhaps unnecessary to add that responsibility for statements contained in *So Worthy a Friend* is mine alone.

To all my friends, worn out, I fear, by my constant enthusiasms and propounding of theories, I say: thank you—here is my book.

# BOOK ONE

Mr. WILLIAM

# SHAKESPEARES

COMEDIES,
HISTORIES, &
TRAGEDIES.

Publiſhed according to the True Originall Copies.

LONDON
Printed by Iſaac Iaggard, and Ed. Blount. 1623.

# CHAPTER I

## *The Monument without a Tomb*

### 1.

TO KEEPE *the memory of so worthy a Friend, & Fellow aliue,* there appeared in London at year's end, 1623, a book entitled MR. WILLIAM SHAKESPEARES COMEDIES, HISTORIES, & TRAGEDIES. This folio volume, dedicated 'To The Most Noble and Incomparable Paire of Brethren. William Earle of Pembroke, &c. Lord Chamberlaine to the Kings most Excellent Maiesty. And Philip Earle of Montgomery, &c. Gentleman of his Maiesties Bed-Chamber,' gave to the world and everlasting renown the greatest single book that has appeared in English, excepting only the Bible. Although scholars have battered at the texts of the thirty-six plays thus presented for more than two hundred years, they have failed to dislodge a single one from the citadel of Shakespeare's fame.

The men responsible for this huge and remarkable undertaking had all been known to the late author. The folio was printed 'at the Charges of W. Jaggard, Ed. Blount, I. Smithweeke, and W. Aspley.' Of this syndicate of publishers and printers, the most important was undoubtedly Edward Blount, the friend and literary executor of Christopher Marlowe, a friend of Marlowe's patron, Sir Thomas Walsingham, and one of the most distinguished publishers of his own or any time; for from his shops had issued *Hero and Leander;* Daniel's *A Defence of Rhyme,* and the first English translations of Montaigne's *Essays* and *Don Quixote.* He also held the copyright to *Pericles* (the only play which the scholars, after much study, conjecture and sifting of evidence internal and external, have been able to add to the canon of Shakespeare's work).

John Smithweeke, afterwards master of the Stationers' Company, had been a publisher since 1597. Among the books that came from his press in St. Dunstan's churchyard were *Romeo and Juliet* and *Hamlet,* and he held, in addition, the copyrights of *Love's Labour's Lost* and *The Taming of the Shrew.*

3

William Aspley, a publisher since 1598, had issued *Much Ado About Nothing,* and *Henry IV,* Part Two, and had had a share in the publication of Shakespeare's *Sonnets* in 1609.

William Jaggard, printer to the City of London at the Sign of the Half-Eagle and Key, situated in the Barbican, a narrow street in Cripplegate, where the folio was printed, had used Shakespeare's name, without permission, for a medley of sonnets and songs entitled *The Passionate Pilgrim* in 1599; and more recently, in 1619, had printed a series of single volumes of the plays, including *A Midsummer Night's Dream, The Merchant of Venice, Henry V, King Lear,* and *The Merry Wives of Windsor.* Jaggard died before the Shakespeare folio was off the press, and while the colophon names him as one of the four at whose 'charges' the book was printed, his son's name, Isaac Jaggard, appears, with Blount's, on the title page.

## 2.

To two other members of the syndicate, John Heminge and Henry Condell, vestrymen of St. Mary Aldermanbury and fellow actors in the company to which he had belonged, Shakespeare in 1616 had bequeathed twenty-six shillings, eight pence apiece for the purchase of rings to remember him by; and they were now, in 1623, the sole survivors of the once-renowned theatrical group which had borne, successively, as one nobleman died and was succeeded by another as patron and protector, the proud titles of Lord Leicester's Servants, Lord Strange's Men, the Lord Chamberlain's Servants, and finally, after the accession of James I, the King's Men. For all of these in turn Shakespeare had been the chief dramatist as well as an occasional actor; and as additional homage, Heminge and Condell placed his name first in the list of 'the Principall Actors in all these Playes,' to the compilation of which they brought not only reverence for their great friend, as will be seen, but the practical contribution of twenty plays in manuscript, the property of the King's Men, which otherwise might have been lost.

Although a distinguished publisher and a great poet were associated in this unprecedented literary and business venture, a sense of the fitness of things dictated that these two veterans of the theater, Heminge and Condell, who perhaps knew Shakespeare better than anyone else, both as man and as playwright, should pen—or at least sign—the two dedications which grace the opening pages of the folio, that to the Earl of Pembroke and his brother, and a second, 'To the great Variety of Readers.'

That Heminge and Condell contributed much, and were much used, is equally clear. Their first dedicatory epistle, after acknowledging old favors to themselves—presumably grants of money and protection to the company—sets forth Shakespeare's relationship to the two earls and the esteem in which he had been held by them, which no doubt was flattering to their Lordships and at the same time gave to the public at large, whether titled or not, a snobbish reason to buy. The authors of this epistle were not under the ordinary compulsion to flatter and fawn, and nothing more, and it is well and movingly written: *'Since your L*[ordships] *haue beene pleas'd to thinke these trifles some-thing, heeretofore; and haue prosequuted both them, and their Author liuing, with so much fauour: we hope, that (they out-liuing him, and he not hauing the fate, common with some, to be exequutor to his owne writings) you will vse the like indulgence toward them, you haue done vnto their parent. There is a great difference, whether any Booke choose his Patrones, or finde them: This hath done both. For, so much were your L*[ordships'] *likings of the seuerall parts, when they were acted, as before they were published, the Volume ask'd to be yours. We haue but collected them, and done an office to the dead, to procure his Orphanes, Guardians; without ambition either of selfe-profit, or fame: onely to keepe the memory of so worthy a Friend, & Fellow aliue, as was our* SHAKESPEARE, *by humble offer of his playes, to your most noble patronage.'*

Masters Heminge and Condell follow the literary convention of their time, which made it necessary to refer to modern works brought to the press as 'trifles,' but it is apparent from their phraseology that all concerned knew that in the present case, at least, the 'trifles' were treasures.

The propriety of this dedication to the Earl of Pembroke and his brother was perhaps greater than will ever be known, at least beyond conjecture. Their mother was the famed Countess of Pembroke—'Sidney's sister, Pembroke's mother,' in William Browne of Tavistock's poem, and the 'Muse of the Poets of our time,' in Marlowe's phrase. Her eldest son, William Herbert, was surrounded from his boyhood by renowned authors. His tutor was the poet Samuel Daniel, author of *A Defence of Rhyme*, written at the instigation of the Countess and dedicated to the young Earl (who succeeded to his father's title in 1601 when he was twenty years old). It was perhaps inevitable that his Lordship should become a patron of poets himself, and he won at length the more enduring title of 'the greatest Maecenas to learned men'—in an age when poets were learned. It is at least possible that he was the 'M^r. W. H.' to whom Shakespeare's *Sonnets* were dedicated.

### 3.

The dedication to their Lordships written, Heminge and Condell proceeded to collaborate on the second, 'To the great Variety of Readers.' Here their names had a somewhat different value, for affixed to this advertisement they were a promise, if not a guarantee, of authentic texts from the repertoire of the King's Men— the two actors, perhaps at the urging of the publisher-bookseller syndicate which brought out the folio, certainly imply as much. First they challenge the common or bookstall variety of reader to pick up, but not let go, the Shakespeare volume, in language that is different from the earlier dedication, but perhaps commercially and psychologically correct: 'From the most able, to him that can but spell: There you are number'd. We had rather you were weighd [i.e., as to your judgment]. Especially, when the fate of all Bookes depends vpon your capacities: and not of your heads alone, but of your purses. Well! It is now publique, & you wil stand for your priuiledges wee know: to read, and censure. Do so, but buy it first. That doth best commend a Booke, the Stationer saies.'

The exhortation to buy concluded, Heminge and Condell again offer a reverent view of their departed friend, and of his works: 'It had bene a thing, we confesse, worthie to haue bene wished, that the Author himselfe had liu'd to haue set forth, and ouerseen his owne writings; But since it hath bin ordain'd otherwise, and he by death departed from that right, we pray you do not envie his Friends, the office of their care, and paine, to haue collected & publish'd them; and so to haue publish'd them, as where (before) you were abus'd with diuerse stolne, and surreptitious copies, maimed, and deformed by the frauds and stealthes of iniurious impostors, that expos'd them: euen those, are now offer'd to your view cur'd, and perfect of their limbes; and all the rest, absolute in their numbers, as he conceiued them. Who, as he was a happie imitator of Nature, was a most gentle expresser of it. His mind and hand went together: And what he thought, he vttered with that easiness, that wee haue scarce receiued from him a blot in his papers.'

This particular bit of information was one which the old actors were in the best position to give, for the manuscript sheets of Shakespeare's plays went to his company, not to a printer, and they had seen them and handled them for some thirty years. When Ben Jonson, who was himself concerned in the publication of the folio, read this passage over, perhaps at the Sign of the Half-Eagle and Key, and in the presence of Heminge and Condell, he ventured to remark that he could have wished Shakespeare had blotted (i.e., revised) more, for which he was severely censured. 'I remember,' he wrote later, 'the Players have often mentioned it as an honour to *Shakespeare*, that in his writing (whatsoever he penn'd) hee never blotted out line. My answer hath beene, would he had blotted a thousand. Which they thought a malevolent speech. I had not told posterity this, but for their ignorance, who choose that circumstance to commend their friend by, wherein he most faulted. And to justifie mine owne candor, (for I lov'd the man, and doe honour his memory (on this side Idolatry) as much as any.)'

### 4.

In 1623, Ben Jonson was the greatest living man of letters in England. He bestrode the Elizabethan and Jacobean periods like a colossus. Poet, playwright, scholar and critic, his patrons were a king (James I, who upon hearing him speak a grace in verse gave him a hundred pounds) and an earl (Pembroke, who sent him twenty pounds each New Year's Day with which to purchase books). His friends were the supreme writers of his time; and the new and younger writers deemed it felicity merely to see him and hear him speak—witness their verses in his honor. Blunt, honest, learned and wise, he attacked the pretensions of poetasters and the frauds of partisan critics—'*Nothing* in our Age, I have observ'd, is more preposterous, then the running *Iudgements* upon *Poetry*, and *Poets;* when wee shall heare those things commended, and cry'd up for the best writings, which a man would scarce vouchsafe, to wrap any wholesome drug in; hee would never light his *Tobacco* with them'—and he laid down the law, which must stand as long as earth's foundations, that: 'To judge of Poets is only the facultie of Poets; and not of all Poets, but the best.'

Such was the man whom we are about to hear praise Shakespeare, in a commendatory poem prefixed to the First Folio which sounds the organ note in the choir of contemporary praise. As it is one thing to pay tribute—which many have done—to illustrious predecessors who lived hundreds or thousands of years before, and another for a great poet to lavish praise on a contemporary, particularly one who was known to him, Jonson's poem, 'To The Memory of My Beloued, The Avthor, Mr. William Shakespeare: And What He Hath Left Vs,' is without parallel in ancient or modern literature:

> *To draw no envy* (Shakespeare) *on thy name,*
> *Am I thus ample to thy Book, and Fame:*
> *While I confess thy writings to be such,*
> *As neither* Man, *nor* Muse, *can praise too much.*
> *'Tis true, and all men's suffrage.*

All were now praising him, whether they understood him or not, or from whatever motive; but he will speak as an expert in his own and Shakespeare's craft. The panegyrics of publishers, booksellers and others, although they perhaps had a citizen's right to state their views, were not for Jonson—nor was the blind adulation of the actors (whose reproof rankled):

> *But these ways*
> *Were not the paths I meant unto thy praise:*
> *For silliest Ignorance on these may light,*
> *Which, when it sounds at best, but echo's right;*
> *Or blind Affection, which doth ne're advance*
> *The truth, but gropes, and urgeth all by chance;*
> *Or crafty Malice, might pretend this praise,*
> *And think to ruin, where it seem'd to raise.*

Nor will he praise Shakespeare as William Basse, another poet, had done, who bade

Renowned Spenser, lie a thought more nigh
To learned Chaucer, and rare Beaumont lie
A little nearer Spenser to make room
For Shakespeare in your threefold, fourfold Tomb.

Instead, touching on this conceit only to reject it, he gives Shakespeare a literary resurrection, with such apostrophes to his risen spirit as few have ever received, and fewer merited:

*I, therefore will begin. Soul of the Age!*
*The applause! delight! the wonder of our Stage!*
*My Shakespeare, rise; I will not lodge thee by*
Chaucer, *or* Spenser, *or bid* Beaumont *lie*
*A little further, to make thee a room:*
*Thou art a Monument, without a tomb.*

### 5.

Shakespeare, he continues, still addressing the spirit of his late friend, as once Chapman addressed slain Marlowe's, lives on—

*while thy Book doth live,*
*And we have wits to read, and praise to give.*
*That I not mix thee so, my brain excuses;*
*I mean with great, but disproportion'd Muses:*
*For, if I thought my judgment were of years,*
*I should commit thee surely with thy peers,*
*And tell, how far thou didst our* Lily *outshine,*
*Or sporting* Kid, *or* Marlowe's *mighty line.*
*And though thou hadst small* Latin, *and less* Greek,
*From thence to honour thee, I would not seek*
*For names; but call forth thund'ring* Æschylus,
Euripides, *and* Sophocles *to us.*

He names the beginners of the Elizabethan drama; Shakespeare overtook the innovators, then surpassed them, and finally took his place with the greatest of the ancients, only to surpass them, too:

*Triumph, my* Britain, *thou hast one to show,*
*To whom all* Scenes *of* Europe *homage owe.*
*He was not of an age, but for all time!*

Jonson, the classical scholar, cannot resist a slight dig at Shakespeare's lack of scholarly attainments; although his candor, for the present, is so great that he cannot hold back one jot of his praise. (Later, when age and misfortune had soured him, and too much praise of Shakespeare had aroused his envy, he had other things to say.) The barb about '*small* Latin, *and less* Greek' has been the source of much mischief. Perhaps in comparison with Jonson's enormous knowledge of those tongues, Shakespeare's Latin was small, his Greek smaller; but this does not tell us much, for it may have been considerable compared with other men's. Later writers took Jonson at his word; but this is a small sacrifice, considering what else we get in his poem:

> *Sweet Swan of* Avon! *what a sight it were*
> *To see thee in our waters yet appear,*
> *And make those flights upon the banks of* Thames,
> *That so did take* Eliza, *and our* James!
> *But stay, I see thee in the Hemisphere*
> *Advanc'd, and made a Constellation there!*
> *Shine forth, thou Star of* Poets—

an unexpected confirmation of the approval of two monarchs, and a significant reference to Shakespeare's birthplace.

### 6.

That all, or any, of the men concerned in the publication of Shakespeare's plays—the Earl of Pembroke, whose name is linked to the King himself in the dedication; Blount, the friend of statesmen and writers; Heminge and Condell, members of Shakespeare's theatrical company for thirty years; and gruff Ben Jonson—should have been a party or parties to a gigantic fraud, and no one the wiser, including the various publishers and printers of Shakespeare's plays previous to the folio; the Stationers' Company, with which the works were registered; the booksellers of London, and the printers and apprentices of the Half-Eagle and Key—passes understanding or belief; and the various theories which seek to ascribe Shakespeare's art to someone else—never, let it be remarked, to another commoner like himself, but always to a dark and titled lord—must now be seen for what they are: without substance, like an empty glove held in a gloved hand.

# CHAPTER II

## The Father of the Man

### 1.

THERE are no lords, real or supposed, in William Shakespeare's genealogy. He came, not from the nobility or gentry who, left idle by the toil of others, kept beautiful and inconsequential records of themselves, but from the great heart of humanity. His pedigree is uncertain. Such ancestors as can be mustered for him performed undistinguished but perhaps necessary labors in the workaday world, and they left few records, chiefly of baptisms and burials, debts and fines. The Shakespeares that are known to history, whether immediately related to the poet or not, were mostly artisans, or workers, although here and there some of them exhibited a particular skill, such as weaver, turner or robber (the earliest William Shakespeare on record, of Clopton in Gloucestershire, while in pursuit of his chosen calling, had the misfortune to be hanged in 1248).

The origin of the name Shakespeare is military and occupational, i.e., a spearman in the ranks; but no warlike original progenitor, shaking his spear in the twilight of antiquity, has been found. Through three centuries to the sixteenth, Shakespeares by the hundreds, if we include the families of those mentioned, appear briefly, and disappear, in the old records; yet the diligent and never-ceasing examination of parish registers, subsidy rolls, muster rolls, deeds and wills, under all the variant spellings of the family name, leads no further back in William Shakespeare's genealogy than his father's father, one Richard Shakespeare of Snitterfield, four miles northeast of Stratford-upon-Avon.

### 2.

Richard Shakespeare was a tenant farmer, holding two farms of Robert Arden of Wilmcote, a substantial farmer who had eight daughters. His annals are brief. His birth date is unknown. He was independent. He was fined twelve pence for crowding the

11

common pasture with his cattle, perhaps because he brought other men's cattle in to batten there; a Thomas Atwood of Stratford, making his will, left 'vnto Richarde Shakespere of Snytfelde my four oxen which are nowe in his keping.' He was ordered to mend the hedges between his land and that of one John Palmer, a tithe gatherer, with whom brushes were regular. He witnessed a will for a dying Stratford friend, and helped make an inventory of the goods of a deceased Snitterfield blacksmith, acts which indicate a good repute. Nevertheless, a hint of trouble charges the last record we have of him: 'that every tenaunte for his parte doe make his hedges and ditches betwixt the end of the lane of Richard Shakespere, and the hedge called Dawkins hedge, before the feast of St. Luke, sub pene three shillings four pence.' By 1561 he was dead. A bond of that year, drawn up in connection with the administration of his goods, values them at thirty-nine pounds, seventeen shillings.

Richard Shakespeare had two sons, Henry and John. It is not clear which was the older. Henry continued to farm at Snitterfield, while John went to live in Stratford, where his father had other friends besides the Thomas Atwood who willed him his oxen. But it was John who was bonded as the administrator of his father's 'goodes catals [chattels] and debtes.'

Henry Shakespeare carried his father's independence a step further. He stayed away from Court Leet, the local court held periodically by the lord of the manor, at which attendance was mandatory, and was fined the usual two pence. He refused to pay tithes, would not accept the verdict of the ecclesiastical court against him, was threatened with excommunication, and was excommunicated; remaining obdurate, he won the sobriquet of 'contumacious.' Perhaps he was. In an argument with one Edward Cornwaile, he thwacked that worthy and 'drew blood,' for which he was fined three shillings, three pence; Cornwaile was fined two shillings, which indicates how the court felt about the matter.

In the last year of his life Henry Shakespeare was fined thrice: four pence, for absenting himself from court; two shillings, six pence, 'for not laboring with teemes for the amending of the Queenes highe-wayes at the dayes appointed, according to the forme of the statute'; and two shillings for not repairing a ditch, a family failing.

His wife's name was Margaret, which is all that is known of her.

### 3.

It cannot be said for certain when John Shakespeare left Snitterfield for Stratford, but he came to maturity there at a time of renewed vigor and prosperity for the ancient town on the Avon, and there a dream of gentryhood gradually possessed him.

In 1553, Stratford was incorporated as a borough and granted a government closely resembling that of the previously suppressed Guild of the Holy Cross, a lay body which had governed the town from time out of mind. The new governing body or corporation consisted of fourteen aldermen and fourteen burgesses; the aldermen elected other aldermen, the entire group elected burgesses. Once a year aldermen and burgesses elected, from among the former, a high bailiff, who became the chief officer of Stratford.

The corporation in session splashed Stratford with bright colors. Bailiff, aldermen and burgesses wore expensive gowns denoting their rank; and a little Lord Mayor's procession was enacted as two sergeants-at-the-mace attended the bailiff and the chief alderman from their homes to the Guild Hall, in the heart of Stratford.

This, in brief, was the organization of the highest stratum of the Stratford government. A step down were two chamberlains, elected by the entire body from the burgesses. The chamberlains collected rents owing to the corporation, audited accounts, and allocated money for the repair of public buildings.

At the foot of the ladder to municipal advancement were four constables and two ale-conners, the latter for the supervision of staple foodstuffs such as bread and ale. These last were chosen from the more 'able' and 'discreet' citizens of Stratford, who were thus enabled to join, and if their abilities warranted, to rise in the corporation hierarchy.

John Shakespeare was to rise to the top.

In addition to the governing body, the new charter provided for a Market Day every Thursday and two Fairs annually; for the reinstitution and support of a free grammar school for the children and youth of Stratford; and for the re-establishment and support of an almshouse 'for twenty-four paupers,' it being, apparently, an unshakable tenet of the faithful that the poor shall be always with them, and who, by a coincidence, always are.

**4.**

In 1561 we find John Shakespeare a member of the Mystery, Craft, or Occupation of the Glovers, Whittawers, and Collar-Makers of Stratford, the glovers' guild, by apprenticeship.

He was also married.

These are the probabilities. He was apprenticed at fourteen, perhaps to Thomas Dickson, glover, of Bridge Street, Stratford, whose wife Joan was the daughter of a neighbor of Richard Shakespeare in Snitterfield. He served the usual seven years, and became a freeman of Stratford by 'redemption,' after which he could marry and open his own shop. That he was certainly a glover by trade, and not anything else, is seen by his mark, a compass and dividers, affixed to documents. He is termed 'glouer' in a Court of Record entry of the year 1556. (The case of Christopher Marlowe's father offers an interesting parallel. John Marlowe was born ten miles from Canterbury, and joined the Brethren of the Assumption of Our Lady, of the Crafts and Mysteries of Shoe-Makers, Coriours and Cobbelers of Canterbury, the shoemakers' guild, by apprenticeship.) Since in his trade or craft of glover and whittawer (bleacher) John Shakespeare made constant purchases of sheep, lamb and kid skins, we find him adding to his income by selling the wool by-products.

**5.**

John Shakespeare's wife Mary was the youngest of the eight daughters of Robert Arden of Wilmcote, from whom Richard Shakespeare had rented land. In 1556, 'secke in bodye,' Arden made his last will and testament, in which he bequeathed his soul to God and all the company of heaven—this was in the reign of Philip and Mary, of pious memory—and left to his daughter Mary 'all my lande in Willmecote, cawlide Asbyes and the crop apone the grounde sowne and tyllide as hitt is and six pounds, thirteen shillings, four pence of monye to be payde orr ere my goodes be devydide.' This bequest of cash, before the division of his goods, appears like a loving touch, and may have had something to do with Mary's recent or pending marriage; but perhaps it sprang from a distrust of his second wife, to whom he left a similar sum, on condition that she suffer another daughter, Alice, to enjoy half his copyhold in Wilmcote 'quyetlye.' And as though to make certain that his provisions would be carried out, he appointed Alice and Mary full executors.

There is no evidence that Robert Arden was ever anything more than a prosperous husbandman, as another early document terms him; and the most that can be said of Mary's immediate forebears is that they were descended, but not in the main line of descent, from the Saxon Earls of Warwick, a claim never put forward by her family and which, if put forward, could probably have been matched by scores of other families in Warwickshire. Nevertheless, the union of John Shakespeare and Mary Arden accelerated his rise to social and political prominence, and from tradesman to gentleman in one generation. He applied, at length, for a coat of arms, and the College of Arms granted it.

### 6.

John Shakespeare's climb follows the usual pattern. We find him first, in 1552, occupying a house in a modest location at the extreme edge of Stratford, on a street which trailed off into a country road leading to Henley-in-Arden. On the twenty-ninth day of April in that year, together with two others, he was fined twelve pence for heaping offal outside his dwelling, the result of routine emptying of chamber pots, contrary to a court ordinance. The item is interesting, not because of the fine and its circumstances, but because this early record definitely places him in a house on Henley Street.

In 1556 we find him the owner of that house, with its adjacent garden. The house was one of three buildings standing so close together that they could be made into one; in 1575 he acquired the other two, with their gardens and two orchards. (One of them was pulled down in 1594 during a fire.)

These timbered and gabled dwellings are now known as The Birthplace, and tradition says that the middle house is the house where William Shakespeare was born; but tradition must be wrong because when John Shakespeare acquired the middle house William was eleven years old. To confound tradition even further, in 1556, when John Shakespeare purchased the first of his Henley Street properties, he also acquired a house with a garden and meadow in Greenhill Street, likewise at the extreme edge of town, and no man knoweth whether he ever went to live there, or what use he made of it, for it does not reappear in the subsequent business records of the Shakespeare family.

In any event, we now find him a member of the glovers' guild, married and the owner of two houses, thus amply fulfilling the Stratford corporation's definition of an officeholder—'able' and 'discreet.' In September, 1556, the corporation, meeting in the Guild Hall on Walkers' Street, elected him ale-conner, and further enjoined upon him, by oath, that 'in everything else you shall well and truly behave yourself.'

John Shakespeare carried out his duties satisfactorily; he did well and truly behave himself. The following year he was chosen a burgess, by vote of the incumbent aldermen and burgesses. In the memorable year of 1558, when Elizabeth came to the throne, he was elected a constable; while in his house on Henley Street, with its rush-strewn floors, low ceilings and darkening beams from open fireplaces, a house beginning to overflow with chests and coffers, bedsteads, heaps of linen, and brass, pewter and silver tableware and candlesticks, in a room hung with painted cloths depicting Biblical events, his first child was born and christened Joan (perhaps for Mary Arden's sister Joan or for Joan Dickson, wife of the glover with whom John Shakespeare got his start). She died in infancy.

John Shakespeare continued to be prominent in Stratford affairs. He became court 'affeeror,' an official who decided what fees, fines or punishments should be imposed in cases not covered by statute; he became one of the two chamberlains for the borough. In disbursing corporation money, he paid four pounds to one Allen 'for techyng y^e chylder.'

Once more a child was born, to die in infancy—Margaret, who lived five months, named, perhaps, for her Aunt Margaret, Henry Shakespeare's wife.

## 7.

It is while John Shakespeare was a borough chamberlain that we get a hint as to his religious beliefs. Partisan writers have made him out to be Protestant, Puritan and Catholic; it is possible to do the same for a great many of his contemporaries, and not be any wiser as to the truth.

The beginnings of Elizabeth's reign are in a twilight era of religion. Her father, Henry VIII, had broken with Rome; her half brother, Edward VI, died before the Reformation could be carried out; her half sister Mary had reinstituted the Catholic religion, as it was usually done in those days, with fire and sword. The 'new learning,' which brought with it discussions of the Bible, made men question whether a wafer was truly the body of Christ; and many a brave but overzealous man and woman, devout in all else, perished in flames because they would not accept the doctrine of transubstantiation. Others, in their wills, set aside two or three shillings 'for faggots with which to burn heretics.'

Elizabeth herself was a Protestant monarch, perhaps from policy; but this did not prevent her from flirting with Catholic princelings and harrying the Puritans. One of her earliest edicts, the Act of Uniformity of 1559, shows clearly what she expected in the strangely merged spiritual and temporal realm: 'All who shall be found non-comformable in the smallest matter shall be immediately apprehended and cast into prison.' The struggle of those years was a political one, chiefly between the Pope and the English sovereign. A papal bull excommunicated Elizabeth and her 'heretical' followers; a Parliamentary Act made it high treason 'to publish or put into use the Pope's bulls.'

So here were ideas only dimly comprehended by the masses of English people, whose new clergy were more like informers and inquisitors serving the state rather than God; and opposing them were 'religious caterpillars' swarming over the realm, and plotting and complotting with adherents of the old religion in secret. The age tried everyone by its discords, but most of all, perhaps, the devout English Catholic, whose dilemma was loyalty to his Protestant sovereign and obedience to the Pope—two irreconcilables. In the absence of specific declarations of faith, the old or the new, as in a will, where the testator bequeathed his soul to God *and* the company of heaven, only political allegiance or forthright acts revealed the Catholic or Protestant.

As chamberlain of the borough of Stratford, John Shakespeare financed the defacing of religious images and frescoes in the Guild Chapel; and he spent a total of six pounds, fifteen shillings and five pence in a thorough overhauling of the Protestant vicar's house. In all this he expressed the predominantly Protestant views of the Stratford corporation, which had dismissed the Catholic vicar appointed under Queen Mary, and which continued the work of remodeling the Guild Chapel by removing the altar and taking down the rood loft and installing a communion table and benches for worshipers. The copes and vestments previously worn by Catholic priests were sold, the moneys thus obtained going to the corporation. A corporation memorandum lists blue, red and tawny velvet vestments among the religious articles dispensed with.

### 8.

Although John Shakespeare's rise in the Stratford hierarchy was a steady one, dissension sometimes shook the corporation. At a turbulent meeting in the Guild Hall in 1565, Alderman William Bott, who lived across the street at New Place, was reported to have spoken 'evell woordes' about the high bailiff and others; and worse, 'that ther was never a honest man of the Councell or the body of the corporacyon of Stratford.' Perhaps Bott had got wind of the agenda of this meeting in advance, for he cautiously—or perhaps defiantly—stayed away, and being sent for, refused to appear and defend himself. He was thereupon expelled, and his place was taken by John Shakespeare.

John Shakespeare had served eight years as a burgess, with several other community offices on the side, when he became an alderman. He had shown uncommon zeal, perhaps uncommon abilities, in all his public duties. He had come to the notice of many influential townsmen, and had made firm friends of several, among them Alderman Adrian Quiney, whose grandson would one day marry his granddaughter. Three years later, in 1568, he reached the summit of prestige and power in Stratford when the assembled aldermen and burgesses elected him high bailiff. He thus became, for one year, the chief officer of the corporation, a judge of the Court of Record, and a Queen's officer as justice of the peace. On days when the corporation council sat he donned a gown of scarlet trimmed with fur, and was escorted to meeting by a sergeant-at-the-mace.

The records now begin to term him 'Master John Shakespeare' and 'Magistro Johanne Shakespeare,' titles appertaining to gentlemen, which made him eligible for the coat of arms for which he longed.

9.

The dream of a coat of arms stimulated John Shakespeare's imagination to reveries of his ancestors, of whom no trace has been found beyond his father. He saw in his mind, and set down on paper, redoubtable forebears who 'for thyre valieant & faithefull service' were 'advaunced & rewarded by the most Prudent Prince king Henry the seventh of famous memorie.' Upon the somewhat less entranced scrutiny of officers of the College of Arms, who could find no such advancement, John Shakespeare's brave and virtuous forebears dwindled to a grandfather; but perhaps because no grandfather rewarded by Henry VII can be found in the records, 'grandfather' subsequently became 'great grandfather,' which made it somewhat more difficult to track down, and gave him, since he had other claims, the benefit of the doubt. The other claims were that he was an officer of the Crown, and that he had married the daughter and heiress of Robert Arden, now termed by him and others a gentleman of reputation and credit.

These matters he presented to Robert Cook, Clarenceux king-of-arms, whose visitation committee fortunately turned up in Warwickshire as John Shakespeare became high bailiff. Cook, apparently, drew up a patent, at least in draft form, and tricked out the Shakespeare coat of arms with its device of a spear and the motto, 'Non Sans Droit'—Not Without Right. Of this, more later, for it was many a weary year before the College of Arms in London granted it.

# CHAPTER III

## *The Birth and a Portent*

### 1.

A MAN who desires a coat of arms needs a son to carry his gentryhood on, and it must have been galling to John Shakespeare's pride to have seen his first two children born girls, whatever may have been his joy in their babyhood and grief at their untimely deaths. But sometime in the second week after Easter, 1564, pride and joy overflowed: a son was born. Properly swaddled and festooned, this precious child was carried the length of Stratford from Henley Street to Holy Trinity Church, standing by the river Avon in the 'old town,' and there, on Wednesday, April 26, baptized and christened William by the Rev. John Bretchgirdle, late M.A. of Oxford and the first Protestant vicar of Stratford. Present, no doubt, were John Shakespeare's friends of the glovers' guild and the corporation, including Alderman William Smith, and his Henley Street neighbor, another William Smith, haberdasher, either of whom may have stood godfather to the Shakespeare heir.

The Stratford parish register, like others for this period, does not record births and deaths, but baptisms and burials. The entry for April 26 is terse: 'Gulielmus filius Johannes Shakspere.' Custom dictated that children be baptized the first Sunday or other holy day after birth, when attendance at church was likely to be greatest; yet April 26 was a Wednesday, an indication that the child was sickly, making prompt baptism an urgent matter for his infant soul, which hovered precariously between heaven and hell. Tradition has made April 23 the birth date, but without warrant from any discoverable source.

For two and a half years William Shakespeare was an only child. In October, 1566, a brother was born and christened Gilbert, godfathered probably by Gilbert Bradley, glover, of Henley Street; and in April, 1569, a sister was born and christened Joan, in memory of the Shakespeares' first child.

## 2.

It was during John Shakespeare's tenure as high bailiff, in the signal year 1569, that a blast of trumpets announced the arrival in Stratford of a troupe of players.

Into the streets swarmed artisan and artificer, housewife and apprentice, with children at their heels, and dogs barking; and saw the actors in bright liveries, on horses gaily decked, making their way to the Guild Hall where the corporation sat, to pay their respects to the town's chief magistrate and request permission to give performances.

Thus it was that the first theatrical company ever to be welcomed in Stratford was greeted by Master John Shakespeare (which hardly makes him a Puritan):

Sirrah, go see what trumpet 'tis that sounds.
How now! who is it?

                              An it please your honour,
Players that offer service.

Bid them come near. Now, fellows, you are welcome.

We thank your honour.

The players identified themselves as the Queen's, which assured them of an honorable reception. Etiquette required that they perform first for members of the corporation and their families in the cool and spacious Guild Hall; after which, with another blast of trumpets to fire the imaginations of the young, they set forth to the inn where they were to lodge—the Swan, the Bear, or the Angel (the last-named on Henley Street)—where public performances were given on a stage erected in the courtyard.

Again in that decisive year a troupe of players came with the bright sound of trumpets and gay caparisons—this time, the Earl of Worcester's Men; and John Shakespeare as high bailiff welcomed them in his gown of scarlet trimmed with fur. Like the Queen's Men before them, they performed first in the Guild Hall, and were rewarded (as the corporation accounts show):

| | |
|---|---|
| Item payd to the Quenes Pleyers | ix$^s$ |
| Item to the Erle of Worcesters Pleers | xij$^s$ |

William Shakespeare was then five years old.

# CHAPTER IV

## Boyhood and Education

### 1.

THOSE who beguile themselves by invoking coroneted shades cannot have given any thought to the logic of art. The facts of Shakespeare's art demand a boy born and bred in a country town, who journeyed to the city on the Thames, liked it for a time, and then returned to the brighter and quieter streets, the leafier paths, of Stratford-upon-Avon. In reading him, we breathe the air of spacious Warwickshire, watered by the long-flowing and leisurely river which parts the shire in two and whispers fruitfulness to both; strolling in Warwickshire, garden and grove of England, and nest of larks, we breathe in the images impressed on the mind of Shakespeare as a boy, which he gave back to the land as a man.

### 2.

Stratford was a market town—the names of the oldest streets show it: Rother Street, from the Anglo-Saxon *hreother*, meaning cattle; Swine Street; Sheep Street; Corn Street; Wood Street—market places where the livestock and produce of surrounding villages went on sale, in a cacophony of hawkers' cries and animal squeals, the pipes and the tongs and bones of entertainers, the tuneful mending of pots and pans in adjacent Tinkers Lane. The houses were cross-timbered, with tiled or thatched roofs, almost every one with its own garden or orchard stretching away beside or behind it. They stood on unpaved streets, with here and there a scatter of cobblestones; and in them dwelt the trade guildsmen of the town, some bearing a surname for their occupational specialty—the coopers, wheelwrights, shoemakers, dyers, butchers, glovers, tilers and thatchers. Many of them carried on a profitable sideline in malting, for home consumption and to supply the taverns and inns of the snug little town, the Crown, the Bear, the Angel, and the Swan. Next to the Swan lived Henry Field, tanner, whose son

22

Richard was apprenticed to a printer and stationer in London in the summer of 1579. William Shakespeare and Richard Field were almost the same age; although they went different ways, one to a seven years' apprenticeship, the other to school, their paths converged in London. Perhaps when he saw Field depart, Shakespeare had the thought for the first time:

I hope to see London once ere I die.

On Henley Street, besides glovers, there was a blacksmith shop and the house of a tailor; one day he saw

a smith stand with his hammer, thus,
The whilst his iron did on the anvil cool,
With open mouth swallowing a tailor's news;
Who, with his shears and measure in his hand,
Standing on slippers,—which his nimble haste
Had falsely thrust upon contrary feet—
Told of a many thousand warlike French,
That were embattailed and rank'd in Kent.

### 3.

The streets and lanes of the town led to country roads and paths through the fields. Slipping out betimes from the house on Henley Street he might wander toward Arden woods by Henley and Clopton roads, or by the Back Lane toward Evesham and Shottery, seeing the grained ash and the barky fingers of the elm, enringed with ivy, flutter their leaves of light and thinnest sound; and daisies pied and violets blue, and lady-smocks all silver-white, and yellow cuckoo-buds, sowing the meadows with color and fragrance—dew in their chalices, first pearls, then flowers' tears. A red-hipped bumblebee droned on a thistletop; the tense and timid deer quivered in the Clopton deer park; the lark, intense as his own spirit, catapulted to heaven's gate, shooting arrows of silver song at cloud-capped towers and all the castles of dream.

In the opposite direction, Back Bridge Street led him past the Bear and the Swan, with their memories of players, to Butt Close by the river, where townsmen practiced archery against the coming of a foreign foe; and so to Clopton Bridge which spanned the Avon with fourteen arches and put the wanderer on the road to Banbury straight ahead, or Shipston to the right, Tiddington to the left.

Treading the strewn fragments of Roman road that led to antique times, he wandered with his thoughts. Downstream, past the willows that rose like mist, stood the parish church with its vaulted bone house, set like a tomb among tumbledown graves, where disinterred skeletons were thrown in grotesque heaps of reeky shanks and yellow, chapless skulls to make room in the churchyard for the newly dead. This was a spot he skirted in horror; the horror of it never left him. Not only sad mortality, but chapel bells, called him back to earth, to town and school.

### 4.

The Guild of the Holy Cross, whose 'beginning was from the time whereunto the memory of man reacheth not,' stood in the very center of Stratford where Church Street, Chapel Street, Walkers' Street and Tinkers Lane formed a crossroads upon which the tide of the town's life flowed. It was a lay fraternal organization, more important in the life of Stratford than the distant parish church by the river, outside the borough limits. It had maintained a chapel, a grammar school and an almshouse, until its dissolution under Henry VIII; and it was there, after the charter of 1553, that Stratford took up the snipped strands of its municipal affairs again with the newly formed corporation. It is with the grammar school that we are concerned.

By the Charter of 1553 Edward VI had decreed: 'We, moved by extraordinary love and affection to the end that we bring up the youths of our kingdom in the aforesaid county of Warwick so that the coming generations shall derive from a childhood more cultured and imbued of letters than was accustomed in our times, and that, when they will have come to a more advanced life, they shall go forth more learned, undoubtedly appreciating the English Church of Christ (whose changes in the land we now are carrying out), taught no less in literary affairs than in precedence for the benefit of all our kingdom, we do in reality and to the full create, erect, found, ordain, make, and establish a certain Free Grammar School with one Master to endure forever in the aforesaid village of Stratford-upon-Avon. And thus we wish and, by these presents, do command it to be established and observed inviolably forever; and that the aforesaid School by us thus founded, created, and established shall be named, called, and designated forever as the King's New School of Stratford-upon-Avon.'

Thus the King received credit and the townsmen received back what they had themselves created and long maintained—until the Crown interfered—through the Guild of the Holy Cross. The school became once more an adjunct of the Guild Chapel, and the bells of the chapel tower, which scattered the larks of sound at sunrise and sunset, chimed the hours and quarter hours, and tolled for the passing of townsmen and for their burials, also called Stratford boys to school.

Its provisions and curriculum can be approximated by comparing it with a similar school attended by Shakespeare's great contemporary, Christopher Marlowe, the son of a Canterbury shoemaker, who was born two months before the Stratford glover's son and heir. The King's School, Canterbury, so called for Henry VIII, under whom it was suppressed and then re-established, after he had rifled its coffers, provided a pre-university education for boys between the ages of nine and fifteen 'with minds apt for learning,' some of them destined for holy orders. The school was an adjunct of Canterbury Cathedral. A statute decreed that boys would not be admitted as students 'before they have learned to read and write and are moderately versed in the first rudiments of grammar.' In the absence of a private tutor, boys received their pre-King's School education from a clerk of the Canterbury corporation, 'or one for him.' A religious of the cathedral was probably the substitute pedagogue.

The cathedral statute referred to gives the broad outlines of the education received by the King's School scholars, who were to attend four or five years, 'until they have obtained a moderate acquaintance with the Latin grammar, and have learned to speak in Latin and write in Latin.'

### 5.

We have seen that Chamberlain John Shakespeare disbursed four pounds to one Allen 'for techyng yᵉ chylder.' This must refer to children of pre-grammar school age, who were taught the alphabet, Lord's prayer and catechism, as well as the rudiments of Latin grammar, by a cleric of the Guild Chapel; and it may be that the 'chylder' included young William Shakespeare—certain it

is that the son of the high bailiff who was for one year afterwards
chief alderman after relinquishing that high office, and finally a
veteran alderman with a long record of public service behind him,
would be likely to receive whatever education the borough offered.
And this would include the King's Grammar School.

The masters of the King's New School during the time William
Shakespeare was likely to have been a student there—i.e., between
1571 and 1579—were Oxford graduates, men of considerable
scholastic attainments as well as accomplished Latinists. They had
not only to pass muster with the Stratford corporation; they were
licensed to teach by the Bishop of Worcester, who had the ecclesiastical administration of the parish of Stratford; and they received at
least the nominal approval of the lord of the manor, the Earl of
Warwick. A teacher who could negotiate successfully with this formidable and finicky aggregation might be fit to tutor a king's son.

These paragons of learning, at least as regards the race of school-
masters, had as guides not only their own grammar school and
university education, but the precepts for teaching laid down in
several notable books. One of them was *The gouernor*, by Sir
Thomas Elyot, the friend of More and Erasmus. By seven a boy
was already studying Greek and Latin, with Latin a medium of
conversation as well. For supplementary reading, Elyot recom-
mended Aesop's *Fables*; Homer, Virgil, Ovid, Horace, Lucan and
Hesiod—in the original tongues; and for recreation, walking, running, tennis, wrestling and swimming; and music—in moderation.
Roger Ascham's *The Scholemaster* was another famous book for
teachers. As the former tutor of Princess Elizabeth his theories
commanded respect. 'In writing this booke,' he declared, 'I haue
had earnest respect to three speciall pointes, trothe of Religion,
honestie in liuing, right order in learning.' As regards Latin, he
advocated translations from good authors, and gentleness instead
of the usual birching for errors committed. When a boy did well,
he wrote, 'let the master praise him, and saie here ye do well. For
I assure you, there is no such whetstone, to sharpen a good witte
and encourage a will to learninge, as is praise.'

· After the Geneva *Bible*, 'Translated According to the Ebrue and
Greke,' perhaps the most important book conned by a grammar
school boy was William Lily's *A Short Introduction of Grammar*

'compiled and set forth for the bringing up of all those that intend to attain to the knowledge of the Latine tongue.'

Item, Lily: 'In nouns be two numbers, the singular and the plural. The singular number speaketh of one, as *lapis*, a stone.'

Item, Shakespeare: '*Evans*. William, how many numbers is in nouns? *William*. Two. *Evans*. What is *lapis*, William? *William*. A stone.'

Lily quotes Horace; Shakespeare's Chiron exclaims:

> O! 'tis a verse in Horace; I know it well:
> I read it in the grammar long ago.

William Shakespeare had not only learned to make a quill pen, from the strongest wing feathers, cleaning and cleaving them with a penknife—as another textbook specified—but he learned to write.

### 6.

The Stratford Grammar School was directly over the Guild Hall. Thus a schoolboy absorbed not only an education but, given perception, was enabled to observe something of the government of the town and to see how the world wags.

Across the street from the school, at the corner of Chapel and Walkers' Streets, stood New Place, once the town residence of Sir Hugh Clopton, benefactor of Stratford and sometime Lord Mayor of London. It was known as the 'great house.' William Shakespeare, seeing it every day, wove his own particular dream around it. In it there now lived William Bott, lawyer and ousted alderman, whose place in the corporation had been taken by John Shakespeare.

### 7.

The tradition that William was withdrawn from school because of his father's financial difficulties has a basis in certain facts; although in the absence of proof that he ever was enrolled, there can be no proof that he was withdrawn. He received an education somewhere, and it was probably at the King's Grammar School that he received it. But between 1578 and 1580 John Shakespeare leased, mortgaged or actually conveyed (sold) most of his wife's land in Wilmcote and Snitterfield. Forty-eight acres mortgaged to Edmund Lambert, Mary Shakespeare's brother-in-law, were forfeited when John Shakespeare failed to make good the mortgage. He tried, through court action, to get this particular parcel of land back, or at least obtain an additional sum on it. The litigation dragged on for two decades, straining family relations and draining his resources.

But even if we accept the tradition as true, it does not explain certain results in his immediate family.

## 8.

At seventeen, Christopher Marlowe went from the King's School, Canterbury, to Corpus Christi College, Cambridge, on a scholarship which, for other holders, usually led to holy orders. He became, instead, a poet and playwright.

Why did not William Shakespeare's ambitious father send him to Cambridge?

Why, if John Shakespeare needed William's assistance, was he not apprenticed?

A mile across the fields from Stratford, by a footpath branching off from Back Lane, in a double 'messuage' or dwelling at Shottery, the answer to both questions may be found.

# CHAPTER V

## *The Cottage over the Fields*

### 1.

VERY good company, and of a very readie and pleasant smooth Witt,' perhaps wise beyond his years as well, William Shakespeare at seventeen took the footpath over the fields to Shottery to call on his father's friend, Richard Hathaway, husbandman, drawn thither by Hathaway's daughters, Anne and Catherine, aged, respectively, twenty-five and eighteen years.

Richard Hathaway was not long for this world. Perhaps he remained in ignorance of the true bent of his visitor's affections, if any, or of those in his household toward the visitor. Already in ill-health, and beginning to decline, it probably mattered little to him which of his two eligible daughters Will Shakespeare favored, so long as he favored one of them. On September 1, 1581, 'sicke in bodie but of perfecte memorye,' he made his will, leaving the sum of six pounds, thirteen shillings and four pence apiece to Anne and Catherine, to be paid to each 'att the daye of her maryage.'

Anne received her dowry under unusual circumstances. On her marriage day she was a full twenty-six years to her husband's eighteen, and beginning to swell with child.

### 2.

To understand this extraordinary denouement, it will be necessary to reconstruct the Hathaway household.

Richard Hathaway had married twice. Five children were born to him by his first union, of whom three were still alive—the unmarried girls, and an unmarried son, Bartholomew, aged twenty-seven. The fact that these three mature but unwed children were still under his roof suggests paternal tyranny. After the death of his first wife, Hathaway married again, and was blessed with five more children, of whom four were still alive when William Shakespeare began to be a caller. The oldest of these was twelve, the youngest only three.

Hathaway appears to have loved the offspring of his two unions equally. The amounts bequeathed to Anne and Catherine were also left to the others; in the case of the youngest child, the sum was increased to ten pounds, 'to be paide vnto him att the Age of Twentie yeares.'

Nevertheless, it was a household with two sets of children and a stepmother.

### 3.

There is a hint of trouble in Hathaway's injunctions to his second wife and his oldest son, to whom he left the use of certain pastures and meadows: 'that if the saide Joane my wife shall att anie tyme or tymes att after my decesse goe about to disanull to take a waye from my saide sonne Bartholomewe the aforsaid half yarde lande with the appurtenances So that he do not enioye the Commoditie and profette of the same Accordinge to the tru meaninge of this my last will and Testament Then my will ys that the said Joane my wife shall geve deliuer and paye vnto my saide Sonne Bartholomewe within one yeare after anie such denyall, or discharge the Some of ffortie poundes of lawfull Englyssh money.'

### 4.

The one most likely to find the Hathaway household irksome would be Anne. Bartholomew could go away, if he so desired (which is exactly what he did after his father's death); an unmarried girl could not.

There was the rub—perhaps she had even heard her stepmother remark that it was time she was married; nor would it have been necessary for her stepmother to remark this—in such things women understand each other, and a look would have sufficed.

There was also the question of the money left her by her father, which she could get only if she married.

### 5.

Now comes the personable son of the former high bailiff of Stratford, to entertain the two Hathaway girls with talk of poetry and the theatrical companies, which were performing in the borough with greater frequency of late. Perhaps he read to them, which would have been more than mere entertainment, for with such a responsive audience, William Shakespeare would see ever more clearly where his ambitions tended; his enthusiasm would be contagious, and be reflected back.

Catherine is a shadowy figure in all this. Anne is not, particularly in view of what happened. Her heart must have been lighter in her side every time she saw the youth from Stratford coming over the fields—he was young, to be sure, younger than herself, younger even than Catherine; but old for his years. He brought tidings of the busy borough and of the world outside, of books, and great and glamorous events.

She marked him for her own.

### 6.

By the summer of 1582 her father was dead. She had no fear of her stepmother. It could have been love at first sight; but it could have been something else. Given a woman of twenty-six, and a youth of eighteen, plus a seduction, and it is not difficult to determine who was the seducer.

In the heat and very midsummer of that year, in the sweet-smelling meadows of Shottery, Anne Hathaway clung gratefully to William Shakespeare with all the pent-up ardor of her spinster-hood.

# CHAPTER VI

## *The Marriage of William Shakespeare*

### 1.

IF ANNE'S lover was equally grateful or responsive, he failed to show it. It was only after his mistress had begun to swell with child by him that he did what true love would have dictated he do at once—he married her; but whether by compulsion —from his father, who had his reputation to maintain; from her brother and others, together with the pleadings of his paramour— must remain in the realm of conjecture.

These are the facts.

On November 28, 1582, there appeared before the chancellor of the ecclesiastical court of Worcester Fulke Sandells and John Richardson, husbandmen, the 'Trustie ffryndes and neighboures' of Richard Hathaway, one of them a supervisor, the other a witness, of his will. By their appearance in this court (which had ecclesiastical jurisdiction over the parish of Stratford) they bound themselves in the sum of forty pounds, individually and together, in accordance with canon law, to guarantee the marriage of Hathaway's daughter. Whatever pressures were exerted were taking effect: William Shakespeare and Anne Hathaway were to marry— in a church, that is, for according to common law, by their cohabitation they were already man and wife.

### 2.

The marriage bond drawn up by the court clerk reads as follows: 'The condicion of this obligacion ys suche that if herafter there shall not appere any Lawfull Lett or impediment by reason of any precontract consanguinitie affinitie or by any other lawfull meanes whatsoeuer but that William Shagspere on th'one partie, and Anne Hathwey of Stratford in the Dioces of Worcester maiden may lawfully solemnize matrimony together and in the same afterwardes remaine and continew like man and wiffe according vnto the lawes in that behalf prouided, and moreouer if there be not at this present

32

time any action sute quarrell or demaund moved or depending before any iudge ecclesiasticall or temporall for and concerning any such lawfull lett or impediment. And moreouer if the said William Shagspere do not proceed to solemnizacion of mariadg with the said Anne Hathwey without the consent of hir frindes. And also if the said William do vpon his own proper costes and expenses defend & save harmles the right Reverend father in god Lord John bushop of Worcester and his offycers for Licencing them the said William and Anne to be married togither with once asking of the bannes of matrimony betwene them and for all other causes which may ensue by reason or occasion therof that then the said obligacion to be voyd and of none effect or els to stand & abide in full force and vertue.'

### 3.

There is nothing unusual about the bond except the phrase 'with once asking of the bannes,' instead of thrice, which may have been due to the interesting condition of the bride, earlier glossed over by the word 'maiden' (a term for the party of the second part to show that she was not a widow).

All that the Bishop of Worcester and his officers were interested in was the avoidance of complaints because of a precontract with a third party or consanguinity (blood relationship) or any of a number of reasons which would make a marriage not binding, thus bringing the church into disrepute.

Two trusty friends and neighbors of Richard Hathaway are seen acting for Shakespeare and his eager bride. It is true that as supervisor and witness of Hathaway's will they were involved in the matter of the payment of Anne's dowry of six pounds, thirteen shillings and four pence; were they the first to insist on a church wedding after learning the facts? Common-law marriages raised eyebrows then as now.

But why this one-sided representation? Why weren't John Shakespeare's trusty friends of the corporation present?

### 4.

I think Alderman John Shakespeare sat, during these negotiations, in his house in Henley Street, a stunned man. He was too shrewd not to have observed differences in his son which set the youth apart. He must have had ambitions for him; the university certainly—perhaps divinity or law.

The dream was over.

It was not Mary Arden Shakespeare alone, with her Catholic heritage, who insisted on a church marriage to ensure the legitimacy of William's offspring. Legitimacy—that was a point that Alderman Shakespeare, with his visions of gentryhood and a family coat of arms, would appreciate. His pride, too, demanded a church wedding—he would not have people say he was too poor for that. The question was: where? Not Stratford, for the townsfolk to gape.

He received Sandells and Richardson, and arrangements were made.

He bowed his head.

### 5.

In one of the half dozen churches in the environs of Stratford, perhaps at Temple Grafton, whose register has disappeared, the marriage of William Shakespeare and Anne Hathaway was celebrated. It must have been a solemn, not to say grim, proceeding: the mature and pregnant bride, an orphan; the youthful bridegroom; the bride's friends, the officiating priest. Their voices come down to us:

*I William take the(e) Anne to my wedded wyfe, to haue and to hold from thys day forwarde, for better, for worse, for richer, for porer, in sickenes, and in healthe, to loue and to cheryshe, tyll death vs departe: according to Godes holy ordinaunce, and therto I plight the(e) my trouth.*

They unclasp, then clasp hands again, at the direction of the priest.

*I Anne take the(e) William to my wedded husbande, to haue and to holde, from this day forwarde, for better, for worse, for richer, for poorer, in sickenes, and in health, to loue, cherish, and to obey, till death vs departe.*

Now William Shakespeare repeats after the priest the irremediable declaration:

*With this ring I the(e) wed: with my body I the(e) worship: and with all my worldly goodes, I the(e) endow.*

Anne Hathaway had married the alderman's son. She had thrown off the yoke of her stepmother. Her child would be a

Shakespeare. It would be legitimate. 'Be frutiful and multiply,' saith the Lord; to which the priests say 'Amen' if they get their fee. If not, they have their revenge: 'bastard' or 'notha' in the parish register after a hapless infant's name.

### 6.

In the bitter winter of 1582 William Shakespeare brought his bride to the trio of houses on Henley Street, in accordance with the antique custom which lodged the eldest son and his wife under the parental roof as a visible sign of succession and inheritance. But more was involved than mere custom: none could say with certainty that Master John Shakespeare had disapproved of the marriage. Outwardly, at least, there was peace.

The newlyweds were given the 'back' of the middle house, a separate little dwelling, cross-timbered outside, which projected into the garden and had its own entrance there. There was a kitchen and parlor on the ground floor, which was heated by a large open fireplace. The bedroom, with a window on the garden, was upstairs. A small stairway in the upper story joined the 'back' to the front house.

The household to which the newlyweds came contained four Shakespeare children besides William: Gilbert, sixteen; John, thirteen; Richard, nine, and Edmund, two. A year before Edmund's birth another child of John and Mary Shakespeare had died— Anne, aged seven and a half. Now another Anne had come to that house of memories.

Mary Arden Shakespeare bestirred herself to establish harmony: wifely admonitions to the alderman, her husband, motherly advice to her erring son; well-intentioned efforts to make her daughter-in-law comfortable. Perhaps quizzical looks passed between Gilbert and Joan as they took the measure of their sister-in-law. The newcomer ingratiated herself by ministering to the infant Edmund.

### 7.

Marriages are made in heaven, but must be endured below.

William Shakespeare had not only married against his inclinations, but very probably found himself in the ignominious position of a husband whose wife, being eight years older, and swelling with all the complacencies of her pregnancy, treated him like a son or younger brother. The memory of Shottery meadows in September could only rankle; bright summer and autumn had given way to a bleak and uneasy season; the first drafts of discontent, loathing and regret were writ large in the cogitations of that winter and early spring:

> If thou dost break her virgin knot before
> All sanctimonious ceremonies may
> With full and holy rite be minister'd,
> No sweet aspersion shall the heavens let fall
> To make this contract grow; but barren hate,
> Sour-ey'd disdain and discord shall bestrew
> The union of your bed with weeds so loathly
> That you shall hate it.

Six months after his marriage, on May 26, 1583, 'Susanna daughter to William Shakespeare' was baptized. There was no exegesis to this brief text in the parish register. The child was legitimate.

Why Susanna? First-born daughters were usually named for their mothers. Susanna does not occur in the family, and is not to be found among the Shakespeares' neighbors. It suggests 'the chaste Susanna' of the Bible. Was the name chosen by the bitter father, as a constant reminder to the child to be chaste—as her mother had not been? If so, it proved ironic.

### 8.

In his first important act in the world of men and women—the toilers at trades and the bearers and upbringers of children, who grow old imperceptibly, their memories a homespun cloth sparsely embroidered with bright moments—William Shakespeare had met with complete and overwhelming failure. He probed himself, but could find no answer in the sour-eyed disdain of his conjugal relationship. He turned to books, and books told him what he needed to know. His troubled spirit was subtly lighted by a gradual awareness that he was not as other men. This secret knowledge of intellectual and creative powers, at once gratifying and disturbing, brought with it the desire and the dream of complete realization, somewhere, sometime. The provincial youth who was to become the greatest poet who ever lived, and the most understanding of men, began now to evaluate himself differently; and in the process his mind stored itself with the richest treasure-trove of images, and observations of the world and its complex inhabitants, ever to come from a single pen. Thus, in time, he turned his temporary defeat into an eternal triumph.

What was the secret? It is not necessary to look for lords between the lines. If we acknowledge the possibility of a youth possessing exquisite sensibilities, intuition and great perceptive powers, logic suggests the probability of another endowed with more exquisite sensibilities, subtler intuition and greater perception. Given the existence of poets, logic must grant the possibility of a poetic genius surpassing all. Thus at every stage in the history of creative art the possibility has existed of an artist who would tower among his own kind because of a combination of sensitivity, perception and creative powers to a superlative degree. That combination appeared in William Shakespeare as England began to glow with the tardy brightness of the Renaissance. The catalyst was Ovid.

## 9.

In his Old Court chamber in Corpus Christi College, hearing the bells of St. Bene't's Church and the more ancient St. Botolph chiming the hours away, and under their flights of sound a subtler music, Christopher Marlowe translated Ovid's *Amores*. It is a literary coincidence worth noting, that two such men as William Shakespeare and Christopher Marlowe, born within two months of each other, should have been, at the same period in their lives, under the spell of the Latin poet; and this on the eve of their appearance in London, one to revolutionize the English drama, the other to give it and to posterity the greatest works of art in that medium.

The fascination of Ovid for a young poet is apparent in Marlowe's translations. Ovid rehearses the great names of bards and heroes, gods and nymphs; Rome rises in marble from his lines, Troy in flames; Jove pursues the daughters of men, and Jason seeks the Golden Fleece. He also praises earthly love, with great charm (but sometimes so realistically that Marlowe's translations were ordered burned by the Archbishop of Canterbury and the Bishop of London):

Then came *Corinna* in a long loose gown,
Her white neck hid with tresses hanging down,
Resembling fair *Semiramis* going to bed,
Or *Lais* of a thousand wooers sped.
I snatched her gown—being thin, the harm was small,
Yet striv'd she to be covered there withal.

He excuses his occupation—

Envy, why carpest thou my time is spent so ill,
And terms't my works fruits of an idle quill?—

and proclaims the eternity of verse:

when Flint and Iron wear away,
Verse is immortal, and shall ne'er decay.

The theme is constant:

Let base, conceited wits admire vile things,
Faire *Phoebus* lead me to the Muses' springs.
About my head be quivering myrtle wound,
And in sad lovers' heads let me be found.

# CHAPTER VII

## Farewell to Stratford

### 1.

IT IS THE beginning of William Shakespeare's mysterious period; the whole of the next year, after the birth of his daughter, is a blank so far as records of him are concerned; but lest the worshipers of lords should step in and nod their foolish heads wisely, it should be added that the period is no more mysterious and no more blank than is to be expected, for we are as yet dealing with an unknown youth in a provincial town.

Perhaps he assisted his father—such is the tradition; perhaps he made a first, tentative visit to London, calling on his boyhood friend Richard Field, 'sonne of Henry FFeilde of Stratford vppon Aven,' who four years before had 'put him self Apprentis to george byshop citizen and staconer of London for vij yeres,' and who had agreed to serve the first six with Thomas Vautrollier, Huguenot printer of Blackfriars, to learn 'ye art of printinge.' Of this, more later. Three theatrical companies visited Stratford in 1584—the Earl of Oxford's Men, the Earl of Warwick's and the Earl of Essex's. Perhaps he accompanied one of these to London.

Certain it is that he read, and that he stored his mind with bright images in this somber time, gazing from his window at the apples and roses of the garden and orchard, or walking cloaked in his thoughts amid the sounds and sweet airs that gave delight and hurt not.

### 2.

He had incentive enough, and troubles enough, to bid him fly; nevertheless, there is a tradition that he left Stratford because of poaching difficulties. He was (says Richard Davies, rector of Sapperton, Gloucestershire, a century later), 'much given to all unluckinesse in stealing venison & Rabbits particularly from Sᵣ Lucy who had him oft whipt & sometimes Imprisoned & at last made Him fly his Native Country to his great Advancemᵗ. but his reveng was so great that he is his Justice Clodpate and calls him a great man & $y^t$ in allusion to his name bore three lowses rampant for his Arms.'

Vague as it is, it was expanded a few years later still by Nicholas Rowe, Shakespeare's first biographer, to the following: 'He had, by a Misfortune common enough to young Fellows, fallen into ill Company; and amongst them, some that made a frequent practice of Deer-stealing, engag'd him with them more than once in robbing a Park that belong'd to Sir *Thomas Lucy* of *Cherlecot,* near *Stratford.* For this he was prosecuted by that Gentleman, as he thought, somewhat too severely; and in order to revenge that ill Usage, he made a Ballad upon him. And tho' this, probably the first Essay of his Poetry, be lost, yet it is said to have been so very bitter, that it redoubled the Prosecution against him to that degree, that he was oblig'd to leave his Business and Family in *Warwickshire,* for some time, and shelter himself in *London.*'

Rowe, taking his cue from the Rev. Richard Davies, turned to Shakespeare's work, and discovered the identity of Justice Clodpate: 'Amongst other Extravagances, in *The Merry Wives of Windsor,* he has made him [Falstaff] a Dear-stealer, that he might at the same time remember his *Warwickshire* Prosecutor, under the Name of Justice *Shallow;* he has given him very near the same Coat of Arms which *Dugdale,* in his Antiquities of that County, describes for a Family there.'

The Lucy coat of arms bore three luces, or pikes; Slender, in referring to Justice Shallow, gives him a dozen white luces; Evans pronounces it 'louses'; and Shallow himself states that 'The luce is the fresh fish.'

Unfortunately for the foregoing account, however, while Sir Thomas Lucy did indeed live at Charlecote, near Stratford, he did not have a deer park; and deer stealing, in any event, was not an offense against the owner of a park, but against the Crown, for which the punishment was abjuration—that is, perpetual exile from the realm. The tradition is wrong legally, and may therefore be wrong otherwise; especially since a more likely prototype of Justice Shallow will make his appearance.

It is possible—more, probable—that Shakespeare, in common with other country youths, in his younger days snared rabbits. The rabbits grew into deer with his reputation. In *The Winter's Tale,* the facts of his own case seem to be stated clearly enough: 'I would there were no age between sixteen and three-and-twenty, or that youth would sleep out the rest; for there is nothing in the between but getting wenches with child, wronging the ancientry, stealing, fighting.' But even this is inconclusive; for it is the business of a dramatist to observe life.

### 3.

A year elapsed after the birth of Susanna before Anne Shakespeare conceived again. She bore twins, baptized February 2, 1585, perhaps with their father absent; for the parish register's spelling is 'less precise than on the previous occasion: 'Hamnet & Judeth sonne & daughter to Williā Shakspere,' although not too much can be made of this, considering the vagaries of Elizabethan orthography. The children were sponsored by Hamnet Sadler, baker of High Street, and his wife Judith. They are the last of Anne Shakespeare's offspring.

With this record from the parish register, William Shakespeare disappears from Stratford, his brief reconcilement with his wife over. It is possible that he was a visitor in 1592; but a decade was to pass before he resolved to resettle in Stratford. He returned, wealthy and renowned, to purchase New Place, the 'great house' across the street from the King's Grammar School, and help his father acquire a coat of arms.

### 4.

He was twenty-one years old. The tradition that takes him at once to London and the theater is well attested.

John Ward, vicar of Stratford, 1662-1681, wrote in his diary, presumably after inquiries: 'hee frequented $y^e$ plays all his younger time.'

John Aubrey, indefatigable compiler of notes concerning the great men of his own and the preceding age, wrote (*circa* 1681, with a wreath in the margin of his manuscript as a mark of homage): 'Wm. being inclined naturally to Poetry and acting, came to London I guesse about 18. and was an Actor at one of the Play-houses and did act exceedingly well: now B. Johnson was never a good Actor, but an excellent Instructor. He began early to make essayes at Dramatique Poetry, which at that time was very lowe; and his Playes tooke well: He was a handsome well shap't man: very good company, and of a very readie and pleasant smooth Witt.' Aubrey is not always accurate, and it is possible that he allowed his enthusiasm to make his pen run, at least as regards that bit about acting.

The Rev. Richard Davies also noted: 'From an Actor of Playes, he became a Composer.' And a Mr. Dowdall, in a letter to a cousin, tells how he visited Stratford, talked to the parish clerk—'aboue 80 y$^{rs}$ old'—and got from him the story that Shakespeare ran away to London 'and there was Rec$^d$ Into the playhouse as a serviture, and by this meanes had an oppertunity to be w$^t$ he afterwards prov'd.'

### 5.

Nicholas Rowe also recounts the tradition that the poet ran away from Stratford, and that upon coming to London 'he was receiv'd into the Company then in being, at first in a very mean Rank'—an echo from Dowdall and the other sources previously quoted; 'but his admirable Wit, and the natural Turn of it to the Stage, soon distinguish'd him, if not as an extraordinary Actor, yet as an excellent Writer. His Name is Printed, as the Custom was in those Times, amongst those of the other Players, before some old Plays, but without any particular Account of what sort of Parts he us'd to play; and tho' I have inquir'd, I could never meet with any further Account of him this way, than that the top of his Performance was the Ghost in his own *Hamlet*.' The last sounds like a sly guess or jest.

It is a pity that Rowe did not track down the identity of the 'Company then in being,' for it would not only have told us something about Shakespeare's early career in London—it might have saved scholars many laborious but inconclusive researches, and readers the tedium of reading them without becoming any the wiser. But more than making up for this lapse is Rowe's characterization of his subject which, while it echoes Aubrey's, may have come from other sources as well: 'Besides the advantages of his Wit, he was in himself a good-natur'd Man, of great sweetness in his Manners, and a most agreeable Companion; so that it is no wonder if with so many good Qualities he made himself acquainted with the best Conversations of those Times. Queen *Elizabeth* had

several of his Plays Acted before her, and without doubt gave him
many gracious Marks of her Favour.' Those who know that frigid
and frugal monarch may doubt this—at least in so far as the Marks
were marks; for she never gave anyone money when her approval
sufficed.

There were others who were less chary. Rowe says: 'What Grace
soever the Queen confer'd upon him, it was not to her only he ow'd
the Fortune which the Reputation of his Wit made. He had the
Honour to meet with many great and uncommon Marks of Favour
and Friendship from the Earl of *Southampton,* famous in the
Histories of that Time for his Friendship to the unfortunate Earl
of *Essex.*'

And now comes Rowe's summation, giving the quintessence of
Shakespeare's character as a man, as it lived on in men's thoughts
of him: 'What particular Habitude or Friendships he contracted
with private Men, I have not been able to learn, more than that
every one who had a true Taste of Merit, and could distinguish
Men, had generally a just Value and Esteem for him. His exceeding Candor and good Nature must certainly have inclin'd all the
gentler Part of the World to love him, as the power of his Wit
oblig'd the Men of the most delicate Knowledge and polite Learning to admire him.'

### 6.

Such was Shakespeare the man as his century drew to a close.
There seems to be no doubt in these writers' minds that their illustrious subject was anyone but William Shakespeare of Stratford-
upon-Avon.

BOOK TWO

# CHAPTER I

## A Portrait of William Shakespeare

### 1.

THE allusions by his contemporaries, and in tradition, offer the materials for a composite portrait of a man whom it must have been a delight, as it undoubtedly was an honor, to know and to meet on intimate terms. He is 'gentle Shakespeare,' 'friendly Shakespeare,' civil, upright in his dealings; 'a handsome well shap't man: very good company, and of a very readie and pleasant smooth Witt'; and at length, in the first biographical synthesis of his character, 'a good-natur'd Man, of great sweetness in his Manners, and a most agreeable Companion.'

Stroke by stroke, this is Heminge and Condell's 'so worthy a Friend.'

### 2.

From the engraving in the First Folio, which was probably copied from a painting, William Shakespeare, pallid and aloof, gives back the curious gaze of generation after generation of scholars and worshipers. There is the high, intellectual forehead, framed in life, it is conjectured, by auburn hair; and beneath thin eyebrows, the small but penetrating hazel eyes, the straight, aristocratic nose, nostrils sensitive and flaring; and a mouth which, while shaped like a Cupid's bow, is nevertheless firm and determined in its sweetness.

He looks out, as generation follows generation, detached and enigmatic, distant and Olympian, a lone figure, towering in men's thoughts, a monument and a man. Love and unparalleled homage are his, and the rituals of worship, whose harmony is marred by recurrent heresies, as when small sects question if he ever lived, or if it was indeed he who wrote. Nor is it to be wondered at that his godhead is questioned. Ordinary men cannot measure his solitary greatness, or their minds encompass the infinite variety of his thought.

### 3.

The hierarchy of major and minor poets exists without him, for he exists alone.

Had he been only the author of the songs in his plays, or of the two narrative poems to which he put his name, his degree in the hierarchy of poets would have been a high one.

Had he been only the author of his sonnets, his degree would have been higher still, one of the highest—such greatness is in them, such lines and stanzas and complete poems illumine the dark depths of this enigmatic sequence.

It is when we come to his plays that we see his unique position.

In his multitudinous characterizations, populating the theater as a god a world; in his sympathies and understanding of human motives and actions; and in his imagery and versification, brightness upon brightness, and harmony following harmony, he is without a peer; and this in comedy, tragedy and history (the chronicle plays of kings). Finally, since we are dealing with a dramatic poet, his dramas remain actable as century follows century; and they can also be read.

### 4.

The Folio engraving is, for the present, the only authentic representation of Shakespeare that we have. It is accompanied in that work by the following tribute to the man and his likeness:

> This figure, that thou here seest put,
>     It was for gentle Shakespeare cut;
> Wherein the Graver had a strife
>     With Nature, to out-do the life:
> O, could he but have drawn his wit
>     As well in brass, as he hath hit
> His face, the Print would then surpass
>     All that was ever writ in brass.
> But, since he cannot, Reader, look
>     Not on his Picture, but his Book.

Despite the conventionality of some of the phrasing, common to portrait-verses of the time, Ben Jonson, who wrote this, approves the portrait of his friend, however inadequate as art or as a likeness it appears to us. The emphasis, however, is on Shakespeare's wit, i.e., his work. Let us turn, therefore, as Jonson advises, to Shakespeare's book, wherein that work is contained.

# CHAPTER II

## *Shakespeare and His Master*

### 1.

THERE are no movements; only artists.

An artist is one who creates works of art.

The work of an artist is his autobiography. It is interesting, but not essential, to know the facts of his birth and death. His work tells us that he lived.

An artist is not one who creates fragments. If we are to give place and praise to fragments, let it be those of the masters, who have so busied themselves in the endeavors of art as to have left fragmentary works behind, in addition to their other works; and such fragments, as a rule, as lesser men cannot achieve.

The work of lesser men—that is, much that is usually considered art—is merely a medium for remembrance. The part-artist reminds us of experiences we have had, but he does not create them for us. We respond to him occasionally because at times we need very little to stir us—the race goes steeped in memories.

A work of art, on the other hand, offers us a new experience. That is the difference between first-rate work and all the other categories and degrees.

It is not subject matter that differentiates one work from another, but feeling and form. It is never an 'original' idea, chiefly because there are no original ideas. The race is so old, it is inconceivable that a newcomer can have a thought which has eluded our tragic and thoughtful species. That which puerile minds call original is usually only novel, and often only bizarre.

It is not the length, but the depth of works that makes them great. The world is so much with us, only intensity can penetrate and affect our overfreighted minds; and that intensity must have a form.

Feeling and form are all; and that man is most an artist who fuses these two into an indivisible one.

In the art of poetry, Shakespeare is the supreme artist, and Christopher Marlowe was his master.

### 2.

Christopher Marlowe appeared in London in the summer of 1587 after a troubled and troublesome sojourn of six years at Cambridge, during which he absented himself considerably, at least once on government service in counter-espionage against the Catholics. Cambridge was glad to see the last of him, particularly as it was clear he did not wish to be ordained after his course in divinity. That illustrious but surprised mother of poets would even have sent him out into the world bare of honors if the Privy Council had not intervened to request 'that he should be furthered in the degree he was to take this next Commencement: Because it was not her majesties pleasure that anie one emploied as he had been in matters touching the benefitt of his Countrie should be defamed by those that are ignorant in th'affaires he went about.'

Christopher Marlowe, M.A., was a true type of the Renaissance man—scholar, poet, adventurer, scorning religion yet apprehensive of salvation:

> I do repent, and yet I do despair;
> Hell strives with grace for conquest in my breast;
> What shall I do to shun the snares of death?

He rejected Christianity, and fell in love with the pagan world symbolized by Helen; and he can be traced in anonymous works by the light of burning Troy.

He was the greatest of the young Elizabethans. Without Shakespeare he would have stood first in that age, so often in a new form is the innovator the master. He came brimful of poetry, steeped in reading, able to take a plain sentence in Holinshed, viz.: 'He was tall of stature, and well proportioned,' and instantly transmute it to:

> Of stature tall, and straightly fashioned,
> Like his desire, lift upwards and divine.

He had read the classics as well as the Bible; he had translated Ovid, and adapted Virgil in a first play about Aeneas and Dido. He was sure of himself and ambitious; his face glowed with 'the

quenchless fire' of his protagonists—those already portrayed and
those to come—and he took admiration as his due. He came, tinged
with cynicism from his contact with ecclesiastics, and full of incau-
tious contempt for the writers of his day, and at twenty-three began
that brief and spectacular career in which he revolutionized the
theater and English poetry with it.

### 3.

However Shakespeare met Marlowe, evidence exists in his work
of friendship, affection and admiration for his great contemporary,
to be presented in its proper place. His own spirit began to glow
with the 'quenchless fire' of Marlowe's ardor. Through him he
discovered a new world, peopled by the sleeping populace within
books. A quill dipped in ink brought kings and renowned deeds out
of the limbo of printed words into light and life. It was years
before he closed the door of the tiring room behind him; but the
study door swung open anew.

Shakespeare would have been Shakespeare without Marlowe;
but he would have been a different Shakespeare, modeled on someone else, someone without Marlowe's vision and splendor: Lily,
Kyd, Peele, Greene or Nashe—all admirable and estimable authors; but no master among them. Fortunate is that writer who
finds, at the outset of his career, a great contemporary or forerunner worthy of imitation, that he may learn to fashion his lines,
at least, on an acceptable model. No writer ever begins by himself,
out of himself, and Shakespeare was fortunate in having Marlowe
to inspire and guide him. Marlowe's blank verse, lyrical and pulsing
with life, gave Shakespeare the structure and movement of his own.

Marlowe began by insulting his contemporaries in a prologue
scorning rhymed verse, in which many plays were then written:

> *From jigging veins of rhyming mother wits,*
> *And such conceits as clownage keeps in pay,*
> *We'll lead you to the stately tent of War*
> *Where you shall hear the Scythian* Tamburlaine
> *Threat'ning the world with high astounding terms;*

and then he showed them how to write iambic pentameter, in
which a few had been attempted:

Your Majesty shall shortly have your wish,
And ride in triumph through *Persepolis*.

And ride in triumph through *Persepolis?*
Is it not brave to be a King, *Techelles?*
*Usumcasane* and *Theridimas*,
Is it not passing brave to be a King,
And ride in triumph through *Persepolis?*

O my Lord, 'tis sweet and full of pomp.

# CHAPTER III

## *'The Flower of Cities All'*

### 1.

A DESCRIPTION of London, made for Queen Elizabeth in 1588 by William Smith, Rouge Dragon Pursuivant of the College of Arms, gives the following statistics: 'This roiall & famous Citty standeth on y$^e$ north side of the River of Thamise, which River is there a thousand foote brode; over which there is a goodly Bridge of stone, which hath 20 arches, y$^t$ are 60 foote in height, 30 in thickness, & distant one from another 20 foote. On both sydes of the Bridge, are howses builded, in such sort that it seemeth rather a continuall street than a Bridge. London is 3 myles long (accompting Westminster withall), and is two myles brode, reckoning Southwark and its bridge. It is devyded into 26 wardes, and hath 108 parish churches w$^{th}$in the walles & xi w$^{th}$out y$^e$ walles, but yet w$^{th}$in the liberties, which is in all 119. Westminster lyeth at y$^e$ West end of London, lyke the suburbes, and was of late by Quene Elizabeth made a Cittie.' It was a metropolis of violent contrasts where splendor and poverty, horror and beauty, were juxtaposed: the heads of traitors grinned from London Bridge, a snowfall of swans dappled the Thames.

Marlowe and Shakespeare's audience was the spectator of the pride and pageantry of Tudor England: queen, court, ambassadors, in resplendent dress; noblemen and cardinals, mayor and corporation, all attended by pages and servingmen, esquires and soldiery, wearing bright liveries and badges. This audience had seen the burning of heretics in Smithfield; it still saw, at Tyburn, daily, the condemned in clusters on ladders, pushed off, momentarily strangled by their halters, then cut down; and as breath and blood began to function again, their bellies slit open and their bowels ripped out and thrown upon a fire at the gallow's foot, before the victims fell as dead of horror as of the hangman's incision.

It was an audience that saw beheading and quartering—dripping heads, hewn limbs and skewered torsos set up on London Bridge and the gates of the city as a terror and warning. It saw the marble palaces on the riverside, where the nobility and gentry, and the proud and grasping prelates, shored up the goods of the world, while the poor swarmed in their hovels or filled the nightmare prisons of the city. It saw bawds and brawlers trudging behind carts, to which their hands were tied, their backs bare and bleeding from the lashes of beadles at crossroads. It saw, when it left the city for the suburbs, the swarms of ragged, misbegotten, misshapen beggars and dwarfs, and amputated soldiery, whining at the gates. It heard, but heeded not, the cries of the mad folk chained and beaten in Bedlam.

It was an audience for strong fare—revenge, torture, inhuman wrongs and inhuman grief. To criticize an Elizabethan play for its horrors is to rip its pages from the context of its time.

### 2.

Plays were first performed in the yards of the great inns of the city, on stages made of planks laid over barrelheads. The yard, and the balconies surrounding the yard, provided accommodations for spectators. (When the first theater was built, it was constructed like an innyard without the inn.)

There were troubles.

By a proclamation of 1559, the second year of Elizabeth's reign, the mayors of incorporated towns and justices of the peace had been empowered to license theatrical performances, save for plays dealing with 'matters of religion or of the gouernaunce of the estate of the common weale.' The City of London, whose corporation was made up of substantial businessmen with puritanical leanings, opposed plays on the grounds that they lured apprentices and servants from their work; that the large gatherings at performances called for special policing to prevent disorders; that they spread infection in time of plague; and that they were, in general, sinful.

In this they were aided and abetted by the clergy.

Ever since theatrical representations had left their swaddling clothes behind in the churches where they began, the clergy had been an enemy to the people's theater, as distinct from ecclesiastical or moral mummery. The clergy as a class, having made it their business to treat this world merely as a preparation for the next, must by the inexorable logic of their profession frown upon any form of merriment or pleasure here below. It is not due to them that the theater started up at all, or that it became a permanent part of community life.

The Elizabethan preacher's logic went like this: 'the cause of plagues is sin, if you look to it well: and the cause of sin are plays: therefore the cause of plagues are plays.' This is puerile stuff; but there were plagues, there was plenty of superstition, along with the dirt, and the Lord Mayor of London and his council were made to hearken—by their predilections, willingly. The players were often ordered out of the city; and wandering after uncertain livelihood in the provinces, were picked up as vagrants or masterless men. They thereupon sought and obtained the protection of various noblemen, who procured them licenses to act, and whose liveries or badges they afterwards wore. As the 'servants' of a nobleman they were immune to the hostility of provincial clergy and constables, as regards their persons; but this was not in itself a guarantee of receipts. They returned from some of these excursions tattered and impoverished, to plead with their protectors for the right to perform in London.

The Privy Council, sometimes to satisfy a great nobleman, sometimes by the intercession of the Queen herself, directed the Lord Mayor to permit plays to be presented within the city. Occasionally the troupes put on plays in the innyards in defiance of Lord Mayor and Privy Council.

Elizabeth, who was fond of plays for her 'solace,' gave her protection to a company known as the Queen's Men, who thus achieved the status of royal servants. To molest her troupe aroused her Tudor ire. At length, in 1581, in order to offset the interference of the London government, her Privy Council empowered the Master of the Revels to authorize or 'put down' all performances, not only in the metropolis, but everywhere in England, which gave back to the Crown the powers granted to communities in 1559.

Royalty, nobility and literacy were thus on the side of the players; and opposing them was the Puritan corporation assisted by the clergy. It was not satisfactory for the players.

3.

When Marlowe and Shakespeare came to London, plays were

still being presented in the innyards, but three theaters for professional troupes had been built outside the city and its meddlesome jurisdiction, yet close enough to draw crowds.

The first was *The Theatre*, in the Liberty of Shoreditch, built by James Burbage in 1576. Burbage was the right man to build the first theater for public entertainment in England. He was pugnacious, and ever ready to defy City corporation and Privy Council whenever they sought to interfere. He had been a carpenter; he approached the project with a practical eye and mind. He had been a theatrical manager, in charge of the Earl of Leicester's company. And he had been an actor. The needs of actors and audience were considered in his design.

The Theatre, judging by contemporary allusions, was either polygonal or circular, 'vast,' with three galleries, one above the other, surrounding a 'yard.' It was built of wood, with the exterior of lime and plaster. The yard was open to the sky, but the galleries were roofed. The stage, with a tiring house at the rear, projected into the yard. The action, as a result, could not have been observed in its entirety except by 'groundlings' at the apex of the stage; so that a good speaking voice was probably a better recommendation for an actor than any marked dramatic ability. The decorations were ornate; a preacher at Paul's Cross thundered against the Theatre as 'the gorgeous playing place' as soon as it was erected. The materials used in the construction of the Theatre were afterwards pulled down and used in the construction of *The Globe*, a venture financed by Cuthbert and Richard Burbage, sons of James, and various actors of the Lord Chamberlain's company, among them John Heminge and William Shakespeare; of which, more later.

The second was *The Curtain*, so-called not because of any connection with a theater curtain, but taking its name either from a curtain (a species of battlement) in the city wall, or from *cortina*, a court or close. As the Curtain, like the Theatre, was built expressly for the showing of plays, it may be assumed that its general construction and appearance were like its nearby prototype, which it followed by a year. We do not know for certain who the original owner was; probably the Henry Lanman who, in 1585, agreed to divide the profits of both theaters with James Burbage, a logical business procedure, since the overflow from one playhouse usually found accommodation in the other. Thus a monopoly was established which was broken in 1587 by the erection of *The Rose* in the Liberty of the Clink, Southwark, across the river from London, a region where other amusements flourished, including bowling and bear-baiting, dicing and prostitution.

The Rose took its name from its location, Rose Alley and Maiden Lane, in the parish of St. Saviour's. It was a circular building, said to have been more magnificent than those erected in Shoreditch, of timber, with an exterior of lath and plaster, a thatched roof, and complete with galleries, which were partitioned and could be curtained off for private performances, i.e., of gallants and their ladies; or so the preachers said. Its builder was Philip Henslowe, dyer, pawnbroker, tenement owner, and collector of rents from Bankside brothels for the Bishop of Winchester. His interest in the theater was that of a businessman; he saw it solely as a source of revenue, with the examples of the Theatre and the Curtain before him.

The Rose had the advantage of being close to the Surrey end of London Bridge, and citizens could come to performances on foot or in the boats of the watermen, who now added their protests to those of the players whenever theaters were shut down because of brawls or plague. There was another theater in Surrey which lacked this advantage of proximity to the metropolis, and as a consequence did not prosper. It was located at Newington Butts, where once the English yeomen practiced archery. It was a mile from the bridge, too far for pleasure seekers who came on foot. It fell into disuse. Little is known of it, save that Shakespeare acted there, and that both his and Marlowe's plays were performed there when Henslowe, repairing the Rose, sent his companies temporarily to Newington.

This is a Puritan view of theatrical entertainment: 'In the playhouses at London it is the fashion of youthes to go first into the yarde and to carry theire eye through euery gallerie: then like vnto rauens, where they spye the carion thither they flye and presse as nere to the fairest as they can: instead of pomegranates they giue them pippines, they dally with their garments to passe the time, they minister talke vpon al occasions, and eyther bring them home to theire houses on small acquaintance or slip into tauerns when the plaies are done; he thinketh best of his painted sheath, and taketh himselfe for a jolly fellow, that is noted of most to be busyest with women in all such places.'

4.

Marlowe's *Tamburlaine* was 'sundrie times shewed vpon Stages in the Citie of London. By the right honorable the Lord Admyrall, his seruantes.' The Admiral's Men also acted at the Theatre and the Rose. They may have met at either place—Marlowe, the most famous dramatic poet of the day, and Shakespeare, as yet an obscure but extremely personable actor. Perhaps for a time they were even employed by the same company, a supposition which cannot be proved or disproved; but if so, both would have come to the attention of Charles Lord Howard of Effingham, the Lord Admiral, the company's protector; and through him to other noblemen. What this might imply for an actor is problematical; but for a playwright it is at least probable that the nobleman for whose company he wrote might tender him some patronage to eke out the fees of the producers—four or five pounds for a play, even a collaboration.

The writers of Elizabeth's reign were prolific as well as gifted, and they were prolific because they had to be to live, which concentrates an author's mind wonderfully. Playwriting was their livelihood as well as profession. That it was more the former than the latter is indicated by their indifference to great works which, being handed over for production, and paid for, ceased to be their concern; unless, perhaps, as actors in them. A species of scholastic snobbery incomprehensible to later times made them see their slightest verses through the press, while disdaining to print their dramatic works. The theatrical companies, on their part, jealously guarded the scripts thus obtained, lest printers get hold of them; but they could not prevent copyists in the theater from making garbled versions by a species of shorthand and selling them to the printers. The printers found it profitable to publish the new plays; the book-buying public, growing ever larger, was alive to the merits of the new literature long before the authors of it.

Whether Marlowe and Shakespeare had a patron at the start—it is unlikely that they struggled for long, if at all, without assistance in an age remarkable for patronage of writers—we know that subsequently each had one: the former, Thomas Walsingham, afterwards Sir Thomas, the kinsman of Elizabeth's principal secretary; the latter, the Earl of Southampton. There is no record and no tradition of poverty for either, and no hint of it in their works; which is unusual, considering the struggles and plaints of their fellow dramatists and the ends which overtook some of them.

## 5.

The mere treatment of any subject reveals the personality of the writer. The hold that Marlowe has on the imaginations of men is due to a conception of his character which was first projected by his verse. New-found records of arrests and the last violent act which ended his career at twenty-nine have not altered the portrait, in Peele's beautiful phrase, of 'the Muses' darling.' The style is all.

It is so with Shakespeare. There is a strain which runs through all the plays in the canon which announces they are his, or in part his, and which tells us what their author was. This personal mark is all the more extraordinary when it is considered that his versification changed from the early Marlovian 'drumming decasyllabon,' which can be drummed out with the fingers, to a five-foot line which is more like speech than verse, which flows like prose, and yet has for its pulse and center the basic measure of iambic pentameter, bright with unforced images, and subtle with a native pause and caesura.

He appears prolific only because so much of what he wrote is so good. Thirty-seven plays, and a hand in one or two others not in the canon; two narrative poems and a sequence of sonnets; a sprinkling of songs throughout the plays—it appears like a great deal. Yet if this mass of work is spread out over the thirty years he spent in writing it, it no longer appears so. Thomas Heywood claimed for himself an entire hand or at the least 'a maine finger' in two hundred and twenty plays that he could remember.

London was unable to provide a playgoing public sufficiently large to support a long run, so that every company was a repertory company, offering new plays frequently to attract audiences. The pay for dramatic compositions was small, not only because repertory can set no great store by any single work, but because the competition in Shakespeare's day was enormous, the proof being the great number of plays which have come down, and the allusions to, and the bare titles of, a great number which have not.

Shakespeare can never be understood by setting him apart from his time and from all other writers.

More popular than *Tamburlaine* was a Senecan drama entitled *The Spanish Tragedie*, but equally well known by the name of its protagonist who had given London a proverbial phrase: 'Hieronimo is mad again.' Its author was Thomas Kyd. Murder, madness, groans and ghosts pervade its scenes—'English *Seneca* read by Candlelight yeelds many good sentences, as *Blood is a beggar*, and so forth,' Thomas Nashe sneered when he saw it; yet out of such beginnings came the drama of revenge climaxed by *Hamlet*.

Two such men as Marlowe and Shakespeare, in London to write for the theater, and eager to succeed, could have evaluated the contents and drawing power of *The Spanish Tragedie*—more, it is most probable that as professionals they did—and then decided that they could outhorror its horrors by a collaboration. For now come a play and an attack which can be made to fit such an hypothesis.

## 6.

It is an immutable law of the scholarly world—viz., that any good scene in an anonymous play was written by Shakespeare; and another, that inferior scenes in his acknowledged works are by other hands than his. Thus, to suit an editor's taste and predilections, scenes and sometimes whole plays are rejected—in the case of *Titus Andronicus*, on the ground that it is too full of horrors to be by gentle Shakespeare. It is, however, no more full of horrors than the canonical histories and tragedies. Titus is the ancestor and prototype of Lear. The horrors, however, are of a special kind.

The play starts with the clash of factions seeking the Roman crown, and the slaughter of a captive prince at the tomb of the Andronici where Titus's fallen sons are being interred. Over their bones he chants a Marlovian elegy:

> In peace and honour rest you here, my sons;
> Rome's readiest champions, repose you here in rest.

The mother of the slain prince is Tamora, Queen of the Goths. She has pleaded for his life in vain; now she vows revenge. The

Roman emperor is enamored of her dark beauty and marries her. Thus the means are provided her. Titus has a daughter, beautiful and loving—Lavinia, who greets him thus:

> In peace and honour live Lord Titus long;
> My noble lord and father, live in fame!

Tamora and her two remaining sons encompass the destruction of the Andronici, two of whom are executed for a murder done by them, another banished; while Lavinia herself falls victim to the ghastliest vengeance ever penned, and which only playwrights twenty-five years old could pen: her husband is killed before her eyes, and she is raped by Tamora's sons, who cut out her tongue and lop off her hands so that she may not be able to tell or write the names of her ravishers and maimers, yet live in dishonor. Titus, half mad with grief for his sons, now beholds his daughter:

> What fool hath added water to the sea,
> Or brought a faggot to bright-burning Troy?

By means of Ovid's *Metamorphoses*, Lavinia reveals what happened to her—

> Ravish'd and wrong'd, as Philomela was,
> Forc'd in the ruthless, vast, and gloomy woods.

She is shown how to write in the sand with a staff, and Titus and his kinsmen learn the names of those who bereft her of honor, speech and hands.

Now the theme turns backward to the opening scene, to become revenge revenged. Tamora's sons are slain, their heads baked in pastry, their mother invited to a feast. There, grief-mad Titus kills his daughter:

> Die, die, Lavinia, and thy shame with thee;
> And with thy shame thy father's sorrows die!

He then kills Tamora, and is killed by her husband. The Andronici triumph again as Titus's banished son returns with an army of Goths and becomes emperor.

If the intention of the authors of *Titus Andronicus* was to match the popularity of *The Spanish Tragedie*, they succeeded so well that twenty-five years later it was still remembered and praised—

from the stage—in conjunction with it: 'Hee that will sweare, *Ieronimo,* or *Andronicus* are the best playes, yet, shall passe vnexcepted at, heere, as a man whose Iudgement shewes it is constant' (Ben Jonson, in his Induction to *Bartholomew Fair*).

## 7.

**The** attack occurs in Robert Greene's *Perimedes the Blackesmith,* printed in 1589: 'latelye two Gentlemen Poets, made two mad men of Rome beate it out of their paper bucklers: & had it in derision, for that I could not make my verses iet vpon the stage in tragicall buskins, euerie worde filling the mouth like the faburden of Bo-Bell, daring God out of heauen with that Atheist Tamburlan.'

Perhaps *Titus Andronicus* was introduced on the stage by a prologue which continued Marlowe's formula for antagonizing other dramatists; although the reference to derision may hark back to the prologue to *Tamburlaine.* Greene says: 'I but answere in print, what they haue offered on the Stage.' No prologue to *Titus* has come down, but that is no proof that it did not have one when the play was produced.

*Titus Andronicus* is a good point from which to appraise the powers of Marlowe and Shakespeare, for the play embodies their individual styles to a remarkable degree.

Marlowe's language, from *Tamburlaine* on, is the language of a poet who died young. His blank verse moves with majestic and melodic rhythms to intoxicate the mind—his own as well as ours; for he sometimes lets himself be carried away, and is lost, as a result, in his own musical mazes:

'What is beauty?' saith my sufferings then?
If all the pens that ever poets held,
Had fed the feelings of their masters' thoughts,
And every sweetness that inspir'd their hearts,
Their minds, and muses on admired themes;
If all the heavenly Quintessence they 'still
From their immortal flowers of Poesy,
Wherein as in a mirror we perceive
The highest reaches of a human wit—
If these had made one Poem's period,

And all combin'd in Beauty's worthiness,
Yet should there hover in their restless heads,
One thought, one grace, one wonder at the least,
Which into words no virtue can digest.

He drew from inexhaustible stores of harmony, lighted by images of the antique world. He gave English blank verse its form and movement; and left it to others to develop his creation. His destiny was a high one: he influenced Shakespeare, until Shakespeare developed his own idiom. He wrote at least one masterpiece, and left, besides, great fragments loaded with rifts of ore.

Marlowe can be imitated; Shakespeare cannot. Shakespeare's characters speak blank verse as though it were the language they were born to speak. It is indicative of his high art that he was able to express so much and so well within the limitations of the Elizabethan theater. There were no women on the stage, their roles being played by boys and youths who shaved before performances.

*Titus Andronicus* points the direction which Shakespeare was to take as the supreme moralist and teacher of mankind. Even the assorted horrors of this play may have been an allegory on the cruelty of his time; while Aaron's speech in defense of his color is a forerunner of Shylock's in behalf of his race:

Coal-black is better than another hue,
In that it scorns to bear another hue.

Those who, in this troubled age, ask whether he was prejudiced have not read him aright; there was—and there remains—only a Christian 'problem' of precept and practice, the commentary on which flashes forth in Marlowe and is constant in Shakespeare.

# CHAPTER IV

## The Beginning of the Book

### 1.

THE advance and repulse of the Spanish Armada brought to England a period of universal exultation, followed by an extraordinary upsurge of national consciousness and patriotism fused by hatred of the Roman church. The young theater began to reflect the spirit of the times with plays about England's long struggle with the papacy, and the feats at home and abroad of her warrior-kings.

Such a play is *The Troublesome Raigne of Iohn King of England*, like *Tamburlaine* in two parts, 'As it was (sundry times) publikely acted by the Queenes Maiesties Players, in the honourable Citie of London.' Its prologue states:

> *You that with friendly grace of smoothèd brow*
> *Have entertained the* Scythian Tamburlaine,
> *And given applause unto an Infidel:*
> *Vouchsafe to welcome (with like courtesy)*
> *A Warlike Christian and your Countryman.*
> *For Christ's true faith endur'd he many a storm,*
> *And set himself against the Man of* Rome.

The play links Marlowe and Shakespeare again in this shadowy early period of their careers, for Shakespeare afterwards rewrote it, compressing its ten acts into five, and giving it the title of *The Life and Death of King John*. It is therefore not improper to discuss the Marlowe apocrypha here because of Shakespeare's possible participation in it, the use he made of it, and its influence on him. That influence, considering Marlowe's revolutionary spirit, went beyond playwriting; it gave Shakespeare, who was in all things conservative—save, of course, his marriage—ideas which could not fail to enlarge his humanity. As regards religion, Marlowe's writings and Marlowe's ordinary talk illumined the medieval night:

65

> I count Religion but a childish Toy,
> And hold there is no sin but Ignorance;

and not content with writing it, he was reported to have said: 'That the first beginning of Religioun was only to keep men in awe.'

From table talk to the stage was but a step. It would have been perilous to attack the English church; but jibes at religion in general were slipped in and were overlooked in the general detestation of Rome which the Marlovian drama now embodied, and which met with the approval of audiences recently aroused to keep their land from becoming a fief of the Pope, to be piously handed over to the King of Spain and his mercies. For this was the age which saw the Massacre of St. Bartholomew's Eve, the Marian fires in Smithfield, and the extirpation of great and noble races in the Western world whose lives were valueless since they were heretics, but whose possessions, by a recurrent coincidence of the religious wars, were not:

> What? bring you Scripture to confirm your wrongs?

These were thoughts for Shakespeare to ponder. Religion has not checked, but rather inflamed the passions of men; and this is not to be wondered at, since in all ages, and in all lands, priests have blessed the poison and daggers of assassins, the plottings of factions, and the battle flags of nations marching to war. Yet there never was a time, until perhaps our own, when the church could not have ranged its power and prestige, while it had both, on the side of brotherhood—had it so desired. The concept of heresy reveals the political roots of religion. It is a totalitarian concept: death to those outside the fold.

## 2.

The prologue is not in itself sufficient proof that Marlowe wrote *The Troublesome Raigne;* it may mean only that it and *Tamburlaine* were shown in the same theater. But much of it is in Marlovian tones; witness Act I wherein Falconbridge muses of his royal father, and then blurts out he is Richard's bastard son:

> Methinks I hear a hollow Echo sound
> That *Philip* is the Son unto a King;

> The whistling leaves upon the trembling trees
> Whistle in consort I am *Richard's* Son.

Typical also of Marlowe is the sprinkling throughout *The Troublesome Raigne* of particular classical allusions which he had made or was to make famous elsewhere:

> Must *Constance* speak? let tears prevent her talk;
> Must I discourse? let *Dido* sigh and say,
> She weeps again to hear the wrack of *Troy.*

But what is most typical of Marlowe is the hatred expressed in this play for the religion of Rome. John's character was not a lovable one; his appeal lay chiefly in his defiance of the Pope. He bids the Bastard ransack the religious houses, and this is the scene as Falconbridge reports:

> My Lord, I have performed your Highness' charge:
> The ease-bred Abbots and the bare-foot Friars,
> The Monks, the Priors, and holy cloistered Nuns,
> Are all in health, and were my Lord in wealth,
> Till I had tithed and told their holy hoards.

> Why so, now sorts it, *Philip*, as it should:
> This small intrusion into Abbey trunks,
> Will make the Popelings excommunicate,
> Curse, ban, and breathe out damned orisons,
> As thick as hailstones 'fore the spring's approach,
> But yet as harmless and without effect,
> As is the echo of a Cannon's crack
> Discharged against the battlements of heaven.

### 3.

When John seeks sanctuary in Swinstead Abbey, a monk, with the encouragement of the abbot, resolves to kill him 'and be canonized for a holy Saint' for the deed. The king is poisoned, and dying, prophesies England's final break with the Pope:

> Since *John* did yield unto the Priest of *Rome*,
> Nor he nor his have prospered on the earth;
> Curst are his blessings, and his curse is bliss.

> But in the spirit I cry unto my God,
> As did the Kingly Prophet *David* cry,
> (Whose hands, as mine, with murder were attaint)
> I am not he shall build the Lord a house,
> Or root these Locusts from the face of earth;
> But if my dying heart deceive me not,
> From out these loins shall spring a Kingly branch
> Whose arms shall reach unto the gates of *Rome*,
> And with his feet tread down the Strumpet's pride,
> That sits upon the chair of *Babylon*.

This was proper flattery from the Queen's players to her royal father. The drama ends with a plea for national unity:

> Let *England* live but true within itself,
> And all the world can never wrong her State;

which Shakespeare transformed to the clarion

> Come the three corners of the world in arms,
> And we shall shock them. Nought shall make us rue,
> If England to itself do rest but true.

### 4.

Shakespeare's version of *The Troublesome Raigne* shows him no Catholic. *King John* is as antipapal as its predecessor. He could even have chosen, had he been finicky on the subject, another version of the king's death, which makes no mention of Swinstead Abbey and monkish regicides; for Holinshed relates first that John died of an ague at Newark Castle, and then gives the account which the author of *The Troublesome Raigne* chose.

What is more important than Shakespeare's religion is Shakespeare's superior gift of characterization, as revealed in his version of this play. Falconbridge, from his first blunt utterance, wins King, Queen and audience.

> He hath a trick of Coeur-de-Lion's face,

Elinor exclaims; he bears his father's face proudly, and though he might insult his brother for looking like a Falconbridge, he persuades his mother, in a charming and gallant speech, to be glad that she let Richard lie with her:

Now, by this light, were I to get again,
Madam, I would not wish a better father.
Some sins do bear their privilege on earth,
And so doth yours; your fault was not your folly:
Needs must you lay your heart at his dispose,
Subjected tribute to commanding love,
Against whose fury and unmatched force
The aweless lion could not wage the fight,
Nor keep his princely heart from Richard's hand.
He that perforce robs lions of their hearts
May easily win a woman's. Ay, my mother,
With all my heart I thank thee for my father!

Did ever bastard son talk so to his mother? Knighted Sir Philip Plantagenet by John, he becomes the prop of king, play and all, so winning are his masculine ways in the mincing throngs of courtiers and nobles on the stage.

The classical allusions of the first Constance go back into the study whence they came. Shakespeare's Constance is a woman, who parleys with the Pope's legate and a king thus:

You hold too heinous a respect of grief.

He talks to me, that never had a son.

You are as fond of grief as of your child.

Grief fills the room up of my absent child,
Lies in his bed, walks up and down with me,
Puts on his pretty looks, repeats his words,
Remembers me of all his gracious parts,
Stuffs out his vacant garments with his form:
Then have I reason to be fond of grief.

The learned disputation between Prince Arthur and Hubert in *The Troublesome Raigne* becomes, under Shakespeare's treatment, that scene in Act IV which remained unsurpassed for pathos, even in his later work. This he was able to perform after a few years of apprenticeship in the theater. What Marlowe lacked throughout his brief career, Shakespeare had from the start: absent from them though he was, his roots were in a home where there were children of his own.

# CHAPTER V

## *Exegesis upon a Duel*

### 1.

WHERE did Shakespeare and Marlowe live in London? The surmise that it would be near the playhouses is borne out by the addresses which have come down to us in certain legal documents: Marlowe in the Liberty of Norton Folgate, adjacent to Shoreditch and the Theatre and the Curtain; Shakespeare in Shoreditch itself, St. Helen's, Bishopgate, and the Liberty of the Clink, Bankside, where stood the Rose.

First, Marlowe. In 1589 Marlowe was living in Norton Folgate, as was his friend, Thomas Watson, one of the most renowned of the Elizabethans. Watson is of interest to us because, together with Marlowe, he provided a scene from life for *Romeo and Juliet;* while a sentence spoken in that scene offers a clue to the authorship of *Henry VI*, Part One.

On September 18, 1589, between two and three o'clock in the afternoon, William Bradley, of Gray's Inn Lane's End, Holborn, had strayed so far as to find himself at the other end of London 'in a certain alley called hoglane in the parish of St. Giles without Creplegate,' and there crossing swords with Christopher Marlowe.

Marlowe was not his real quarry, however, but Marlowe's friend, Watson. A few minutes later Watson appeared. 'Whereupon the aforesaid Christopher Morley drew back & ceased to fight. And thereupon the aforesaid William Bradley, seeing the same Thomas Watson thus intervening there with his sword drawn, spoke to him in the following English words, that is to say *(Art thowe nowe come then I will haue a boute w^{th} thee).'*

Watson, fresh for the fray, shortly after drove his sword home. The consequence was that he and Marlowe were taken to Newgate and enrolled as follows: 'Thomas Watson lately of Norton ffowlgate in Middlesex County, gentleman, & Christopher Marlowe lately of the Same, yoman, who were brought to the Gaole the

70

xviij^th day of September by Stephen wyld, Constable, both on Suspicion of murder.'

So much for two of Marlowe's addresses at year's end, 1589. A coroner's jury found Watson had slain Bradley in self-defense. Marlowe was quickly released on a recognizance, and Watson received the Queen's pardon.

## 2.

The report of the coroner, from which the above account of the duel was taken, is in legal Latin, save for that single sentence, the taunt by Bradley, when Watson hove into view: *Art thowe nowe come then I will haue a boute w^th thee.* Now this particular remark by Bradley, heard by the throng which saw the duel in Hog Lane, probably became current in Shoreditch and its environs —" 'Art thou now come,' quotha," etc.—as the story was told and retold for a nine days' wonder. It was indeed an unusual salutation—not 'Have at thee,' as a gentleman might say; but spoken in the manner of one who had a grudge, one who had gone out of his way to make this moment: 'Art thowe nowe come then I will haue a boute w^th thee'; and this spoken, falling dead.

From the duel to a play is no great leap for an era in which men went from plays to duels.

In Act I, Scene V, of *Henry VI*, Part One, Lord Talbot sees the approach of Joan of Arc, and exclaims:

Here, here she comes. I'll have a bout with thee.

Shakespeare might have written this line and the scene in which it is embedded after hearing the tale of the duel as it was told by Marlowe and Watson, or by others. He might even have been present in Hog Lane and seen the duel begin, the intervention of Watson, Marlowe fall back, and Bradley's death. It is like the duel in *Romeo and Juliet*, which seems drawn from life, wherein Tybalt challenges Romeo, and is challenged by Mercutio, who gets his death's wound when Romeo intervenes. Marlowe himself, of course, is a type of Mercutio.

There does not appear to be much of Shakespeare in *Henry VI*, Part One, however; and by a species of braggadocio peculiar to himself, Marlowe becomes the likeliest person to have written the line and the passage in which it is contained. This is all the more probable since much of the play is in his manner (not the manner of an imitator, of whom there were now many). The opening is assuredly his:

> Hung be the heavens with black, yield day to night!
> Comets, importing change of times and states,
> Brandish your crystal tresses in the sky;

as is the ending—

> Thus Suffolk hath prevail'd; and thus he goes,
> As did the youthful Paris once to Greece;
> With hope to find the like event in love,
> But prosper better than the Trojan did.

### 3.

There is, however, another hand in *Henry VI*, Part One: perhaps more than one. Act I, Scene II, lacks the vigor and movement of the opening scene; several other scenes are equally pedestrian; while the rhymed couplets of Act IV are unlike both Marlowe and Shakespeare. We do not know what kind of blank verse Watson wrote, unfortunately, for his plays have disappeared. Who could have written the couplets?

Lord Strange's players opened the season at the Rose on February 19, 1592, with a repertory which included Greene's *Friar Bacon and Friar Bungay*, Marlowe's *Jew of Malta*, and *Henry VI*, Part One. In *Pierce Penilesse*, published the same year, Nashe indicates how enthusiastically *Henry* was received: 'How would it have ioyed braue *Talbot* (the terror of the French) to thinke that after he had lyne two hundred yeares in his Tombe, hee should triumphe againe on the Stage, and haue his bones newe embalmed with the teares of ten thousand spectators at least, (at seuerall times) who, in the Tragedian that represents his person, imagine they behold him fresh bleeding?'

There are better scenes, and some more stirring to the English heart, than the death of Talbot—why, then, did Nashe choose this one, written in rhymed couplets, if it was not by his friend and boon companion, Greene, whom he habitually praised?

Before the year was out, Part Two and Part Three had been written and produced. The link between Shakespeare and Marlowe, and Shakespeare and Greene, so far as the sequels are concerned, is of a different order. This we know from the sources of the two new parts, and from Greene's direct attack on Shakespeare who, it appears, was not only an actor in Lord Strange's troupe, but an adapter of plays.

# CHAPTER VI

## *The Riddle of* Henry VI

### 1.

THE common historical source of *Henry VI*, One, Two and Three, is Holinshed's *Chronicles*. No remarkable deviations from Holinshed's text are apparent in these plays. The playwrights found the turmoils loosed on England by York and Lancaster to their taste, and they did little more than turn the prose of the chronicler into blank verse. For here were princes, cardinals and nobles who bragged of their high birth and illustrious descent, and with the breath left to them after so bragging, broke their oaths to the king and to each other, connived with ruffians and assassins, and in their efforts to attain power and possessions, hacked and hewed their way to the throne itself, quartering their arms and their opponents with equal zest. Not even Shakespeare could show the heart of man more villainous than history showed it; the best he could do was to improve the structure and versification of the metrical version of these bloody annals.

### 2.

We have seen that Part One was, for the most part, a Marlovian work, with some portions probably by Greene, to the whole of which Shakespeare may have given what the scholars like to call a few 'master touches.'

Part Two, however, is a revised version of an earlier play entitled *The first part of the Contention betwixt the two famous Houses of Yorke and Lancaster*. *The Contention* begins where *Henry VI*, Part One, left off. Part Two and *The Contention* open and close with the identical lines and scenes.

Part Three is likewise based on an earlier play, *The True Tragedie of Richard Duke of Yorke*. *The True Tragedie* begins where Part Two and *The Contention* left off. And once again, Part Three and *The True Tragedie* open and close with the same lines, same scenes. A scholarly thesis that the *Contention* and *True*

74

*Tragedie* are merely surreptitious theater copies of Part Two and Part Three falls to pieces on examination.

The title page of *The Contention* does not state by whom it was performed; the title page of *The True Tragedie* tells it was performed by the Earl of Pembroke's Men, for whom Greene was, according to Nashe, 'chief agent of the companie, for he writ more than four other,' until Marlowe supplanted him. Greene, therefore, cannot be left out of any reckoning of the authorship of the two source plays of *Henry VI*; nor can his collaborator, Lodge.

The style, i.e., the personality, of Marlowe and Shakespeare is apparent in their work; but this cannot be said for the lesser men who clustered about them. In their writing for the stage, Greene and Lodge, excellent poets though they were, could only attain to imitations of Marlow, and seem never to have developed an idiom of their own. They fade into obscurity just when the theater is undergoing a new birth, with Marlowe's great work done and Shakespeare emerging into full stature.

## 3.

Marlowe's hand in *The Contention* is everywhere evident, in the versification and typical echoes from his previous works. Even the relationship between the Duke of Suffolk, William de la Pole, and Queen Margaret is patterned on that of the Earl of Mortimer and Queen Isabel in Marlowe's *Edward II* (also produced by Pembroke's Men).

Item, *Edward II:*
    Tell *Isabel* the Queen I looked not thus,
    When for her sake I ran at tilt in France,
    And there unhorsed the Duke of *Cleremont.*

Item, *Contention:*
    I tell thee, Poull, when thou didst run at Tilt,
    And stol'st away our Ladies' hearts in *France,*
    I thought *King Henry* had been like to thee.

Item, *Henry VI,* Part Two:
    I tell thee, Pole, when in the city Tours
    Thou ran'st a tilt in honour of my love,
    And stol'st away the ladies' hearts of France,

I thought King Henry had resembled thee
In courage, courtship, and proportion:
But all his mind is bent to holiness,
To number Ave-Maries on his beads;
His champions are the prophets and apostles;
His weapons holy saws of sacred writ;
His study is his tilt-yard, and his loves
Are brazen images of canoniz'd saints.

This expansion of a speech in *The Contention* shows how much Shakespeare had learned from Marlowe as regards versification, and other things.

### 4.

The conjuring scene in *The Contention* is written with Marlowe's favorite words and lines, and in revising it, because Marlowe's hallmark was on it, Shakespeare not only showed wisdom, but left evidence for all but scholars to perceive how completely untenable the copyist theory is. Part of the conjuring scene in *Henry VI*, Part Two, is in prose. Is it not most unlikely that a copyist hack in the theater would set down in smooth iambic pentameter what had come to his ears as plain prose?

The copyist theory breaks down again in the death of Suffolk by water, as it was prophesied (once more I choose what I believe to be lines by Marlowe):

A Sworder and banditto slave,
Murthered sweet Tully.
Brutus' bastard-hand stabbed Julius Caesar,
And Suffolk dies by Pirates on the seas.

In *Henry VI*, Part Two, the movement of these lines becomes:

A Roman sworder and banditto slave
Murder'd sweet Tully; Brutus' bastard hand
Stab'd Julius Caesar; savage islanders
Pompey the Great; and Suffolk dies by pirates.

With these emendations, a telltale half line of the original is dropped, indicating, if anything, that the copyist theory has been stated in reverse by the scholars.

So much for the verse; what of the prose in *The Contention?*
Who among the university wits writing for the companies then in
being could have written the Jack Cade scenes with their earthy
humor and tolerance of the common man? Who but Shakespeare,
who came from the class of artisans, who had studied them in
Stratford and London, while his colleagues of the theater were
cloistered in colleges studying books?

### 5.

When Suffolk brings Queen Margaret to England in *The Contention,* after having espoused her in Henry's behalf in France,
he tells the king that he has brought

> The happiest gift that ever Marquess gave,
> The fairest Queen that ever King possesst;

but in *The True Tragedie* she has been too long a wife, and too
often aggrieved; she is no longer a woman but a warrior, and worse
than a warrior—what we find her as York is taken on the field:

> Look, York! I dipt this napkin in the blood
> That valiant Clifford with his rapier's point
> Made issue from the bosom of thy boy;
> And if thine eyes can water for his death.
> I give thee this to dry thy cheeks withal.

To which York replies:

> Oh Tigers heart wrapt in a woman's hide!
> How couldst thou drain the life-blood of the child,
> To bid the father wipe his eyes withal,
> And yet be seen to bear a woman's face?

The powerful scene in which these passages occur has the emotional overtones which men have come to associate with Shakespeare. He is not like Marlowe; it cannot be said, by a trick of
words and images and rhythms used over and over: *this is his.*
It is something felt, rather than perceived, throughout his work;
an unmistakable manner in which facility is secondary; the manner
of a man who achieved maturity, while his colleagues did not—
whose horizon went beyond the margins of the classics to circum-
scribe the world.

# CHAPTER VII

## *'There Is an Vpstart Crow . . .'*

### 1.

THE emergence of William Shakespeare from obscurity to fame coincided with the eclipse and death of Robert Greene, M.A., Oxford and Cambridge, one of the most versatile writers of the period as well as one of the most prolific: 'In a night & a day would he haue yarkt vp a Pamphlet as well as in seuen yeare, and glad was that Printer that might bee so blest to pay him deare for the very dregs of his wit,' Nashe wrote idolatrously of his friend. Sometimes, however, his profligacy ran ahead of his ability to produce; he sold a play to the Queen's Men, and when the Queen's Men went into the provinces, he sold it to my Lord Admiral's: 'his only care was to haue a spel in his purse to coniure vp a good cuppe of wine with at all times.'

Poet, playwright, romancer and pamphleteer, Robert Greene was a proud figure with his red beard 'like the spire of a steeple,' expensive doublet, and 'a very faire Cloake with sleeues, of a graue goose turd greene.' This was in his heyday; by midsummer, 1592, he was on the downgrade: 'Who in London hath not heard of his dissolute, and licentious liuing?' a Puritan asked; 'his beggarly departing in euery hostisses debt; his infamous resorting to the Banckside, Shorditch, Southwarke, and other filthy haunts: his obscure lurkinge in basest corners: his pawning of his sword, cloake, and what not, when money came short.'

Thus we find him in September, 1592, his apparel pawned, the Great Pox syphilis racking his bones, his body covered with sores, on his deathbed in a shoemaker's house near Dowgate by the river. He had been picked up in the street. It is the setting for his eclipse: a stranger's house—Greene's last audience a shoemaker and his wife—no friend near, not even Nashe, who may not have known where to find him. He has two visitors before the end: his mistress and their sickly son, whom they have named Fortunatus. They, too, are in want, and they leave him uncomforting and uncomforted.

He is still able to write, and he scribbles a story of 'the follie of youth, the falshood of make-shifte flatterers, the miserie of the negligent, and mischiefes of deceiuing Courtezans'—his own story.

He pens a letter to his deserted wife: 'That I haue offended thee highly I know, that thou canst forget my iniuries I hardly beleeue: yet perswade I my salfe if thou saw my wretched state, thou couldest not but lament it: nay, certainely I knowe thou wouldest. Al my wrongs muster themselues about me, euery euill at once plagues me. For my contempt of God, I am contemned of men: for my swearing and forswearing, no man will beleeue me; for my gluttony, I suffer hunger: for my drunkennesse, thirst: for my adulterie, vlcerous sores.'

He writes still another epistle, '*To those Gentlemen his Quondam acquaintance, that spend their wits in making plaies, R.G. wisheth a better exercise, and wisdome to preuent his extremities.*'

He had with him at the end, unrelinquished when all else was, several of his typical, didactic tales, the last of his manuscripts. The letter to his wife, the epistle to his 'Quondam acquaintance,' are shuffled with these. On September 3, he died; the next day his last benefactors, the shoemaker and his wife, saw him buried. On September 5, the house where he died had a visitor: Gabriel Harvey, the Puritan before mentioned, who drew from his hosts an account of Greene's death; and some time afterwards, another, Henry Chettle, a printer and writer, who picked up Greene's manuscripts.

### 2.

On September 20, the register of the Stationers' Company received the following entry: 'William wrighte Entred for his copie, vnder master watkins hande vppon the perill of Henrye Chettle a booke intituled Greenes *Groatsworth of wyt bought with a million of Repentance.*'

'Vppon the perill of Henrye Chettle' is a most unusual phrase. Thus it was foreseen from the start that the manuscript now being prepared for the press would make trouble.

William Wright, publisher, brought the book out at once, while Greene's sudden and tragic end was still on men's tongues. Revealing and pathetic as the autobiographical portions were, the real sensation was caused by the section addressed to the dead writer's 'Quondam acquaintance.' Four men are chiefly concerned; two are certainly Marlowe and Shakespeare; the third is probably Nashe; the fourth may have been Lodge.

Marlowe is first: 'Wonder not (for with thee wil I first begin) thou famous gracer of Tragedians, that *Greene,* who hath said with thee (like the foole in his heart) There is no God, shoulde now giue glorie vnto his greatness: for penetrating is his power, his hand lyes heauie vpon mee, hee hath spoken vnto mee with a voice of thunder, and I haue felt he is a God that can punish enemies. Why should thy excellent wit, his gift, bee so blinded, that thou shouldst giue no glorie to the giuer?'

Nashe is next: 'With thee I joyne young Juvenall, that byting satyrist, that lastlie with mee together writ a comedie. Sweete boy, might I advise thee, be advised, and get not many enemies by bitter words; inveigh against vaine men, for thou canst do it, no man better; no man so wel.'

Lodge follows: 'And thou, no lesse deserving then the other two, in some things rarer, in nothing inferiour; driven (as my-selfe) to extreame shifts; a little have I to say to thee; and were it not an idolatrous oth, I would sweare by sweet S. George thou art unworthie better hap, sith thou dependest on so meane a stay'— that is, the theater; for now he addresses all three, warning them not to put their trust in the players, for he had done more than they in the theater, only to be neglected at the end: 'Base minded men all three of you, if by my miserie you be not warnd: for vnto none of you (like mee) sought those burres to cleaue: those Puppets (I meane) that spake from our mouths, those Anticks garnisht in our colours. Is it not strange, that I, to whom they all haue beene beholding: is it not like that you, to whome they all haue beene beholding, shall (were yee in that case as I am now) bee both at once of them forsaken?'

Bitter, bitter were his thoughts when he wrote this, for all his late-won piety—the ink has laved his bitterness, steeping it black. He has attacked the players, and admonished those who wrote for them; now, plumbing the depths of his bitterness, he excoriates a writer who is also a player: 'Yes trust them not: for there is an vpstart Crow, beautified with our feathers, that with his *Tygers hart wrapt in a Players hyde,* supposes he is as well able to bombast out a blanke verse as the best of you: and beeing an absolute

*Johannes fac totum,* is in his owne conceit the onely Shakescene in a countrey.'

Three things should be noted here: Shakespeare was an actor 'beautified with our feathers'; he was a writer of blank verse; and he was an adapter of other men's work, a *'Johannes fac totum'* who could do all or anything in the theater. Such was the acknowledgment of his position and powers at the age of twenty-eight, Greene's venom aside.

### 3.

Greene's blast in 1589 against 'that Atheist Tamburlan' was ineffectual. Tamburlaine was historical; he was, in any case, an infidel. But for Marlowe himself to be accused of atheism in print for all to read was fraught with peril from the spiritual and temporal powers, to whom conformity was the outward sign of loyalty. Considering what we know of Marlowe's temperament, and Kyd's account of his 'rashnes in attempting soden pryvie iniuries to men' when aroused, it is not improbable that he went at once to the man responsible for the publication of Greene's book and belabored him with words, if not with his fists. Chettle was a stranger to him at the time; when Marlowe was through with him, Chettle wanted no more of him, as we shall see.

Shakespeare did not have Marlowe's combative spirit. Painful as it was to his proud and sensitive nature to be termed 'an vpstart Crow,' a *'Johannes fac totum,'* and even more derisively, 'the onely Shake-scene in a countrey,' he appears to have taken these insults in silence. But he had friends who were openly outraged by these remarks, and who did not hesitate to protest in his behalf. With this pressure exerted upon him, it appears that Chettle sought Shakespeare out and offered an explanation face to face.

Together with these direct and indirect protests, rumors started up. One of them was to the effect that Chettle himself had forged the manuscript; another, that Nashe had done so. Nashe defended himself at once, and in doing so characterized Greene's book in such a manner as to indicate that he did not believe it to be his late friend's work: 'a scald, triuial, lying pamphlet, cald *Greens groats-worth of wit* is giuen out to be of my doing. God neuer haue care of my soule, but vtterly renounce me, if the least word or sillable in it proceeded from my pen, or if I were any way priuie to the writing or printing of it.' This appeared in the second edition of *Pierce Penilesse,* published about a month and a half after Greene's death—that is, in the middle of October.

Chettle also wrote an explanation, and offered it to Nashe, who was about to put his pamphlet through the press again. Nashe wisely rejected it. It appeared in a book entitled *Kind-Harts Dreame,* which the title page describes as 'Conteining fiue Apparitions, with their Inuectiues against abuses raigning. *Deliuered by seuerall Ghosts vnto him to be publisht, after* Piers Penilesse *Post had refused the carriage.*'

### 4.

The contrast between Marlowe and Shakespeare's characters is nowhere so apparent as in Chettle's appraisal of the two men which appeared in the winter of 1592:

'*About three moneths since died* M. Robert Greene, *leauing many papers in sundry Booke sellers hands, among other his Groats-worth of wit, in which a letter written to diuers playmakers, is offensiuely by one or two of them taken, and because on the dead they cannot be auenged, they wilfully forge in their conceites a liuing Author: and after tossing it to and fro, no remedy, but it must light on me. How I haue all the time of my conuersing in printing hindred the bitter inueying against schollers, it hath been very well knowne, and how in that I dealt I can sufficiently prooue. With neither of them that take offence was I acquainted, and with one of them I care not if I neuer be: The other, whome at that time I did not so much spare, as since I wish I had, for that as I haue moderated the heate of liuing writers, and might haue vsde my owne discretion (especially in such a case) the Author beeing dead, that I did not, I am as sory, as if the originall fault had beene my fault, because my selfe haue seene his demeanor no lesse ciuill than he exelent in the qualitie he professes: Besides, diuers of worship haue reported, his vprightnes of dealing, which argues his honesty, and his facetious grace in writting, that aprooues his Art. For the first, whose learning I reuerence, and at the perusing of* Greenes *booke, stroke out what then in conscience I thought he in some dis-*

*pleasure writ: or, had it beene true, yet to publish it, was*
*intollerable: him I would wish to vse me no worse than I*
*deserue. I had onely in the copy this share, it was il written,*
*as sometimes* Greenes *hand was none of the best, licensd it*
*must be, ere it could be printed, which could neuer be if it*
*might not be read. To be breife, I writ it ouer, and, as neare*
*as I could, followed the copy, onely in that letter I put some-*
*thing out, but in the whole booke not a worde in, for I protest*
*it was all* Greenes, *not mine nor Maister* Nashes, *as some*
*vniustly haue affirmed.'*

### 5.

Chettle's explanation, while it leaves some particulars vague,
carries an over-all impression of credibility. He does not beg abject
pardon of anyone—he even hits back at one of the men whom he
had offended.

He had seen Shakespeare plain. He found him as prepossessing
in real life as he was engaging on the stage. More: men of position
had told him Shakespeare was honorable, and had praised him as
as a writer. He feels regret that he did not tone down Greene's
attack, and his regret rings honestly.

He does not wish to know Marlowe better (after a first encounter?). This, to be sure, is harsh; candor makes him add that
he admires Marlowe's learning, and righteous indignation makes
him state that there was something worse in Greene's letter which
he struck out. What was it? What could have been worse than a
charge of atheism?

He had copied Greene's manuscript, taken out a sentence or two
about Marlowe, put nothing in, registered it with the Stationers'
Company, and seen it through the press. But he does not explain
how the manuscript came into his possession; for Gabriel Harvey
saw it after Greene's death, and he saw it, not at a bookseller's, but
in the house where Greene died. Perhaps another storm would
have broken if Chettle confessed he had played the role of a
literary ghoul or scavenger.

# BOOK THREE

# CHAPTER I

## *Stratford Revisited*

### 1.

THIS was a memorable period in the life of William Shakespeare. He saw and acted in the production of his plays in the innyards of the city, the theaters in the suburbs, on stages in the provinces, and at the court itself for the 'solace' of the Queen. He was the friend of renowned poets, the collaborator of successful dramatists; and his acquaintance had become wider still—in Chettle's phrase, with 'diuers of worship,' that is, a number of men of position and quality, who honored him for his abilities and who respected him for his 'vprightnes of dealing.'

Among that talented and turbulent coterie which provided London with entertainment and England with a national literature, his character stands out, solitary and admired, from this time forth—he was never attacked again, hereafter being named only to be praised. He is not to be found in the vituperative battles of the pamphlets; he stands aloof from the wars of the theaters. He partook of the life of his fellows in the theater without being dragged down to a violent or ignominious end. He had the rewards of the maker—in full measure; the rest was loneliness.

Did his thoughts turn in his solitude to the house on Henley Street, and to the children in that house? We are in a realm of conjecture, uncharted and unchartable. Something drew Shakespeare back to Stratford at the end, in addition to weariness and disillusion—a need, deep-rooted but long denied, for a home. Between this shadowy period and that resettlement in Stratford, there are certain events which fit the pattern of exile and return.

### 2.

What of Anne Hathaway Shakespeare, living in the 'Back' of the middle house, with Susanna, aged nine, and Hamnet and Judith, the twins, now seven? There is no record, not even a tradition, of her ever having gone to London. Had she seen her husband in the years since he departed? Whether she still felt affection for him or not, her thoughts could not but be bitter. Even a brilliant woman, married and a mother, might resent such whole-hearted application to a profession which took her husband from her hearth and home. Anne was thirty-six, burdened with the management of three children, constantly under the eyes and strictures or pity of her husband's family and those outside it. The end of passion is a necessary concomitant of the beginning of passion; the end of love follows the beginning of love; but such reflections, if she had them, could not make her position any more satisfactory, in her own eyes or the eyes of the world—the little world of Stratford. How her husband felt toward her she must have known, only too well.

What thoughts, what mixed emotions, must have been hers when, as is likely, she saw her strange husband on Stratford stages, and heard his familiar voice uttering the unfamiliar lines? If he went to London in 1585, when he was twenty-one years old, by 1587 he might have been in one of the companies which the Stratford Corporation minutes list as having performed at the Guild Hall in that year:

> Item, p^d for mending of a forme that was broken by the *Quenes* players, xvi *d*.
> Item, Gyven to the Quenes players, xx *s*.
> It. Gyven to my lord of Essex players, v *s*.
> It. Gyven to therle of Leycester his players, x *s*.

Thus, Shakespeare's troupe, touring the provinces, in that and subsequent years, and performing in the Guild Hall before the members of the Stratford Corporation and their families, might have presented to townsmen and kin a higher dramatic moment in the course of the action of a given play than the writers of it foresaw. And Shakespeare himself, after his appearances as an actor, would have returned to the bosom of his family, to the hospitality of his mother and father, brothers and sisters, and to the proud and joyful contemplation of his children, if not to the arms of his wife. Dangerous as it is to take a passage not specifically autobiographical and make it fit a biographical hypothesis, a greater danger may lie in resisting such a course. In 1589, when Shake-

speare and Marlowe wrote *Titus Andronicus,* Susanna Shakespeare
was six years old. That love of his daughters which is so evident in
his last years and last works is prefigured in *Titus* by a single line,
so purely Shakespearean that it can hardly be doubted that it is
his; and I cannot but believe that he wrote it after a resumption of
acquaintance with his first-born child, in all the charm, and vivacity
of her little girlhood:

> The cordial of my age to glad my heart.

It is a father's thought; Marlowe was incapable of it.

### 3.

What of John Shakespeare? He had ceased to attend corporation meetings, and another alderman took his place: 'At thys halle
William Smythe & Richard Courte are Chosen to be Aldermen in
the places of John Wheler & John Shaxpere for that m$^r$ wheler
dothe desyre to be put out of the Companye & m$^r$ Shaxpere dothe
not Come to the halles when they be warned nor hathe not done
of Longe tyme.' The probable reason for this will shortly appear.

John Shakespeare was still in business as a glover, dealing in
wool and other commodities on the side. He was still involved in
lawsuits. He was still trying to get back his wife's acres in Wilmcote from her brother-in-law, Edmund Lambert; and after the
death of Edmund in 1587, from Edmund's son, John. A bill of
complaint against John Lambert for trespass, filed in the Court of
the Queen's Bench at Warwick, Michaelmas Term, 1588, reveals
that Mary Shakespeare's nephew was actually in the custody, tech-
nical or otherwise, of the marshal; but even more interesting than
this revelation of family feuding is the fact of William Shakespeare's participation in the suit, and therefore of his presence in
Stratford.

This bill of complaint indicates that John Shakespeare, failing
to get the forfeited land back, had somehow persuaded John
Lambert to pay an additional twenty pounds for it, and 'that
hitherto he has not summoned to justice the said John Lamberte
for the property, nor some part thereof, and besides that he, the
same John Shackespere, and Mary his wife, at the same time with
William Shackspere their son, have always been ready hitherto not
only for covenanting the aforesaid premises but also for delivering

to the same John Lamberte all writings and proofs concerning the same; the aforesaid John Lamberte, however, caring but the least for his aforesaid promise and undertaking, but with scheming and fraudulent intent craftily and cunningly to deceive and defraud this John Shackspere of the aforesaid twenty pounds, has not up to this time paid the same twenty pounds to the aforesaid John Shackespere according to his promise and undertaking, nor has he made satisfaction in part for the same, although for this he was often enjoined by the same John Shackspere afterwards.'

John Lambert's answer to this bill of complaint, if he ever made one, has not been found; but nine years later, the contest was resumed, and another bill of complaint was sworn against him. This, and Lambert's answer to it, will be given in the proper place.

Meanwhile other litigation, not always of his own making, kept John Shakespeare busy. A Henley Street tinker of his acquaintance, a Welshman, having been accused of a felony, got John to go bail for him in the amount of ten pounds; the tinker failed to appear in court, and the ten pounds were forfeited. Master Nicholas Lane of Bridge Town brought suit against John Shakespeare, asserting that John had obligated himself for ten pounds of a sum of twenty-two pounds borrowed from Lane by John's brother Henry. Lane was a formidable antagonist, in or out of court; he struck a Henley-in-Arden man with a crab-tree club and left him for dead. His victim surviving, he got off with a fine. John, with the stubborn streak of the Shakespeares, resisted Lane's suit, was actually arrested, and released when Alderman Richard Hill went surety for him. He had not had enough of courts, however, for in the busy and otherwise memorable year 1588 he brought suit against a John Thompson, and another against a William Greene; and in 1589 he sued to collect a debt from Richard Sutton.

In February, 1591, he was sued by Adrian Quiney, Humfrey Plumley and Alderman Hill for default, while in April of the same year he sued Robert Jones to collect nine shillings, one pence.

The Court of Record at Stratford shows sixty-seven entries concerning him, and it appears from these that he participated in at least twenty-five suits over a period of forty years, a probably charitable estimate. It is impossible to tell at any particular period whether he was ahead or behind in his finances; though he disposed of land, he may have had money to show for it. In any event, he still owned the three houses in Henley Street, and the suit to regain possession of his wife's Wilmcote acres seems somehow part of his forthcoming intensive and successful attempt to achieve a coat of arms and thus establish himself, his son and his grandson in the line of landed gentry.

## 4.

Suits were not his only troubles.

On September 25, 1592, her Majesty's ecclesiastical commissioners for the County of Warwick drew up a list 'of sutch recusantes as have bene hearetofore presented for not comminge monthlie to the churche accordinge to hir Majestys lawes,' and included the name of John Shakespeare. He had not only stayed away from corporation meetings; he had ceased to attend church.

The Queen's commissioners were interested in conformity, as a safeguard against popish plotters, and checking church attendance was an obvious formula. Those who did not conform, if of the old religion, were a danger to the realm, not only in the person of the Queen, against whom plots were continuous, but against the very land itself, for it was now rumored that Spain was preparing another Armada for a second attempt at invasion. The lords spiritual and temporal quite properly took a very serious view of nonconformity, and ordered 'that every person so offending and lawfully convicted shall be committed to prison without bail till they shall conform and yield themselves to come to Church and make written declaration of their conformity. But in case the offenders against the Statute being lawfully convict shall not submit and sign the declaration within three months, they shall adjure the realm and go into perpetual banishment. And if they do not depart within the time limited by the Quarter Sessions or Justices of Peace, or if they return at any time afterwards without the Queen's License, they shall suffer death without benefit of clergy.' My Lord Archbishop is not on record as having protested this particular ruling, but Burghley, the Lord Treasurer, told the Privy Council as follows: 'I favour no sensual and wilful Recusant, but I conclude according to my simple judgment, that this kind of proceeding is too much favouring of the Romish Inquisition, and is a device rather to seek for offenders than to reform.'

It is dramatic to assume that John Shakespeare was secretly a

Catholic, but the truth is probably more mundane. He was growing old; the parish church was far removed from Henley Street. He was involved in continuous litigation, and any public appearance might mean an encounter with a process-serving bailiff. There was the rub. The list that the Queen's commissioners sent to her Privy Council has this significant notation, which has no appeal for partisan writers: 'It is sayd that these laste nine coom not to churche for feare of processe for debtte.' There follow nine names of Stratford worthies, Alderman John Wheeler being first, his son second, and 'Mr. John Shackespere' third. He stayed away from church for the same reason that he stayed away from the Guild Hall when the corporation sat.

The same year, being of substance and in good Stratford repute, he inventoried the goods of two deceased friends: Rafe Shaw, a Henley Street wool-driver (i.e., one who drove his wool to market), and Henry Field, tanner, also a near neighbor, and father of Richard Field, printer. At this juncture of his affairs, the pattern of his son's exile and return achieves its first great climax.

# CHAPTER II

## *The Plague in London*

### 1.

CLOAKED in the fog that rose from the Thames, and billowing like a genie that had risen from the foul gutters and ditches of the city, the plague strode silently over London, followed by soft-footed, busy death.

Men walking in the narrow streets saw darkness like a whirlpool before their eyes; staggered and fell, tongues protruding, turned black and evil-smelling in a moment. Men and women sitting by their hearths felt a stiffening in their limbs, a fire in their vitals, slithered from stools, gasped for breath or lay still.

Over the doors of houses appeared pieces of paper scrawled with the pious ejaculation, 'Lord haue mercy vppon vs,' which propitiated heaven and fulfilled the law's requirement of notice of infection.

Church bells tolled, mixing the gloom of the air with gloomy sound.

Heaped carts creaked to distant graveyards; the flambeaux of the gravediggers and hooded deathsmen flared on the outskirts of the city.

With the plague, the medieval night descended on London. In a carnival of superstition, terror and horror, the inhabitants mixed familiar herbs with grotesque plants, swished vinegary concoctions in parched mouths, as catchpenny pamphlets advised; cowered behind bolted doors where nevertheless death entered, to kneel with those who prayed the prayer of the plague, 'Lord haue mercy vppon vs,' to lie down with the ailing, break crusts with the well and topple those who stood. Shops were silent; streets stretched empty to the gates of the city.

### 2.

Such was London in the summer and fall of 1592, after the Privy Council had ordered certain obvious sanitary precautions to be taken, among them 'that restraint be made of Enterludes of Playes, assemblies of ffencers, or other prophane Spectacles, and of going with Drummes, Proclamacons, or calling of people to the same within this Cittie and Liberties thereof.' With this order, theaters were closed, to reopen only spasmodically and briefly, and always against the opposition of the Puritan corporation and Puritan preachers—who justified God's ways to man with the text, 'the cause of plagues is sin, if you look to it well: and the cause of sin are plays: therefore the cause of plagues are plays.' It was almost a deathblow for the acting companies, for plague hovered fitfully over London for approximately two years.

These two years, between Greene's deathbed attack and the winter of 1594, when the records resume to show Shakespeare an important member of the Lord Chamberlain's Servants who acted before Queen Elizabeth, were for him a prolific period of composition. It is at least as likely that he was in Stratford as that he was anywhere else, for all who could leave the pestilent metropolis did so; and this is the period of the early comedies, with scenes and songs redolent of the country.

# CHAPTER III

## Stratford Townsmen

### 1.

THE son of Henry Field, the widow and son of Rafe Shaw, enter William Shakespeare's story at this point.

A redoubtable figure in Stratford scholastic, ecclesiastic, political and social circles was Alexander Aspinall, M.A., Oxford, who became master of the King's Grammar School in 1582, and who stayed on, in the precincts of the Guild Hall, letting his manifold abilities be felt beyond the confines of the schoolroom, till he became in time, not only schoolmaster to Stratford youth, but chamberlain, alderman and deputy town clerk; and finding time, withal, for business—turning over corporation leaseholds, buying and selling wool, and making malt.

A man with these versatile accomplishments had the respect of fellow townsmen; his fellow townswomen looked up to him with other feelings. Widow Shaw showed him so much attention, having first fixed upon him as a successor to her late lamented spouse, that they were betrothed. Custom now required that Master Aspinall present his lady with a pair of embroidered and perfumed gloves; and as she lived in Henley Street, it is not unlikely that he stopped off in John Shakespeare's shop to make the necessary purchase. In the Commonplace Book of Sir Francis Fane, of Fulbeck, occur these lines, attributed to William Shakespeare, as marking the occasion:

> The Gift is small,
> The Will is all:
> Alexander Aspinall.

Aspinall may have been the prototype of Holofernes, 'the schoolmaster, exceeding fantastical, too too vain,' in *Love's Labour's Lost*. His stepson, Juliyus Shaw, witnessed William Shakespeare's will in 1616.

**2.**

As for Richard Field, the tanner's son who had apprenticed himself for seven years to 'learne ye art of printinge' in London in 1579, by the time William Shakespeare had begun to act and to write, he had served his apprenticeship and was in business for himself. He, too, married a widow, the relict of his employer, Vautrollier, thus inheriting a business ready-made, an accountant for that business, and a home where he and the Widow Vautrollier that was proceeded to make themselves snug.

One of Field's memorable publications in 1589 had been Ovid's *Metamorphoses*, a distinguished piece of printing, perhaps the very publication which Shakespeare and Marlowe used on the stage in *Titus Andronicus* to discover the ravishers of Lavinia, and which Shakespeare was shortly to use by himself as the source of a new work.

The death of Field's father, the inventory of his goods and execution of his will, very probably brought Richard to Stratford in the summer or fall of 1592, where he resumed acquaintance with the Shakespeares. If it was not in Stratford that he saw William again, it was certainly in London. For in the spring of 1593 he printed and published a book by Shakespeare whose typography and format indicate not only his own loving care over the work of a friend, but the author's personal supervision. Field must have rejoiced in Shakespeare's social climb, for the book was dedicated to the Earl of Southampton.

# CHAPTER IV

## Enter the Earl of Southampton

### 1.

HENRY WRIOTHESLEY, third Earl of Southampton, had been something of a prodigy, for a nobleman's son, having entered St. John's College, Cambridge, in the fall of 1585 at the age of twelve. From that 'most famous and fortunate Nurse of all learning' he corresponded with Lord Burghley, the Lord High Treasurer, in elevated Latin strains. He left Cambridge with an M.A. in 1589, and was presented to Queen Elizabeth, whose royal ward he was, his father being dead. At court he met the Earl of Essex, like himself a favorite of fortune, and they became close friends.

A portrait painted in his twenty-first year shows him with a worldly-wise expression in his bright blue eyes, the expression of a man to whom all things of the world had been offered with a bow and a scrape, flattery and obeisance. His features are regular, almost feminine. His cheeks are pink. Thick blond hair is swept back from the forehead, to fall in a cascade behind his back and upon the left shoulder, placed there perhaps by the painter, full of admiration for his Lordship's physical attributes. A thin mustache and a modest, newly begun beard are insufficient to transform the femininity of his features. His figure is slight, and attired so gorgeously that, had he not had servants to wait on him, he might have starved after being dressed, for it is impossible to imagine him bustling about for his dinner in that stiff and fabulous costume. A gorget of red leather, threaded with silver, is partly hidden by a broad white collar edged with lace. He wears a thin satin doublet, white trunks, and knee breeches laced with gold. Garters of purple stitched with silver support his white stockings. Little white silk bows, like four-petaled flowers, decorate the sword belt, embroidered with red and gold; the sword hilt is overlaid with gold. His right hand, in an embroidered and jeweled gauntlet, rests by a white-plumed helmet.

The martial note was not incongruous. He whom the spoiled and primping ladies of Queen Elizabeth's court could not resist was likewise a paragon in the eyes of men, a soldier as well as courtier, sharing adventures against the Spaniard on the high seas with his friend, the Earl of Essex, who at length aspired to the crown of the monarch whose favorite he was, and who mounted a scaffold instead of the throne—with Southampton almost sharing his fate.

Living in his Lordship's 'paie and Patronage' as tutor and friend was John Florio, the translator of Montaigne, who, in a book entitled *Second Frutes, To be gathered of twelve Trees of divers but delightsome tastes to the tongues of Italians and Englishmen,* offers a glimpse of the Earl's household (in a dialogue between 'Master John' and a pupil named 'Henry'): 'What shall wee doo untill it be dinner time?—Let us make a match at tennis.—Agreed, this coole morning calls for it.—And then after dinner we will goe see a plaie.'

Time which dims high deeds has not dimmed the luster of Southampton's fame as a patron of learned men and poets, and it was to him that Shakespeare now dedicated a book, in keeping with the Elizabethan tradition which made a poem a valued work, and a play not.

### 2.

On April 18, 1593, Richard Field registered with the Stationers' Company, upon payment of the customary six pence, 'a booke intitled *Venus and Adonis*,' which he shortly after put up for sale 'at the Signe of the white Greyhound in Paules Church-yard,' the bookshop of one John Harrison. The book was a quarto volume of twenty-nine pages, superbly printed and virtually free of errors The title page bore the following Latin motto, from Ovid's *Amores:*

> *Vilia miretur vulgus: mihi flauus Apollo*
> *Pocula Castalia plena ministret aqua,*

which Marlowe had translated as

> Let base, conceited wits admire vile things,
> Fair *Phoebus* lead me to the Muses' springs.

*Henry Wriothesley,*
*Earl of Southampton*

More interesting than the Latin and learning which this circumstance implies is the dedication of the little volume 'TO THE RIGHT HONORABLE HENRIE WRIOTHESLEY, Earle of Southampton, and Baron of Titchfield,' who must now be considered as one of those 'diuers of worship' among Shakespeare's acquaintance, and very probably his patron. The dedication, though flattering his Lordship, is not fulsome; in contrast to others of the period, it is dramatically brief:

> Right Honourable,
> I know not how I shall offend in dedicating my vnpolisht lines to your Lordship, nor how the worlde will censure mee for choosing so strong a proppe to support so weake a burthen, onelye if your Honour seeme but pleased, I account my selfe highly praised, and vowe to take aduantage of all idle houres, till I haue honoured you with some grauer labour. But if the first heire of my inuention proue deformed, I shall be sorie it had so noble a godfather: and neuer after eare so barren a land, for feare it yeeld me still so bad a haruest, I leaue it to your Honourable suruey, and your Honor to your hearts content which I wish may alwaies answere your owne wish, and the worlds hopefull expectation.
>
> Your Honors in all dutie,<br>William Shakespeare.

Shakespeare here spells his name as he probably wished it to be spelled, as he had spelled it at the baptism of his daughter Susanna. The country images in the dedication may indicate that he was in Stratford.

### 3.

The source of Shakespeare's *Venus and Adonis* is Ovid's *Metamorphoses*. The story there told is the classic myth of the goddess of love playing with Cupid and being wounded in the bosom by one of his arrows just as Adonis appears. Falling madly in love, she renounces Olympus and the company of the gods to follow this beautiful youth around, wooing instead of wooed:

> Backward she push'd him, as she would be thrust,
> And govern'd him in strength, though not in lust.

It is one long paean of praise of physical love, with the imagery
of a country landscape applied to the body:

> 'Fondling,' she saith, 'since I have hemm'd thee here
> Within the circuit of this ivory pale,
> I'll be a park, and thou shalt be my deer;
> Feed where thou wilt, on mountain or in dale:
>     Graze on my lips, and if those hills be dry,
>     Stray lower, where the pleasant fountains lie.'

Shakespeare's rendering of the tale in six-line stanzas reads as
though it had been dashed off swiftly in a frenzy of composition
and then handed over for publication without further ado. The
lines gush forth in a steady spurt, exuberant and sensual, occasionally cloying; here and there they foreshadow the language of
the *Sonnets:*

> 'Torches are made to light, jewels to wear,
> Dainties to taste, fresh beauty for the use,
> Herbs for their smell, and sappy plants to bear;
> Things growing to themselves are growth's abuse:
>     Seeds spring from seeds, and beauty breedeth beauty;
>     Thou wast begot; to get it is thy duty.'

### 4.

Thus, in an unwonted role, the goddess of love woos unwilling
Adonis, and an autobiographical allegory appears:

> 'Ay me,' quoth Venus, 'young, and so unkind?
> What bare excuse mak'st thou to be gone;'

for the story as Shakespeare tells it is essentially that of an older
woman wooing a youth who finds her wooing and her person
equally repugnant, and who is upbraided in terms such a woman
would use, not a goddess:

> 'Art thou obdurate, flinty, hard as steel?
> Nay, more than flint, for stone at rain relenteth.
> Art thou a woman's son, and canst not feel
> What 'tis to love? how want of love tormenteth?
>     O! had thy mother borne so hard a mind,
>     She had not brought forth thee, but died unkind.'

This much proximity to Anne, if the poem was written in Stratford, would have suggested to him.

## 5.

The creative processes are subtle, not mysterious. Perhaps proximity to his wife brought the subject of chastity to his mind anew. The story of Lucrece, who preferred death to dishonor, is in Ovid's *Fasti* (chief source of the poem Shakespeare is about to write); it was in Livy's *History of Rome*, Chaucer's *Legend of Good Women*, and Gower's *Confessio Amantis*. But other memorable tales were told by these authors, and if Shakespeare chose this one, it must have been because it had a special appeal for him. The contrast in Stratford did not elude him—this, and a personal aversion he was unable to shake off:

> I see no more in you
> Than without candle may go dark to bed.

In any event, on May 9, 1594, a year after the appearance of *Venus and Adonis*, a poem entitled '*the Ravyshement of Lucrece*' was registered with the Stationers' Company, this time by John Harrison, who had found the first book sufficiently popular and profitable to negotiate for the right to publish the second; and not content with this, now took over the publication rights of the first as well, as a memorandum in the Stationers' register, under the date '25 Junij' shows:

> Master Harrison Assigned ouer vnto him from Richard ffeild in
> *Senior.*      open Court holden this Day a book called
> *Venus and Adonis.*

With the publication of *Lucrece*, Harrison reissued *Venus and Adonis*. Richard Field printed both.

## 6.

*Lucrece* appeared as a quarto containing 265 seven-line stanzas. Again, unusual care is evident in the printing and presentation of this work, including big margins. And again Shakespeare dedicated his new poem

TO THE RIGHT HONOVRABLE, HENRY Wriothesley, Earle of
Southampton, and Baron of Titchfield:
The loue I dedicate to your Lordship is without end: wherof
this Pamphlet without beginning is but a superfluous Moity.
The warrant I haue of your Honourable disposition, not the
worth of my vntutord Lines makes it assured of acceptance.
What I haue done is yours, what I haue to doe is yours, being
part in all I haue, deuoted yours. Were my worth greater, my
duety would shew greater, meane time, as it is, it is bound to
your Lordship; To whom I wish long life still lengthened
with all happinesse.

Your Lordships in all duety.

William Shakespeare.

The young Earl, twenty at the time *Venus and Adonis* was
dedicated to him, now twenty-one, and appearing, at least on fes-
tive occasions, as his portrait shows him to posterity, had won
Shakespeare over completely by his charm, and perhaps by his
munificence as well. It is at least evident from the new dedication
that whatever intimacy existed between the two men had grown in
the interval between the two books.

## 7.

Did Shakespeare, in their new intimacy, lodge occasionally at
Southampton House, past Newgate beyond the bars, in London,
or at the Earl's baronial residence in Tichfield? In one of the early
stanzas of *Lucrece* he plays on the motto of the Southampton coat
of arms, 'Ung par tout, tout par ung' (one for all, all for one);
while toward the end of the poem there is a description of a
tapestry depicting Troy which he might have seen at the home
of his patron (and which he remembered for *Hamlet* as well):

At last she calls to mind where hangs a piece
Of skilful painting, made for Priam's Troy;
Before the which is drawn the power of Greece,
For Helen's rape the city to destroy,
Threat'ning cloud-kissing Ilion with annoy;
Which the conceited painter drew so proud,
As heaven, it seem'd, to kiss the turrets bow'd.

The lines jet forth from his nimble pen, swift without grace, and monotonous with insistent rhyme. The seven-line stanza quickly grows tedious; the fifth line seems a superfluous prop, like a fifth wheel. But here and there the language turns *Sonnet*-ward, as in this characterization of Hecuba:

> In her the painter had anatomiz'd
> Time's ruin, beauty's wrack, and grim care's reign;

the great mood once attained, the lines move majestically into complete and harmonious utterance:

> For sorrow, like a heavy-hanging bell,
> Once set on ringing, with his own weight goes;
> Then little strength rings out the doleful knell.

Lucrece compares Sinon's treachery with her ravisher's:

> as Priam did him cherish,
> So did I Tarquin; so my Troy did perish.

> Look, look, how listening Priam wets his eyes,
> To see those borrow'd tears that Sinon sheds!
> Priam, why art thou old and yet not wise?
> For every tear he falls a Trojan bleeds:
> His eye drops fire, no water thence proceeds;
> Those round clear pearls of his, that move thy pity,
> Are balls of quenchless fire to burn thy city

—the last line embedding a phrase borrowed from Marlowe.

### 8.

*Lucrece* is less remarkable as poetry than *Venus and Adonis*. It reads like an assignment in which he did not put his heart. It begins abruptly and ends undramatically. The phrase in the dedication, 'this Pamphlet without beginning,' might indicate that Shakespeare was conscious of defects. The poem itself is prefaced by an 'Argument' which gives the background for the events related. The 'Argument' is interesting, aside from its value as exposition. It contains the germ of the plot of *Cymbeline:* the leaders of Tarquin's army meet in his tent, where they praise their wives' supposed virtues; posting to Rome, all find their wives dancing and reveling—all but Collatine, whose Lucretia is discovered spinning among her maids. Out of her virtue and renowned chastity sprang her peril, fate and death.

Elizabethan and Jacobean readers preferred the earlier work. *Venus and Adonis* went through ten editions between 1593 and 1602, while *Lucrece* had only five between 1594 and 1616, the year of Shakespeare's death.

The poem remains interesting for autobiographical reasons, of which the dedication is first. Line 48,

O! rash false heat, wrapp'd in repentant cold,

may have formed itself in Shakespeare's mind originally as a retort to Greene's parody of the famous line in *Henry VI;* although it is hard to think of Shakespeare as nursing a grudge. Near the end of his life he took a romance of Greene's to make into a play, just as for the present he did not hesitate to take a romance by Greene's friend, Lodge. He was impartial.

# CHAPTER V

## Two Plays for 'Diuers of Worship'

### 1.

THOMAS LODGE, M.A. of Oxford, Doctor of Physicke, student of law, ship's doctor, soldier and adventurer, stands forth as a type of Renaissance Englishman. Like Greene, with whom he collaborated in *A Looking-Glasse for London and England*, he was a versatile author—playwright, pamphleteer, novelist (or more accurately, romancer) and poet; and like Greene, hard beset for lack of funds, incarcerated in the Clink for a debt to a tailor, going to sea to shake off his creditors, and replying to ill fortune with poems, tales and plays.

The great choir of singing voices of his time has drowned out his sweet and charming strains. He is remembered for a lyric—

> Love in my bosom, like a bee,
> Doth suck his sweet;

but he has many such lyrics; and for two prose works: his *Defence of Poetry, Music, and Stage Plays*, written as a reply to a Puritan onslaught on these pleasures, and *Rosalynde*, a novel published in 1590 and reprinted in 1592. *Rosalynde* was dedicated to 'the Right Honourable and his most esteemed Lord the Lord of Hunsdon, Lord Chamberlaine to her Maiesties houshold,' the protector and patron of the acting company with which Shakespeare was now to be associated for the rest of his life. Perhaps it was Hunsdon, or another of Shakespeare's noble friends—Southampton, for example —who, intrigued by this tale of banished noblemen and ingenious beauties in the French Forest of Arden, asked him to dramatize it. Proximity to his own Forest of Arden helped.

As always when he worked on a borrowed plot he added characters and incidents of his own invention, besides the habiliments of his great verse. His chief characters, to be sure, are ready-made for his hand: Rosander becomes Orlando—Rosalynde, Rosalind. One has his faithful retainer, Adam—

O good old man! how well in thee appears
The constant service of the antique world,
When service sweat for duty, not for meed!
Thou art not for the fashion of these times,
Where none will sweat but for promotion;

the other has the usurping duke's daughter for companion in exile,
Alinda, whom Shakespeare renamed Celia. Touchstone, Jacques
and Audrey are new additions. Lodge's novel is full of sonnets and
sonnettos, for his characters, like Shakespeare's, whether high or
low, are miraculously endowed with the faculty of dashing off
poems. The wholesale wooings, and wholesale marriages, are trans-
planted en masse to *As You Like It*.

But Shakespeare had also the faculty of absorbing and synthesiz-
ing whatever he read, so that he obtained not only a plot for a
play, but sustenance for his thought. Lodge's prose has an Old
Testament flavor and is full of wise saws. The deathbed advice of
Rosander's father he saved for Polonius: 'chuse a friend as the
Hiperborei do the mettals, seuer them from the ore with fire, and
let them not bide the stampe before they be currant: so trie and
then trust: let time be the touchstone of friendship, and then
frends faithful lay them up for jewels. Be valiant my sonnes, for
cowardice is the enemy to honour; but not too rash, for that is
extreme.'

*As You Like It* is interesting for another reason.

## 2.

Between the publication of *Venus and Adonis* and that of
*Lucrece* an event occurred which shook literary London and reverberated to the provinces. On May 30, 1593, Christopher Marlowe
was stabbed to death in a room of a tavern in Deptford. His slayer
pleaded self-defense, told a story of argument and finally a clash
over the bill, 'that is, *le recknynge*.'

Thus perished Christopher Marlowe, aged twenty-nine years.
His slayer received the Queen's pardon. The poets grieved for
him; the Puritans gloated over his death as a divine judgment for
his blasphemies—'see what a hooke the Lord put in the nosthrils
of this barking dogge.' Quickness of limb and brightness in his
head lay in an unmarked grave in a suburban churchyard across
the Thames from London. He had left behind an unfinished love

poem, *Hero and Leander,* and a famous lyric, *The passionate Shepherd to his love;* George Chapman was to write a continuation of the first, Sir Walter Raleigh had written an equally famous reply to the second—every lady's Commonplace Book had them, Marlowe's

> Come live with me, and be my love,

and *The Nymphs Reply to the Shepherd:*

> If all the world and love were young,
> And truth in every Shepherd's tongue,
> These pretty pleasures might me move,
> To live with thee, and be thy love.

The shepherd was dead. Shakespeare heard the news and mourned. He was two months younger than Marlowe; but while his own career might be said to be just beginning, his great friend and collaborator, the creator of Tamburlaine, Faustus and Barabas, had gone abruptly into the dark at the summit of his fame and powers, with a declaration in his last play that could be his epitaph:

> Base fortune, now I see, that in thy wheel
> There is a point, to which when men aspire,
> They tumble headlong down; that point I toucht,
> And seeing there was no place to mount up higher,
> Why should I grieve at my declining fall?
> Farewell, fair Queen, weep not for *Mortimer,*
> That scorns the world, and as a traveller,
> Goes to discover countries yet unknown.

Thus had he concluded *Edward II,* in verse that had grown in content, deepened with thought. What might he not have done if he had lived?

### 3.

The thoughts of Shakespeare turned backward to their memorable association, and to the works Marlowe had created alone. The scene shifts, from *Edward II.* Barabas is under the balcony, no longer proud over

> Infinite riches in a little room,

but seeking his daughter and his gold in a speech that rang like the speech of a lover:

> But stay, what star shines yonder in the *East?*
> The Loadstar of my life, if *Abigail.*

> Oh girl, oh gold, oh beauty, oh my bliss!

The flag flies over the playhouse—was it 1589? 1590? They are showing *The Massacre at Paris*—the din of St. Bartholomew's Eve fades, the wheel of fortune turns for Guise's fall:

> Yet *Caesar* shall go forth.
> Let mean conceits, and baser men, fear death,
> But they are peasants, *I* am Duke of *Guise:*
> And princes with their looks engender fear.

> Stand close, he is coming, I know him by his voice.

> As pale as ashes, nay then, 'tis time
> To look about.
> > *They stab him.*

'His ghost be with the old Philosophers.'

> Cut is the branch that might have grown full straight,
> And burnèd is *Apollo's* Laurel bough,
> That sometime grew within this learnèd man;
> *Faustus* is gone, regard his hellish fall.

Now the far-off iambic thunder—

> Holla, ye pampered Jades of *Asia:*
> What, can ye draw but twenty miles a day,
> And have so proud a chariot at your heels,
> And such a Coachman as great *Tamburlaine?*

Farther off still, but never forgotten, never to be forgotten, the immature *Dido,* whose lyrical intensity transformed iambic pentameter, the theater and all:

> Then he unlockt the Horse, and suddenly
> From out his entrails, *Neoptolemus*
> Setting his spear upon the ground, leapt forth,
> And after him a thousand Grecians more,

> In whose stern faces shin'd the quenchless fire,
> That after burnt the pride of *Asia*.

The quenchless fire was quenched; and yet would glow forever in books, and in men's minds, like toppled Troy. It shone from the unfinished fragment:

> Where both deliberate, the love is slight;
> Who ever lov'd, that lov'd not at first sight?

It might stand for Marlowe himself. Such were some of the golden strands which Shakespeare, consciously and unconsciously, wove into his own work.

### 4.

George Peele had commented on Marlowe's death in his *Honour of the Garter*, a poem written to commemorate the installation of new knights on June 26, 1593:

> Unhappy in thy end,
> *Marlowe*, the Muses' darling.

Gabriel Harvey had done so, in *A New Letter of Notable Contents*, which appeared three months after the affray at Deptford:

> Is it a Dream? or is the *Highest mind*
> That ever haunted Paul's or hunted wind,
> Bereft of that same sky-surmounting breath,
> That breath that taught the Timpany to swell?

Thomas Edwards referred to Marlowe in the Elizabethan manner of tagging a poet by the name of his subject—his stanza pairs Marlowe with his friend, Thomas Watson, the author of *Amintae Gaudia* (The Joys of Amintas):

> *Amintas* and *Leander's* gone,
> Oh dear sons of stately kings,
> Blessed be your nimble throats,
> That so amorously could sing.

And thus Shakespeare, cogitating the manner of Marlowe's death in the tavern at Deptford, and the Puritan thunder against his supposed atheism (Act III, Scene III, of *As You Like It*):

'When a man's verses cannot be understood, nor a man's good wit seconded with the forward child Understanding, it strikes a man more dead than a great reckoning in a little room.' *Ibid*, Scene IV: 'the oath of a lover is no stronger than the word of a tapster; they are both the confirmers of false reckonings.' And in Scene V comes the astonishing apostrophe to Marlowe in the character of *the passionate Shepherd*, and the quotation of a famous line from *Hero and Leander:*

> Dead shepherd, now I find thy saw of might:
> 'Who ever lov'd that lov'd not at first sight?'

### 5.

Association with the courtly circles of Lord Hunsdon, the Lord Chamberlain, and the Earl of Southampton gave Shakespeare an infinitude of subject matter to draw from.

To begin with, there were the young men themselves, self-centered and foppishly attired, Italianate Englishmen who moved beautifully in a world of their own, half real, half imagined, but all of a piece, with servants to attend them and laws to protect their hereditary prerogatives, forming a convenient barrier against the ills of a world in which a few had everything and the many barely or not enough to live on—a world on which they had turned their well-covered backs, draped and caped.

Their lives formed a pattern of charming excesses, in sport and style, in wit and wooing. They were, for the most part, personable young men, wellborn, well traveled, sometimes well read, and plentifully supplied with money by doting parents or expectant moneylenders. Above all, these were the men who, with sojourns at the two great universities behind them, and apt for learning as well as adventures abroad, brought the Renaissance into Elizabeth's England by their importation of Continental books, music, fashions and manners. To be sure, they sometimes carried their Continental trophies with a ridiculous difference, and Shakespeare could not help satirizing them for it: 'Farewell, Monsieur Traveller: look you lisp, and wear strange suits, disable all the benefits of your own country, be out of love with your nativity, and almost chide God for making you that countenance you are; or I will scarce think you have swam in a gondola.'

Shakespeare had listened to these gallants praising their mistresses as paragons—what matter if the greatest paragon proved only the latest mistress? Their speech, which was also one of their excesses, charmed him; and if he reproved it by Rosalind, it was because it was his business to present life whole: 'The poor world is almost six thousand years old, and in all this time there was not any man died in his own person, *videlicet*, in a love-cause. Troilus had his brains dashed out with a Grecian club; yet he did what he could to die before, and he is one of the patterns of love. Leander, he would have lived many a fair year, though Hero had turned nun, if it had not been for a hot midsummer night; for, good youth, he went but forth to wash him in the Hellespont, and being taken with the cramp was drowned; and the foolish coroners of that age found it was "Hero of Sestos." But these are all lies: men have died from time to time, and worms have eaten them, but not for love.'

## 6.

It was also for these men that Shakespeare had devised a comedy which is apparently original with him, no parent play or plot ever having been found for it, *Love's Labour's Lost*—which is, nevertheless, out of Thomas Lodge's *Rosalynde*. Once more we have sequestered noblemen, this time graced by the addition of royalty; and noble beauties, witty wooings, and sonnets and songs in profusion. The scene is country—the King of Navarre's park; the time—

> bear with me, I am sick;
> I'll leave it by degrees. Soft! let us see:
> Write, 'Lord have mercy on us' on those three;
> They are infected, in their hearts it lies;
> They have the plague, and caught it of your eyes.

*Love's Labour's Lost* is a vast repository of autobiographical jottings. Stratford is brought into the play in the persons of the pedantic, Latin-quoting schoolmaster and the curate, his crony of the Guild precincts—one, 'exceeding fantastical; too-too vain; too-too vain'—the other, 'a foolish mild man; an honest man, look you, and soon dashed! He is a marvellous good neighbor, faith, and a very good bowler.' Perhaps Shakespeare invited Master

Aspinall and the curate of Stratford parish, William Gilbert, hight *Sir* William, 'sir' being a priest's courtesy title, to entertain Southampton and his friends with their learning, it being of an odd brand; just as in the play, Holofernes and Sir Nathaniel amuse their lordships by their strange jargon, which moves Moth to say: 'They have been to a feast of languages, and stolen the scraps.'

A hint of Shakespeare's incipient snobbery enters with Costard the clown:

> Here comes a member of the commonwealth;

he has been too much with lords. Yet in the same passage he satirizes the world to which their lordships belong:

> Pray you, which is the head lady?

> Thou shalt know her, fellow, by the rest that have no heads.

### 7.

Surprisingly, the Dark Lady is here; her name is Rosaline; and there is a quibble on 'will' as a forecast of the punning sonnets:

> Is she wedded or no?

> To her will, sir.

Shakespeare describes her thus:

> A wightly wanton with a velvet brow,
> With two pitch balls stuck in her face for eyes.

More surprising still—there is a hint of the rival poet, on whose name he puns:

> Beauty is bought by judgment of the eye,
> Not utter'd by base sale of chapmen's tongues.

Chapmen is Elizabethan for peddlers.

But if it was not Chapman on whose name he puns in the accepted Elizabethan manner, then another explanation must be sought for what seems to be an allusion to Chapman's *Shadow of Night:*

> O paradox! Black is the badge of hell,
> The hue of dungeons and the scowl of night.

## 8.

While Shakespeare in his work encompasses all, he is perhaps pre-eminently the poet of love, and *Love's Labour's Lost* shows it to profusion, climaxed by this paean of praise:

> It adds a precious seeing to the eye;
> A lover's eyes will gaze an eagle blind;
> A lover's ear will hear the lowest sound,
> When the suspicious head of theft is stopp'd:
> Love's feeling is more soft and sensible
> Than are the tender horns of cockled snails:
> Love's tongue proves dainty Bacchus gross in taste.
> For valour, is not Love a Hercules,
> Still climbing trees in the Hesperides?
> Subtle as Sphinx; as sweet and musical
> As bright Apollo's lute, strung with his hair;
> And when Love speaks, the voice of all the gods
> Makes heaven drowsy with the harmony.
> Never durst poet touch a pen to write
> Until his ink were temper'd with Love's sighs—

Chapman again, for the last two lines seem to be a paraphrase, if nothing more, of two lines in *Shadow of Night:*

> No pen can anything eternal write
> That is not steep'd in humour of the Night—

and Marlowe:

> *Leander* now like Theban *Hercules,*
> Ent'red the orchard of *Th' Hesperides,*
> Whose fruit none rightly can describe but he
> That pulls or shakes it from the golden tree.

With these two echoes, and yet another quotation from Chapman dealing with Marlowe, to be offered in the proper place, the identity of the rival poet in Shakespeare's Sonnet 86 will be given its concluding testimony.

9.

*Love's Labour's Lost* ends in a masque, with their lovesick lordships disguised as Muscovites, to mock the visit of Russian ambassadors to Elizabeth, who were, apparently, as little understood
then as their modern counterparts are now. An earthy song brings
masque and play to a finish, and the beholders and actors down
to earth:

> When daisies pied and violets blue
> And lady-smocks all silver-white
> And cuckoo-buds of yellow hue
> Do paint the meadows with delight,
> The cuckoo then, on every tree,
> Mocks married men; for thus sings he,
> Cuckoo;
> Cuckoo, cuckoo: O word of fear,
> Unpleasing to a married ear!

# CHAPTER VI

## Portrait of an Ideal Wife

### 1.

COMEDY is the observation and criticism of manners. With the comedies, Shakespeare's verse becomes meditative. The speeches every schoolboy is made to memorize instead of enjoy are here. The first sweet songs are sung; the high, melodious instruments of the Elizabethans enter: cases or families of viols—bass, tenor and treble; the virginal, like a keyed lute; the stringed lute itself; violin or rebec, cithern and flute—families of instruments in consort, or lone members in a medley accompanying single voices or a chorus. Hereafter, music and verses are wedded: enter music, and melodious iambics in praise of it.

Now the incomparable craftsman appears, clothing his poetry and thoughts of men in language that survives the fluctuations of current speech, which every generation forms anew. The comedies are the work of a man at peace with himself and the world, due perhaps to temporary withdrawal from London and the strenuous, itinerant life of an actor. Perhaps it was due in part to the appreciation of learned and discerning men.

In this atmosphere he set down, by a series of tentative sketches, the portrait of an ideal wife. It was a subject which, if it did not obsess him, assuredly occupied his thoughts; and it was to reach a climax years later in the most wonderful portrait of a woman ever penned, or ever painted.

### 2.

No man has written about women with more compassion or greater understanding than Shakespeare. Nothing is plainer in his work than that he delighted in their company, admired their virtues, and understood their inconsistent natures. His thoughts of them were constant, and he came to certain conclusions.

In *As You Like It* he had catalogued their humors: 'changeable, longing and liking; proud, fantastical, apish, shallow, inconstant, full of tears, full of smiles, for every passion something, and for no passion truly anything.' This, to be sure, is hard; but it has the merit of truth as far as it goes. His concern was with the relationship of the sexes, particularly the marriage relationship, and the truth of his observation grows as he delves deeper:

> Now tell me how long you would have her after you have possessed her.

> For ever and a day.

> Say 'a day,' without the 'ever.' No, no, Orlando; men are April when they woo, December when they wed: maids are May when they are maids, but the sky changes when they are wives.

He had a wife, and knew something of all wives. He knew something of all husbands too.

3.

Shakespeare's delight in a fair-speaking woman is evident in Adriana's speech to her husband in *The Comedy of Errors:*

> The time was once when thou unurg'd wouldst vow
> That never words were music to thine ear,
> That never object pleasing in thine eye,
> That never touch well welcome to thy hand,
> That never meat sweet-savour'd in thy taste,
> Unless I spake, or look'd, or touch'd, or carv'd to thee.

This is the ideal; it is how he thought it should be, and he thought so all the more intensely because it was not so with the wife of his own bosom. For the artist, there is compensation in all things, whether ill or good: perhaps a part of his understanding, as of his prolificity, is due to her. His prolificity, it may be noted again, is more apparent than real, when it is considered that a certain proportion of the plays ascribed to him is merely adaptation or revision. (*The Comedy of Errors* is based on a play by Plautus, itself drawn from even earlier sources; but it is a subject by which Shakespeare might have been intrigued by the sight of his own twins in Stratford who, although boy and girl, were probably at this period dressed alike to stir his imagination, which made him add to the twin brothers of Plautus twin attendants to quadruple confusion and delight.)

## 4.

*The Taming of the Shrew* is Shakespeare's revision of an earlier play entitled *A Pleasant Conceited Historie, called The Taming of A Shrew,* which had been acted by the Earl of Pembroke's Men, Marlowe's—and probably Shakespeare's—old company. He wafts the characters from Athens to Padua, but sets the Induction on a heath near Stratford. *The Shrew* is an appropriate vehicle, for the development of his theme, and in it the portrait of an ideal wife achieves a certain permanence in Katharina's great speech at the close:

> A woman mov'd is like a fountain troubled,
> Muddy, ill-seeming, thick, bereft of beauty;
> And while it is so, none so dry or thirsty
> Will deign to sip or touch one drop of it.
> Thy husband is thy lord, thy life, thy keeper,
> Thy head, thy sovereign; one that cares for thee,
> And for thy maintenance commits his body
> To painful labour both by sea and land,
> To watch the night in storms, the day in cold,
> Whilst thou liest warm at home, secure and safe;
> And craves no other tribute at thy hands
> But love, fair looks, and true obedience;
> Too little payment for so great a debt.

Transfer, if you will, the 'painful labour both by sea and land' to offices; transform the imagery of the Elizabethan hierarchy to that of the modern commonwealth. Shakespeare has expressed an old-fashioned view; but one, perhaps, not yet out of date. He offers a choice, and has left it to increasingly discordant generations to decide:

> I am asham'd that women are so simple
> To offer war where they should kneel for peace,
> Or seek for rule, supremacy, and sway,
> When they are bound to serve, love, and obey.

## CHAPTER VII

### An Amorous Interlude

#### 1.

SHAKESPEARE'S search for love, which was to reach a dramatic climax in the *Sonnets*, is imperfectly but intriguingly sketched in by a curious little book entitled *Willobie his Avisa, or the true Picture of a modest Maid, and of a chast and constant wife*, which was registered for publication September 3, 1594. It tells the story of an English maid, afterwards a wife, whose constancy was such that she resisted the advances of nobleman, gentleman, foppish foreigner and native adventurer—the author included. All are repulsed and stand amazed at her chastity and wit, particularly the former. The historical Lucrece, as portrayed by Shakespeare, though she ended her life to save her name and her husband's from dishonor, nevertheless had been ravished by Tarquin; no such blot stains the simple annals of this English Lucrece, yclept Avisa. These prefatory verses link the two tales:

> In Lavine Land though Livy boast
> *There hath been seen a* Constant *dame;*
> *Though* Rome *lament that she have lost*
> *The* Garland *of her rarest fame;*
> *Yet now we see that here is found*
> *As great a* Faith *in* English *ground.*

> *Though* Collatine *have dearly bought,*
> *To high renown, a lasting life,*
> *And found, that most in vain have sought,*
> *To have a* Fair, *and* Constant *wife;*
> *Yet* Tarquin *pluckt his glistering grape,*
> *And* Shake-speare *paints poore* Lucrece' *rape.*

#### 2.

The author of *Willobie his Avisa* was Henry Willoughby, the son of a gentleman of the same name, onetime high sheriff for Wiltshire and receiver-general of the Queen's revenues in Dorset and Somerset. He entered St. John's College, Oxford, at sixteen, and was nineteen when the events recorded in his book took place. *Avisa* does more than name Shakespeare; the poet's initials are juxtaposed with those of the author, which happen to be the same as those of Henry Wriothesley, Earl of Southampton. As though to make Shakespeare's identity certain, he is termed a player; he is depicted as an expert on love, and he is reported to have been himself lately in love—in fact, as just recovering. He also quotes some famous lines.

The setting of the tale is the

> wester side of Albion's Isle,
> Where Austin pitcht his Monkish tent;

Austin being St. Augustine, this would be Cerne Abbas, in Dorsetshire.

> At East of this, a Castle stands,
> By ancient shepherds built of old,
> And lately was in shepherds' hands,
> Though now by brothers bought and sold;

this could be the Norman castle at Sherborne inhabited by Sir Walter Raleigh and his half brother, Carew. Sir Walter may be the cavaliero who is one of those repulsed by Avisa. Avisa is a barmaid; her house is the St. George tavern or inn:

> where hangs the badge
> Of England's Saint.

> And there she dwells in public eye,
> Shut up from none that list to see;
> She answers all that list to try,
> Both high and low of each degree;
> But few that come, but feel her dart,
> And try her well ere they depart.

### 3.

They try in vain. Avisa dazzles all comers, her beauty brighter, apparently, than the glittering glasses and shining pewter pots

which her fair hands whisk to the tables. Willoughby is too agitated
to tell his own, or the Earl's, case in verse; he begins in prose:
'H.W. being sodenly infected with the contagion of a fantasticall
fit, at the first sight of *A*, pyneth a while in secret griefe, at length
not able any longer to indure the burning heate of so feruent a
humour, bewrayeth the secresy of his disease vnto his familiar
frend W.S. who not long before had tryed the curtesy of the like
passion, and was now newly recouered of the like infection; yet
finding his frend let bloud in the same vaine, he took pleasure for
a tyme to see him bleed, & in steed of stopping the issue, he
inlargeth the wound, with the sharpe rasor of a willing conceit,
perswading him that he thought it a matter very easy to be com-
passed, & no doubt with payne, diligence & some cost in time to be
obtayned. Thus this miserable comforter comforting his frend
with an impossibilitie, eyther for that he now would secretly laugh
at his frends folly, that had giuen occasion not long before vnto
others to laugh at his owne, or because he would see whether an
other could play his part better than himselfe, & in vewing a far
off the course of this louing Comedy, he determined to see whether
it would sort to a happier end for this new actor, then it did for
the old player. But at length this Comedy was like to haue growen
to a Tragedy, by the weake & feeble estate that H.W. was brought
vnto, by a desperate vewe of an impossibility of obtaining his purpose, til Time & Necessity, being his best Phisitions brought him a
plaster, if not to heale, yet in part to ease his maladye.'

The question whether Henry Willoughby or Henry Wriothesley is meant is complicated by the fact that the author, while
apparently disposing of this H.W. in prose, continues his tale with
an H.W. who engages W.S. in a verse dialogue.

## 4.

### H.W.

What sudden chance or change is this,
That doth bereave my quiet rest?
What surly cloud eclipst my bliss,
What sprite doth rage within my breast?
Such fainty qualms I never found,
Till first I saw this western ground.

But yonder comes my faithful friend,
That like assaults hath often tried;
On his advice I will depend.

### W.S.

Well met, friend Harry; what's the cause
You look so pale with Lented cheeks?
Your wanny face & sharpened nose
Show plain your mind some thing mislikes;
  If you will tell me what it is,
  I'll help to mend what is amiss.

### H.W.

Seest yonder house, where hangs the badge
Of England's Saint, when captains cry
Victorious land to conquering rage,
Lo, there my hopeless help doth lie;
  And there that friendly foe doth dwell,
  That makes my heart thus rage and swell.

### W.S.

Well, say no more; I know thy grief,
And face from whence these flames arise;
It is not hard to find relief,
If thou wilt follow good advice:
  She is no Saint, She is no Nun;
  I think in time she may be won—

a sophistry remembered from *Titus Andronicus:*

She is a woman, therefore may be woo'd;
She is a woman, therefore may be won;

or from *Henry VI*, Part One:

She's beautiful and therefore to be woo'd,
She is a woman, therefore to be won;

or from the more recent *Richard III:*

Was ever woman in this humor woo'd?
Was ever woman in this humor won?

5.

W.S. is assuredly William Shakespeare; are the two H.W.'s Henry Willoughby, or Henry Willoughby and Henry Wriothesley? It seems unlikely that a nineteen-year-old undergraduate would be privy to Shakespeare's affairs, although he could be familiar with his work. The most interesting question remains: if one of the H.W.'s is the Earl of Southampton, what could have brought him into Raleigh's territory? It was Southampton's friend, Essex, who supplanted Raleigh as the Queen's favorite.

Avisa herself is completely baffling. She is a *rara avis,* to be sure, and Avis is a woman's name; but why Avisa? The epistle '*To the gentle & courteous Reader*' states that the name is an anagram, viz., 'Amans. vxor. inuiolata. semper. amanda. *That is in effect. A louing wife, that neuer violated her faith, is alwaies to be beloued.*' It is not illuminating.

But whoever she was, for Shakespeare she was the forerunner of another woman in an inn, this time at Oxford, with whom he was apparently more fortunate than Avisa's suitors were, with the consequences somewhat more serious.

# CHAPTER VIII

## A Night of Errors in London

### 1.

THUS went two years in the life of Shakespeare. Throughout, despite amusing excursions, there is evidence of a deep preoccupation with his craft which, play by play, advanced him to the front rank of Elizabethan dramatic poets, and at length to the unique position which is his so far as English literature is concerned, and perhaps the world's.

By the winter of 1594 he was back in London, where the Lord Chamberlain's Men re-formed their company after the vicissitudes of the plague years.

### 2.

The holiday season of that winter was enlivened by a series of spectacular entertainments, including stage plays, at Greenwich, before Queen Elizabeth and her court, and at Gray's Inn, Holborn, for the amusement of students, benchers and their friends.

On St. Thomas's Eve (December 20) the students at Gray's Inn started their festivities by staging an imitation, slightly satirical, of the Queen's household and government. It began with the 'inthronization' of 'the High and mighty Prince, HENRY Prince of Purpoole,' who marched with his retinue from his lodgings to the great hall of the Inn, where a trumpet shrilled and a king-at-arms read off his sonorous titles: 'Duke of High and Nether Holborn, Marquis of St. Giles and Tottenham, Count Palatine of Bloomsbury and Clerkenwell, Great Lord of the Cantons of Islington, Kentish-Town, Paddington and Knights-bridge, Knight of the most Heroical Order of the Helmet, and Sovereign of the Same; Who Reigned and Died, A.D. 1594.'

It was perhaps a cautious touch to add a note about his ephemeral reign, for the 'inthronization' with its fanfare and observance of courtly rites had almost an air of usurpation. Into the hall there entered a champion in complete armor, on horseback, who rode to the center, and in a voice that boomed and reverberated, challenged 'any Man, of high Degree, or low, that will say that my Sovereign is not rightly Prince of Purpoole.' Throwing down a gauntlet as gage, and looking about him threateningly, he departed. Once more, trumpets shrilled as the horse's hoofs clattered over the floor. Other high-flown speeches followed, and the Prince of Purpoole held court, reading aloud the names, honors and perquisites of his faithful 'nobles,' after which 'His Highness called for the Master of the Revels, and willed him to pass the time in Dancing: So his Gentlemen-Pensioners and Attendants, very gallantly appointed, in thirty Couples, danced the Old Measures, and their Galliards, and other kind of Dances, revelling until it was very late.'

The night concluded with the exit of the Prince from the hall; the flambeaux of his retinue flared in the narrow streets, and trumpets rang out over the rooftops of dark Holborn.

### 3.

This was the first 'grand Night.' The second fell on St. Innocent's Day (December 28). The preparations were somewhat more elaborate; more invitations were issued, and the Lord Chamberlain's company was commissioned to perform a play.

News of the first night's entertainment had spread over the city, and as night fell the hall was crowded to overflowing: 'there was a great Presence of Lords, Ladies, and worshipful Personages, that did expect some notable Performance at that time; which, indeed, had been effected, if the multitude of Beholders had not been so exceeding great, that thereby there was no convenient room for those that were Actors.'

Thirty years before, the students of the Inner Temple had staged a similar night's entertainment, to which Gray's Inn had sent an 'ambassador' with an appropriate retinue. Now, as confusion grew in the Prince of Purpoole's court, there threaded through Holborn a gaily apparelled column of high-spirited young men—the ambassador and attendants dispatched by the Templars. This column arrived at Gray's Inn at nine o'clock, and to the sound of trumpets, marched into the hall and the presence of the prince. The ambassador was flattering to his Highness; 'he declared how his excellent Renown and Fame was known throughout the whole World; and that the Report of his Greatness was not contained within the Bounds of the Ocean, but had come to the Ears of his noble Sovereign, *Frederick Templarius,*' and so forth. The Prince of Purpole made a welcoming speech in reply, the ambassador was given a chair at his side, the crowd pressed forward, and pandemonium broke loose: 'When the Ambassador was placed, as aforesaid, and that there was something to be performed for the Delight of the Beholders, there arose such a disordered Tumult and Crowd upon the Stage, that there was no Opportunity to effect that which was intended: There came so great a number of worshipful Personages upon the Stage, that might not be displaced; and Gentlewomen, whose Sex did privilege them from Violence, that when the Prince and his Officers had in vain, a good while, expected and endeavoured a Reformation, at length there was no hope of Redress for that present.'

In the press and turmoil that ensued, the ambassador from the Inner Temple was swept from his place of honor, and his followers mauled. They took exception to this treatment with no flowery speeches, and left the hall, very much aggrieved, making their way to the exits as best they could, hearing the clamor of the jeering throng. The trumpets were silent. Tattered and bedraggled they made their way back in the darkness to the precincts of Fleet Street.

In the hall the merriment continued unabated: 'Dancing and Revelling with Gentlewomen; and after such Sports, a Comedy of Errors (like to *Plautus* his *Menechmus*) was played by the Players. So that Night was begun, and continued to the end, in nothing but Confusion and Errors; whereupon, it was ever afterwards called, *The Night of Errors.*' One of the players on the overcrowded stage was William Shakespeare.

### 4.

The sequel offered an opportunity to satirize the procedure of the Queen's ministers and the London corporation when faced with problems beyond their control, viz., 'it gave occasion to the Lawyers of the Prince's Council, the next Night, after Revels, to read a Commission of *Oyer* and *Terminer*, directed to certain Noble-men and Lords of His Highness's Council, and others, that they should enquire, or cause Inquiry to be made of some great Disorders and

Abuses lately done and committed within His Highness's Dominions of Purpoole, especially by Sorceries and Inchantments; and namely, of a great Witchcraft used the Night before, whereby there were great Disorders and Misdemeanours, by Hurly-burlies, Crowds, Errors, Confusions, vain Representations and Shews, to the utter Discredit of our State and Policy.' This saved face, and perhaps amused the discomfited Templars. Peace between the two houses was eventually made, for on the next great night the ambassador of the Inner Temple and his train returned, and were suitably honored. That night a watch of armed men was posted at all doors to bar intruders.

### 5.

The next night was the Friday after New Year's Day, that is, January 3, when 'there was a most honourable Presence of Great and Noble Personages, that came as invited to our Prince; as namely, the Right Honourable the Lord Keeper, the Earls of *Shrewsbury, Cumberland, Northumberland, Southampton,* and *Essex,* the Lords *Buckhurst, Windsor, Mountjoy, Sheffield, Compton, Rich, Burleygh, Mounteagle,* and the Lord *Thomas Howard;* Sir *Thomas Henneage,* Sir *Robert Cecill;* with a great number of Knights, Ladies and very worshipful Personages: All which had convenient Places.' The greatest lords of the realm were present, including Shakespeare's patron and his friend.

### 6.

The climax of the festivities at Gray's Inn came with the performance of a masque before the Queen herself, surrounded by her court; afterwards, Elizabeth 'thanked His Highness for the good performance of all that was done; and wished that their Sports had continued longer, for the Pleasure she took therein.'

This was gracious, but cost nothing; and the cluster of jewels which she now presented to the Prince of Purpoole had been paid for by the noblemen of her court, who knew better than to ask her for a contribution. In this she was consistent, for she never gave anything when her hand to kiss or an approving word could be made to suffice.

# CHAPTER IX

## Shakespeare Acts before Elizabeth

### 1.

THE greatness of Queen Elizabeth encompassed even the theater; for had she been other than a lusty, somewhat masculine Tudor princess, albeit a frugal one; had she been, for example, Puritan or pious to the verge of penance, the chief glory of her reign, the drama, might never have quickened into life. But with her temperament and knowledge of books, she who had been the apt pupil of Roger Ascham, and able to make a Latin or English verse herself, *extempore*, if need be—she could only smile and be glad at her flourishing theater; and she saw it flourish more because she smiled. The theater had a unique place in her affections; it could loosen her purse strings. Because of her, her servant, the Master of the Revels, was an official of importance, aside from his role of censor, for he catered to the solace of his royal mistress. This personage was Sir Edmund Tyllney, who lived in a battlemented apartment over St. John's Gate, Clerkenwell, like Chaucer over Aldgate two hundred years before.

### 2.

Her Majesty's festivities of the Christmas season of 1594 had for their heart and center 'twoe seuerall comedies or Enterludes,' allowed by the Master of the Revels, and performed at Greenwich by the Lord Chamberlain's Men December 26 and December 28, probably in the afternoon, since on the latter date the same company performed at Gray's Inn at night. What the two comedies were is not known; it can only be surmised that the second one was *The Comedy of Errors*, and that the players went straight from the performance before the Queen to Holborne, carrying the gear for that play with them.

These two performances before Elizabeth and her resplendent court—all the laced and bejeweled ladies in waiting with their floor-kissing skirts, and all the lords and lordlings with their stockinged legs and beribboned knees—provide specific evidence of Shakespeare as an actor in the Lord Chamberlain's company, whose protector and patron was Henry Carey, Lord Hunsdon, the Lord Chamberlain and cousin of the Queen. More, it reveals Shakespeare's position in that company; for on March 15, 1595, the Privy Council approved payments for the performances at Greenwich, the money being paid over to three of the chief men in the company, shareholders as well as actors.

The document reads: 'To Willm̃ Kempe Willm̃ Shakespeare & Richarde Burbage seruants to the Lord Chambleyne vpon the councelles warr$^t$ dated at Whitehall xv$^{to}$ Martii 1594[1] for twoe seuerall comedies or Enterludes shewed by them before her Ma$^{tie}$ in xpmas tyme laste paste viz$^d$ vpon S$^t$ Stephens daye[2] & Innocentes daye[3] xiij$^l$ vj$^s$ viij$^d$ and bye waye of her ma$^{tes}$ Rewarde vj$^l$ xiij$^s$ iiij$^d$ in all xx$^{li}$.' William Kempe was a veteran trouper, renowned as a comedian, dancer and clown; Richard Burbage, son of the builder of the Theatre, was the greatest dramatic actor of his time.

For the two performances the company received thirteen pounds, six shillings, eight pence—a not inconsiderable sum which was further increased, as the surprising notation about her Majesty's reward shows, by an additional six pounds, thirteen shillings, four pence; making in all the document says, twenty pounds—which is accurate enough for an age without adding machines.

Her Majesty had been amused.

### 3.

Meanwhile, the ransacking of Holinshed went on. Yet another play 'publikely acted by the right Honourable the Lorde Chamberlaine his Seruants' was *The Tragedie of King Richard the Second*. A fateful play, to be bound up with Essex's vain and vainglorious attempt half a dozen years later to seize London and the Queen. The play stayed in the Earl's memory, a precedent and a guide; old as it was by then, and out of use, a bribe to Shakespeare's fellows revived it on the eve of his rebellion, presumably to show

---

[1] Old Style.
[2] Dec. 26.
[3] Dec. 28.

London's citizens that deposition was historical—it had given their forebears Henry IV.

*Richard II* leads to the threshold of Henry IV's reign; and as though impatient to use what he had found, Shakespeare went beyond Holinshed's account of Richard and Bolingbroke to provide a foretaste of Bolingbroke's son, Prince Hal, afterwards Henry V:

> Inquire at London, 'mongst the taverns there,
> For there, they say, he daily doth frequent,
> With unrestrained loose companions.

# CHAPTER X

## A View of the Renaissance

### 1.

THUS did Shakespeare begin to fulfill himself; and bright shone his great mind as England rode out the plague years and Europe wallowed in ignorance, wretchedness and cruelty, a sick continent brutalized by religious wars. Only a scholar, poring over books, and blissfully unaware of teeming populaces beyond the margin of his vellum pages, can believe that the Renaissance was anything more than a scattering of bright candles in the medieval night, a bridge of golden lamps in a darkness not yet altogether lifted from that unhappy 'heartland' of the world. Beyond the lonely lights of art and learning, the peoples of Europe, taxed and tithed, labored for hereditary masters; the old and new nobility, many unable to read or write, kept their retainers as ignorant as themselves; the parasite and hostile monks shuffled like shadows, their hearts shriveled by the fires of the stake; while in and out and around the walled cities, columns of pillaging soldiery wound like snakes, blighting the soil and tumbling the walls, their pennons and banners blessed by priests, and pitiless priests in the councils of invader, conqueror and oppressor.

### 2.

To the House of Fugger, royal merchants and moneylenders of Augsburg whose clients were emperors and kings, came reports of affairs which might affect their manifold enterprises. These 'newsletters,' which poured in as steadily as ticker tape, show Europe as it was in the years memorable for the race, when the horizons of the world were being pushed back.

From Middleburg, October 9, 1592: 'In England the plague is still raging. The Court and others of importance have left London for the country.' From Antwerp: 'Last week 198 people died of the plague in London.'

From Saragossa: 'On the 19th day of October at 5 o'clock of

the evening there were executed here: Juan de Luna, Don Diego de Heredia, Francisco de Ayerbe, Dionysio Perez de San Juan and Pedro de Fuerdes. In the first place, according to old usage, they were led, all except Fuerdes, through the streets of Saragossa on horseback. Don Francisco and Don Diego were in black woollen penitential garb and long black cloaks, the horses being swathed in black saddlecloths. Ayerbe and Dionysio Perez were also led on horseback in black penitential robes, but their steeds had no saddle-cloths. Pedro de Fuerdes was dragged in advance of them on a bundle of straw by two horses. On the market-place a scaffolding had been erected out of boards, and in the midst thereof a small railing; before this they were made to kneel. This scaffolding was covered with black cloth. Don Juan de Luna had his head cut off from the front and Don Diego from the back, Ayerbe and Dionysio Perez merely had their throats cut, then they were laid down and left to die by inches. Pedro de Fuerdes they strangled with a rope.'

From Prague: 'A printed book has been offered here publicly for sale, which a learned Italian from Florence, of the name of Butius Fidelinius, has had printed and dedicated to His Holiness the present Pope. In this volume he adduces over a hundred prob-able reasons why not only the Christians, but also the Turks, the Jews, and in short all peoples, although they may not believe in Christ, shall be saved. But the Christians will most likely experi-ence greater joys and honors after the Resurrection than the un-believers. This book was purchased by many with great amazement and horror.'

## 3.

From Cologne, July 23, 1593: 'It is announced from London on the 17th inst. that 149 people died of the plague that week. It is feared it may spread further.'

From Antwerp: 'Zeeland letters dated Middleburg 19th inst. say that, owing to the great mortality in London, 220 people from that city have taken refuge there, and that English fugitives are arriving at other places also. As the King of Navarre has turned Papist and concluded an armistice for three months, the Queen of England is going to recall all her troops from France.'

From Antwerp: 'Letters of the 10th from London announce that there are about a thousand deaths of plague weekly in the city and outside it some five hundred, and there is no sign of any end to the mortality.'

From Venice, November 12: 'Lisbon letters of the 2nd ult. report that the Portuguese have recently discovered an island in East India which is very rich in mines of copper and other metals.'

### 4.

From Antwerp, January 8, 1594: 'News comes from England of a fresh conspiracy to set up a King in England. Four Jesuits seem to have persuaded a young Earl of the Reformed religion by name Derby that the Pope had chosen him to be King of England. The Pope was minded to confirm him as King and send him a consecrated crown. The Jesuits thought that by means of a rising they could make this gentleman King. But the plot was discovered in time.'

From Middleburg, March 17: 'Great treason has been discovered in England, and some executions have already taken place; among these are Spaniards, Portuguese and Irish. Dr. Lopez may be tried any day. Letters to him have been found from the Count de Fuentes now in Brazil. He wrote to Lopez in the name of the King of Spain and procured him to kill the Queen, by poison or other means, for 50,000 crowns.'

From Antwerp, September 3: 'This evening comes news from Middleburg that the Spaniards in Brittany have captured Brest and destroyed the English warships, taking two of them. They are now lords and masters of this port, and the English will have a bad neighbor, for with a fair wind they can cross from there to England in 24 hours.'

From Antwerp: 'A letter from Paris of the 29th brings news that the King of Navarre all but perished in the palace of Madame de Lioncourt. For as he was returning the salute of one who had made obeisance to him, a youth between seventeen and eighteen years of age essayed to stick a knife into his throat.'

### 5.

The sentence carried out against Jean Chatel, erstwhile student in the College of Jesuits at Clermont, for attempting to kill the King of Navarre, now styled King of France, was as follows:

Clad only in a shirt, and holding in his right hand a lighted candle weighing two pounds, he was made to kneel before the door of Notre-Dame. In this position of public penance, the hot drippings of the candle giving him a foretaste of horrors to come, he confessed that he had planned the inhuman and horrible murder of the King, and that he had wounded him in the face. He likewise confessed that, as result of false and accursed instructions, he had been led to believe that it was permissible to kill kings, the more so as in this instance the King, Henry IV, did not belong to the church and lacked the confirmation of the Pope. He begged forgiveness of God and the King for his diabolical act.

This huggermugger by the river concluded, he was driven through narrow streets to the Place de la Grève in an open cart. Four horses stood there, pawing the cobbled square. The crowd set up a shout, part reprobation, part approbation, for many of the pious believed he was an instrument of God, and in assaulting the King he had acted for the honor of the Church. A *brazier* burned there; from the glowing coals the executioner withdrew a pair of red-hot tongs and proceeded to tear Chatel's arms and legs. A momentary respite followed; the knife with which he had attempted to kill the King was thrust into his right hand; then the hand, still clutching the knife, was lopped off.

Now the four horses were led up, and grouped to sniff the four points of the compass. Bruised, battered, burned and maimed, more dead that alive in the nightmare of his punishment, the youth was tied to the four horses by the legs, arm and bleeding stump, and a gasp of horror floated like a ghost over the Place de la Grève as his limbs dissolved and his torso fell to the ground with a thud. Thus perished this miserable regicide.

The wrath of King and Parliament now turned upon the Jesuits. Members of the Society of Jesus were given fourteen days to leave the kingdom, and the King's subjects were forbidden to send students to Jesuit colleges outside the country. The King also sent an embassy to the Pope to petition absolution.

From Rome: 'The King of Spain has had the Pope informed that he does not oppose the pardoning of the King of France, and that the Pope should act as he thinks best for the honor of God and the Holy Church. Nevertheless His Majesty is resolved to wage unceasing war against Navarre.'

## 6.

Meanwhile, from the mother-city of Christianity, a newsletter to the House of Fugger reported that 'During a procession held yesterday to initiate the forty hours' prayer in St. Agatha's Church, a young Englishman of 25 smote the Sacrament out of an Archbishop's hand with such force that it fell to the ground and the crystal of the monstrance wounded the hand of the criminal. A crowd at once gathered, dashed burning torches in his face, and tried to kill him.' The finale, from Rome: 'Last Monday the Inquisition handed over to the secular power the Englishman who, as already mentioned, insulted the Sacrament. On the Tuesday following he was bound to a cart, his right hand was cut off, and he was then taken through the town. He was frequently smitten with lighted brands by the executioner and finally burnt alive in the Piazza del Capitolio.'

Also from Rome the decree went forth: 'Whereas many new heretical books are being printed, the titles of these have been collected in an Index and their publication has been definitely prohibited.'

# CHAPTER XI

## *The Shakespeare Coat of Arms*

### 1.

WILLIAM'S growing fame and his continuous association with noblemen and other gentlemen, direct tidings
of which must have come to John Shakespeare, reawoke
in the breast of the erstwhile high bailiff of Stratford that dream
of gentryhood which had hovered on the horizon of his thoughts
as a bright and constant cloud.

In the year 1596 he deemed the time propitious for a renewed
appeal, seeing in his grandson, Hamnet, now a stripling of eleven,
the prospect that his name would be carried on, with the hoped-for
designation of 'gentleman' after it. As a matter of fact, his service
as high bailiff entitled him to such an advancement for himself and
his heirs: 'the Herealde must not refuse, to deuise to such a
publique person, vpon his instant request, and willingnes to beare
the same without reproche, a coate of Armes,' according to the
*Blazon of Gentrie;* and the mystery is why the project was allowed
to languish so long.

### 2.

On October 20, 1596, a grant for a coat of arms for the Shakespeare family was drawn up at Derby House, the 'office' of the
College of Arms in London. At the top left occurs the motto

'Non Sanz Droict,' and below the motto, neatly but somewhat stiffly drawn, is a trick of the coat and crest. This grant exists in two states at the College of Arms, one a revised version of the other, and both marred by interlineations, deletions and words missing because of tears in the paper. By comparing the two drafts, and a later effort to impale the Arden arms with the Shakespeare arms, it is possible to arrive at an approximate version of the 1596 grant, as follows:

'To all and singuler Noble and Gentilmen: of what Estate, degree, baring Arms to whom these presentes shall come. William Dethick Garter principall king of Arms sendethe greetinges. Knowe yee that whereas, by the authorite and auncyent pryveleges perteyning to my office from the Queenes most excellent Maiestie and by her highnesse most noble & victorious progenitours, I am to take generall notice & record and to make declaration & testemonie for all causes of Arms and matters of Gentrie through all her maiesties kingdoms, dominions, principalites, Isles and provinces, To the'nd that, as manie gentillmen by theyr auncyent names of families, kyndredes, & descentes have & enioye certeyne enseignes & cottes of arms, So it is verie expedient in all Ages that some men for theyr valeant factes, magnanimite, vertu, dignites & desertes maye vse & beare suche tokens of honour and worthinesse, Whereby theyr name & good fame may be the better knowen & divulged and theyr children & posterite (in all vertue to the service of theyr prynce & contrie) encouraged. Wherefore being solicited and by credible report informed, That John Shakespeare of Stratford vppon Avon in the counte of Warwike, whose parentes & late grandfather for his faithfull & valeant service was advanced & rewarded by the most prudent prince King Henry the seventh of famous memorie, sithence which tyme they have continewed in those partes being of good reputacon & credit, and that the said John hath maryed the daughter & one of the heyres of Robert Arden of Wilmcoote in the said Counte esquire, and for the encouragement of his posterite to whom these achivmentes by the auncyent custome of the Lawes of Arms maye descend. I the said Garter king of arms have assigned, graunted, and by these presentes confirmed: This shield or cote of Arms, viz. Gould, on a Bend Sables, a Speare of the first steeled argent. And for his creast or cognizaunce a falcon his winges displayed Argent standing on a wrethe of his coullers: supporting a Speare Gould steeled as aforesaid sett vppon a helmett with mantelles & tasselles as hath ben accustomed and doth more playnely appeare depicted on this margent: Signefieing hereby & by the authorite of my office aforesaid ratefieing that it shalbe lawfull for the said John Shakespeare gentilman and for his children yssue & posterite (at all tymes & places convenient) to beare and make demonstracon of the same Blazon or Atchevment vppon theyre Shieldes, Targetes, escucheons, Cotes of Arms, pennons, Guydons, Seales, Ringes, edefices, Buyldinges, vtensiles, Lyveries, Tombes, or monumentes or otherwise for all lawfull warrlyke factes or ciuile vse or exercises, according to the Lawes of Arms, and customes that to gentillmen belongethe without let or interruption of any other person or persons for vse or bearing the same. In wittnesse & perpetuall remembrance hereof I have herevnto subscribed my name & fastened the Seale of my office endorzed with the signett of my Arms. At the office of Arms London the xx daye of October the xxxviii[th] yeare of the reigne of our Soueraigne Lady Elizabeth by the grace of God Quene of England, France and Ireland Defender of the Fayth etc. 1596.'

## 3.

While the negotiations for the coat of arms were being carried to a successful conclusion, an event occurred which hung the Henley Street household with black and made the new-gained badge of gentryhood a mockery: Hamnet, the first-born son of the first-born son died—and with his death the hope of an unbroken line of heirs male died, too.

There is nothing to indicate either Hamnet's fatal sickness or the day of his death. Sometime in the second week of August, 1596, he sickened and died, aged eleven and a half years. The Stratford parish register entry of his burial is brief—but how much that is unexpressed is contained in those few words:

August 11 Hamnet filius William Shakspere.

Was Shakespeare present at the burial of his son? It seems
unlikely. A record at Faversham, Kent, reveals that his company
played there, perhaps as Hamnet lay dying: 'Item payde to my
Lorde of Hunsdouns players aboute Lamas bye thappoyntmente
of M$^r$ Saker xvi$^s$.' Lamas is August 1. Lord Hunsdon, the Lord
Chamberlain, had died the previous July, and it was therefore
inappropriate to designate his company by his official title. (In the
following year, Hunsdon's son, George, was appointed Lord
Chamberlain, and the troupe resumed its former designation.)
'Mr. Saker'—what can this be but a town clerk's approximation of
the name of the player who had negotiated for the performance?
The clerk was a little vague concerning the date, too: 'aboute
Lamas,' he wrote down.

# BOOK FOUR

# CHAPTER I

## *Genesis of a Fat Immortal*

### 1.

EVER since the defeat of the Spanish Armada in the stirring days of '88, the English had not ceased to marvel at and admire their own martial and maritime prowess. The thud of archery butts, beating out a steady tattoo of practice; eternal vigilance on shoreline and the seas that girt the island kingdom round; and occasional exploits, such as Raleigh's voyage to Guiana, the raid of Essex and Raleigh on Cadiz, and Essex and Southampton in the Azores, singeing the shoreline and outlying possessions of the Spaniard, kept the nation's patriotism alive, to flare up from time to time with the bonfires of their celebrations.

Plays which held the mirror of their history up to themselves helped the English to keep their patriotism at a complacent pitch, and once more, it seemed, a time had come when playgoers would never tire of dramas dealing with their country's past, that dim but stirring time when English monarchs and the English nobility and yeomanry fought in the waste marches of Scotland and Wales, or streamed forth from crowded harbors in a forest of spears upon the decks of ships to offer battle to the French upon French soil.

Ingenious plots were superfluous when history could furnish such materials. There was a play entitled *The Famous Victories of Henry the Fifth, Conteining the Honorable Battell of Agincourt* which had been 'plaide by the Queenes maiesties Players' sundry times and afterwards achieved print.

The author or authors of this play, which is not distinguished for its construction or language, had gone to Holinshed's *Chronicles* for their 'plot,' and had there noted a passage in the life of Henry IV concerning his son, which charged him 'with riot and other vnciuill demeanor vnseemlie for a prince. Indeed he was youthfullie giuen, growne to audacitie, and had chosen him companions agreeable to his age; with whome he spent the time in such recreations, exercises, and delights as he fansied.'

However inconsiderable as playwrights the author or authors of *The Famous Victories* may have been, perception and a flare for characterization are evident from the use made of this particular passage.

### 2.

The play opens with Prince Henry and two men named Ned and Tom awaiting Sir John Oldcastle, another crony, after a robbery. The prince is impatient; he asks: 'whither shall we goe,' and this dialogue ensues:

Why, my Lord, you know our old hostess at Feversham.

Our hostess at Feversham? 'Sblood, what shall we do there?
We have a thousand pound about us,
And shall we go to a petty ale-house?
No, no; you know the old tavern in Eastcheap;
There is good wine: besides, there is a pretty wench
That can talk well, for I delight as much in their tongues,
As any part about them.

Thus is the stage set for the appearance of a fat immortal who, though strangely named, is recognizable by his wit:

How now, Sir John Oldcastle?
What news with you?

I am glad to see your grace at liberty,
I was come, I, to visit you in prison.

To visit me? Didst thou not know that I am a Prince's son? Why, 'tis enough for me to look into a prison, though I come not in myself, but here's such ado nowadays; here's prisoning, here's hanging, whipping, and the devil and all. But I tell you, sirs, when I am King, we will have no such things; but, my lads, if the old king my father were dead, we would be all kings.

He is a good old man; God take him to his mercy the sooner.

Out of these shadows, and the substance in Holinshed's *Chronicles*, came Shakespeare's *Henry IV* and *Henry V*; and with them, Falstaff and his crew.

# CHAPTER II

## *The English Gargantua*

### 1.

WHETHER it was a source book like Holinshed, or another man's plot or play, Shakespeare, the supreme adapter as well as creator, was able to transform any material, seemingly at will, to suit the needs of his company, seldom outraging his art, and often excelling it. His dramatic predecessors created characters; he alone creates people.

Perhaps his greatest triumph of this order is the fat knight whom he took over, name and all, from the anonymous play; and so transmogrified him that when he says of himself, 'banish plump Jack, and banish all the world,' he speaks for everyone.

It is not only because Falstaff is a cosmos, a tun of man to whom all seasons and all hours are a harvest time. He is also the axletree around whom revolve the proud and imperious men who throng the pages of *Henry IV*, the Atlas who bears aloft the portentous business of battles and of kings—for what would it all be without him but another chronicle play? This seems to have been recognized from the start.

### 2.

There is nothing in the whole range of English humorous writing to equal the creation of Falstaff by Shakespeare. By comparing Falstaff with his predecessor in the anonymous play it is possible to get some notion of Shakespeare's creative method. Shakespeare does not merely take a character and give him better lines to speak, something he could do with ease; or a more complicated psychological motivation, likewise a specialty of his. For the period in which a particular character takes shape in his mind, he becomes that character, and the character develops with all the potentialities of a Shakespeare—yet always along his or her own line of development.

Falstaff as Oldcastle in the anonymous play is already witty; but we have no real notion of the man, not even of his appearance. In Shakespeare's transformation, it is not necessary to see Falstaff on the stage to know him; he fills the mind with his bulk and measureless affability. His true genius, like that of his creator, lies in his language. His sword may cleave to his scabbard, and usually does, in the face of danger; it is his tongue which is lively in defense or offense. He is a juggler of words, a cozener of his opponents' thoughts; his shameless wit is as nimble as he is, in his person, gross.

He is a prodigious consumer of commodities. His beard is streaked with the grease from hundreds of fat capons stored in his capacious belly and washed down by torrents of sack; the fat of capons exudes from his pores; his nose is oily with it, and his eyes glow like wicks, two tiny gleams of gluttony and lechery. He is the English Gargantua:

Item, A capon ................................. 2s. 2d.
Item, Sauce .................................... 4d.
Item, Sack, two gallons ........................ 5s. 8d.
Item, Anchovies and sack after supper ........... 2s. 6d.

There is nothing lean about him but his purse.

### 3.

The scholars are fond of remarking that there are few topical allusions in Shakespeare's plays. The change of name from Sir John Oldcastle to Sir John Falstaff contains a topical allusion, for the change would not have been made had there been no objection from someone, probably the family of the historical Oldcastle, martyred long before by those who claimed spiritual power over him, and who proved it by roasting him to death over a slow fire. Following the protest, and casting about for a new name, Shakespeare remembered, from *Henry VI*, Part One, a minor character named Sir John Fastolfe who, in one of the many alarums and excursions before the walls of Rouen, ran for his life. A pun on Falstaff's earlier designation remains in the text. The scene is his first appearance with Prince Hal:

Is not my hostess of the tavern a most sweet wench?

As the honey of Hybla, my old lad of the castle. And is not a buff jerkin a most sweet robe of durance?

How now, how now, mad wag! what, in thy quips and thy quiddities? what a plague have I to do with a buff jerkin?

Why, what a pox have I to do with my hostess of the tavern?

Well, thou hast called her to a reckoning many a time and oft.

The passage is interesting for yet another reason. We have seen that, in *As You Like It*, Shakespeare quoted a line from Marlowe, and commented on Marlowe's sudden death; in the lines just given, there is an allusion to another poet, John Davies, afterwards Sir John, a writer who accompanied Shakespeare's patron, Lord Hunsdon, the Lord Chamberlain, into Scotland to welcome James, and whom James is reported to have embraced for the delight he took in Davies's work.

'Is not a buff jerkin a most sweet robe of durance?' Is not this a reference to Davies's epigram, *In Katam:*

> *Kate,* being pleas'd, wisht that her pleasure could
> Indure as long as a buff jerkin would.
> Content thee, *Kate;* although thy pleasure wasteth,
> Thy pleasure's place like a buff jerkin lasteth;
> For no buff jerkin hath been oft'ner worn,
> Nor hath more scrapings, or more dressings borne.

The epigrams of Davies were surreptitiously printed with Marlowe's translations from Ovid, and the book containing both was ordered burned by the Archbishop of Canterbury and the Bishop of London. The reference to the buff jerkin was probably inserted to amuse Shakespeare's literary friends, and perhaps his noble ones, to whom the manuscripts of writers found their way.

So much for the lack of allusions in Shakespeare's work—until we come to the next one.

### 4.

Falstaff rises to his greatest heights, literally and figuratively, in a room of the Boar's Head Tavern in Eastcheap, playing king and prince to Hal's prince and king. There are no alarums, no buckram men, to rattle him out of his complacency. He talks as though talking were as great a pleasure to him as consuming capons with sack. He is the most engaging talker in English literature— he delights a prince of the blood and a tavern wench and an Elizabethan audience with its sprinkling of high and low:

*Falstaff.* Well, an the fire of grace be not quite out of thee, now shalt thou be moved. Give me a cup of sack to make mine eyes look red, that it may be thought I have wept; for I must speak in passion, and I will do it in King Cambyses' vein.
*Prince.* Well, here is my leg.                      [*Makes a bow.*
*Falstaff.* And here is my speech. Stand aside, nobility.
*Mistress Quickly.* O Jesu! This is excellent sport, i'faith!
*Falstaff.* Weep not, sweet queen, for trickling tears are vain.
*Mistress Quickly.* O, the father! how he holds his countenance.
*Falstaff.* For God's sake, lords, convey my tristful queen,
          For tears do stop the flood-gates of her eyes.
*Mistress Quickly.* O Jesu! he doth it as like one of these harlotry players as ever I see!

He begins his earnest buffoonery, examining Hal's excesses, criticizing his wasted years and companions, and achieving a climax of self-praise. Then they exchange roles:

*Prince.* The complaints I hear of thee are grievous.
*Falstaff.* 'Sblood, my lord, they are false: nay, I'll tickle ye for a young prince, i'faith.
*Prince.* Swearest thou, ungracious boy? henceforth ne'er look on me. Thou art violently carried away from grace: there is a devil haunts thee in the likeness of a fat old man; a tun of man is thy companion. Why dost thou converse with that trunk of humours, that bolting-hutch of beastliness, that swoln parcel of dropsies, that huge bombard of sack, that stuffed cloak-bag of guts, that roasted Manningtree ox with the pudding in his belly, that reverend vice, that grey iniquity, that father ruffian, that vanity in years? Wherein is he good but to taste sack and drink it? wherein neat and cleanly but to carve a capon and eat it? wherein cunning but in craft? wherein crafty but in villany?

wherein villanous but in all things? wherein worthy but in nothing?

*Falstaff*. I would your Grace would take me with you: whom means your Grace?

*Prince*. That villanous abominable misleader of youth, Falstaff, that old white-bearded Satan.

*Falstaff*. My lord, the man I know.

*Prince*. I know thou dost.

*Falstaff*. But to say I know more harm in him than in myself were to say more than I know. That he is old, the more the pity, his white hairs do witness it; but that he is, saving your reverence, a whoremaster, that I utterly deny. If sack and sugar be a fault, God help the wicked! If to be old and merry be a sin, then many an old host I know is damned: if to be fat be to be hated, than Pharaoh's lean kine are to be loved. No, my good lord; banish Peto, banish Bardolph, banish Poins; but for sweet Jack Falstaff, kind Jack Falstaff, true Jack Falstaff, valiant Jack Falstaff, and therefore more valiant, being, as he is, old Jack Falstaff, banish not him thy Harry's company: banish not him thy Harry's company: banish plump Jack, and banish all the world.

*Prince*. I do, I will.

## 5.

From Oldcastle, Falstaff; and from Ned and Tom—Bardolph, Poins, Peto and swaggering Pistol, who appears spoutingly, brimming over with snatches from old plays:

Down, down, dogs! down fates! Have we not Hiren here?

*Mistress Quickly*. Good Captain Peesel, be quiet; it is very late, i'faith. I beseek you now, aggravate your choler.

These be good humours, indeed! Shall pack-horses,
And hollow pamper'd jades of Asia,
Which cannot go but thirty miles a day,
Compare with Caesars, and with Cannibals,
And Trojan Greeks? nay, rather damn them with
King Cerberus; and let the welkin roar—

Marlowe's mighty line still echoing in Shakespeare's mind.

## 6.

'Banish plump Jack, and banish all the world,' said Falstaff, and the prince replied: 'I will.' In the last scene of *Henry IV*, Part Two, when he is crowned king, he does. Holinshed says: 'he was crowned the ninth of Aprill, being Passion sundaie, which was a sore, ruggie, and tempestuous day, with wind, snow, and sleet; that men greatlie maruelled thereat, making diuers interpretations what the same might signifie. But this king euen at first appointing with himselfe, to shew that in his person princelie honors should change publicke manners, he determined to put on him the shape of a new man. For whereas aforetime he had made himselfe a companion vnto misrulie mates of dissolute order and life, he now banished them all from his presence (but not vnrewarded or else vnpreferred); inhibiting them vpon a great paine, not once to approch, lodge, or soiourne within ten miles of his court or presence.'

The author or authors of *The Famous Victories* told it thus:

> *Ned.* How now, Harry?
> Tut, my Lord, put away these dumps;
> You are a king, and all the realm is yours.
> What, man, do you not remember the old saying?
> You know I must be Lord Chief Justice of England;
> Trust me, my lord, methinks you are very much changed,
> And 'tis but with a little sorrowing, to make folks believe
> The death of your father grieves you,
> And 'tis nothing so.
> *Hen. V.* I prithee, Ned, mend thy manners,
> And be more modester in thy terms,
> For my unfeigned grief is not to be ruled by thy flattering
> And dissembling talk. Thou sayst I am changed;
> So I am indeed, and so must thou be, and that quickly.

And thus Shakespeare:

> *Falstaff.* God save thee, my sweet boy!
> *K. Hen. V.* My lord chief justice, speak to that vain man.
> *Ch. Just.* Have you your wits? know you what 'tis you speak?

*Falstaff.* My king! my Jove! I speak to thee, my heart!
*K. Hen. V.* I know thee not, old man: fall to thy prayers;
How ill white hairs become a fool and jester!
I have long dream'd of such a kind of man,
So surfeit-swell'd, so old, and so profane;
But, being awak'd, I do despise my dream.

Thus did royal Hal assume majesty, banishing plump Jack to break his heart at last. It was not a denouement which pleased any but the moralists in Shakespeare's audience, and the *Epilogue* to Part Two promised restitution of a sort: 'If you be not too much cloyed with fat meat, our humble author will continue the story, with Sir John in it, and make you merry with fair Katharine of France: where, for anything I know, Falstaff shall die of a sweat, unless already a' be killed with your hard opinions; for Oldcastle died a martyr, and this is not the man.'

*The Life of King Henry the Fifth* was already taking shape in Shakespeare's mind; but before he could write it, a greater than the Muses stepped in to request the return of Falstaff to light, to laughter and to love.

# CHAPTER III

## Shakespeare and Justice Shallow

### 1.

THE tradition that Queen Elizabeth asked Shakespeare to write yet another play featuring Sir John Falstaff, and that the play was *The Merry Wives of Windsor*, has its beginnings in the seventeenth century, and is mentioned by at least three writers less than a hundred years after Shakespeare's death.

John Dennis, in the Epistle to his edition of *The Merry Wives*, declared: 'First, I knew very well, that it had pleas'd one of the greatest Queens that ever was in the World, great not only for her Wisdom in the Arts of Government, but for her knowledge of Polite Learning, and her nice taste of the Drama, for such a taste we may be sure she had, by the relish which she had of the Ancients. This Comedy was written at her Command, and by her direction, and she was so eager to see it Acted, that she commanded it to be finished in fourteen days; and was afterwards, as Tradition tells us, very well pleas'd at the Representation.'

Nicholas Rowe may have drawn his information from Dennis, or he may have heard the tradition from the same source as Dennis: 'She was so well pleas'd with that admirable Character of *Falstaff*, in the two Parts of *Henry* the Fourth, that she commanded him to continue it for one Play more, and to shew him in Love. This is said to be the Occasion of his Writing The *Merry Wives* of Windsor. How well she was obey'd, the Play it self is an admirable Proof.'

Charles Gildon, in *Remarks on the Plays of Shakespeare*, says: 'The *Fairys* in the fifth act make a Handsome Complement to the Queen, in her Palace of *Windsor*, who had oblig'd him to write a Play of *Sir John Falstaff* in Love, and which I am very well assured he perform'd in a Fortnight; a prodigious Thing, when all is so well contriv'd, and carry'd on without the least Confusion.'

Gildon does more than call attention to the compliment to the Queen; the passage, which gives the setting of the play, holds a clue regarding the occasion of the first performance of *The Merry Wives:*

> About, about!
> Search Windsor castle, elves, within and out:
> Strew good luck, ouphs, on every sacred room,
> That it may stand till the perpetual doom,
> In state as wholesome as in state 'tis fit,
> Worthy the owner, and the owner it.
> The several chairs of order look you scour
> With juice of balm and every precious flower:
> Each fair instalment, coat, and several crest,
> With loyal blazon, ever more be blest!
> And nightly, meadow-fairies, look you sing,
> Like to the Garter's compass, in a ring:
> The expressure that it bears, green let it be,
> More fertile-fresh than all the field to see;
> And, *Honi soit qui mal y pense* write
> In emerald tufts, flowers purple, blue, and white;
> Like sapphire, pearl, and rich embroidery,
> Buckled below fair knighthood's bending knee.

Taking the tradition, the passage quoted above, and the testimony on the title page of the first edition of the play, that 'it hath beene diuers times Acted by the right Honorable my Lord Chamberlaine's Seruants. Both before her Maiestie, and else-where,' it is most probable that the play was performed before Queen Elizabeth at a festival marking an installation of new Knights of the Garter. Such a ceremony took place at Windsor on May 24, 1597, when five new knights of this order were created. One was Frederick, Duke of Württemberg, whom Elizabeth invariably addressed as 'Our Cousin Mumpellgart,' from a former title, and to whom 'cosen garmombles' in *The Merry Wives* may be a sly reference (his Highness did not attend the installation). The others were Thomas Lord Howard de Walden; Charles Blount, Lord Mountjoy; Sir Henry Lee, and George Carey, Lord Hunsdon, the late Lord Chamberlain's son and himself the successor to his father's honors and office, who rode into Windsor with a great company of men and gentlemen, servants and retainers, all gallantly arrayed in blue coats faced with orange-colored taffeta, and with orange-colored feathers in their hats—among them the company of players who bore the proud title of the Lord Chamberlain's Men.

2.

*The Merry Wives* offers the possibility of further biographical material for a life of Shakespeare. Let us read over the opening of this play. The scene is Windsor—Justice Shallow, Slender, his cousin, and Sir Hugh Evans, a Welsh parson, stand before Page's house:

> *Shallow.* Sir Hugh, persuade me not; I will make a Star-chamber matter of it; if he were twenty Sir John Falstaffs he shall not abuse Robert Shallow, esquire.
> *Slender.* In the county of Gloster, justice of the peace, and *coram.*
> *Shallow.* Ay, cousin Slender, and *cust-alorum.*
> *Slender.* Ay, and *rato-lorum,* too; and a gentleman born, Master Parson; who writes himself *armigero,* in any bill, warrant, quittance, or obligation,—*armigero.*
> *Shallow.* Ay, that I do; and have done any time these three hundred years.
> *Slender.* All his successors gone before him hath done't; and all his ancestors that come after him may: they may give the dozen white luces in their coat.
> *Shallow.* It is an old coat.
> *Evans.* The dozen white louses do become an old coat well; it agrees well, *passant.*

This, if drawn from life, reflects a quarrel with a justice of the peace. But Shakespeare, we know, was not quarrelsome. His reputation as a well-behaved, quite circumspect human being is well attested. There is silent corroboration in his long, smoothly flowing career in a profession sometimes noted for difficult and eccentric characters. In all the vast, feverish and arduous business of repertory—composition, collaboration, acting, prompting, directing, and travel with his company when it took to the road—not a single instance has been recorded of so much as a falling-out with any of his colleagues.

It is therefore a little surprising to find that on November 29,

1596, one William Wayte craved sureties of the peace 'against William Shakespeare, Francis Langley, Dorothy Soer wife of John Soer, and Anne Lee, for fear of death, etc.'—the inoffensive 'etc.' standing for 'and mutilation of his limbs.' It is true that all this is part of a legal formula, but there had been cases where death had in fact followed such a writ of attachment—Shakespeare himself knew of one instance, for seven years before, William Bradley had petitioned sureties of the peace against Thomas Watson and others, and died at the sharp end of Watson's sword in Hog Lane.

It was serious enough, in any case; and William Wayte, the plaintiff, happened to be the stepson of Justice William Gardiner of Southwark, who issued the writ, which gives the affair an interesting turn at the start.

### 3.

Shakespeare's supposed residence at this time was in St. Helen's parish, Bishopsgate. Bishopsgate Street ran north into Shoreditch, where stood the Theatre and the Curtain, and south the width of London to become Grace Church Street, and so over London Bridge into Southwark. What had brought him across London and over the river to become embroiled in an action at law in which it was now necessary for him, as well as his associates of the writ, to appear in court with two bondsmen who would put up good and lawful English money as a guarantee that he, and the others, would keep the peace toward all her Majesty's subjects, and especially toward the plaintiff—or go to jail?

A new theater had recently risen in Paris (or Parish) Garden, St. Saviour's, on the Bankside, where once had stood the great monastery of Bermondsey, dissolved with the other monastic houses by Henry VIII, the properties passing to the Crown and thence to favored noblemen by gift or purchase. The manor of Paris Garden changed ownership more than once since Henry's day; finally a prosperous London goldsmith, noting by the throngs at the Theatre, the Curtain and the Rose that there was profit in plays, leased the manor for a thousand years—little knowing what only a few of them would bring—and obtained a license to build another playhouse. He was strenuously opposed by the Lord Mayor and aldermen, who not only did not want any more playhouses in or near London, but took this opportunity to request that those already standing be 'plucked down,' a phrase indicative of their choler.

The new theater was begun in 1594 and finished in 1595; in the summer of 1596 it was described by a Dutch visitor as the largest and most magnificent in London, with a seating capacity of three thousand. It was called *The Swan,* a name chosen perhaps because of the many swans breasting the curve of the soft-running Thames a few hundred feet away. The Swan made new business for the watermen, for Londoners came to it by water as well as over the bridge, using Paris Garden Stairs or Falcon Stairs nearby. The builder and owner of the Swan was Francis Langley, named with William Shakespeare in Wayte's writ.

4.

As for Dorothy Soer and Anne Lee, nothing is known beyond their names and the fact that on November 29, 1596, in company with the greatest dramatic poet of their time and the owner of the most magnificent theater of their time, they were ordered to keep the peace toward William Wayte, who went 'in fear of death, etc.' because of them. We must turn to Langley for further elucidation, if any. On November 3, three weeks before Wayte flew before his stepfather-justice to start an action of his own, Francis Langley had petitioned sureties of the peace himself, 'against William Gardener and William Wayte for fear of death, etc.' This is the same William Gardiner, stepfather of William Wayte, justice of the peace and of the quorum, who becomes more and more interesting upon closer inspection; for the man was rich, powerful, the host to great personages from London, feared by the poor of Southwark and Bermondsey, and boasted a coat of arms blazoning a griffin *passant* impaling three white luces.

# CHAPTER IV

## *Justice Shallow and Master Slender*

### 1.

JUSTICE GARDINER'S reputation in Southwark was not a savory one; he was, a deponent swore, 'a great rich man in his estate, and one who had still money to lay out upon anything whereby he thought to get advantage, and was given to deal hardly with his poor neighbours in dealing and bargaining with them; and he was one who carried himself very sternly amongst his neighbours, and by such his dealing he was very hardly thought of amongst his neighbours.'

He mixed moneylending with his jurisprudence, and villainy with his moneylending. About a decade before, one William Brooke and Agnes his wife borrowed eighty pounds from him, giving as security a mortgage on the rents of certain houses in their possession. They deposed afterwards that Gardiner, taking advantage of their inability to read, had written 'fourscore' years instead of 'fourteen,' and not content with this, that he absented himself or shut the door of his house to them when payments were due, so that forfeiture would follow and the properties fall into his hands.

This kind of thing he could do without assistance. His villainies, however, were not restricted to strangers, and we also find him acting in concert with his stepson Wayte, who proved a willing helper. A girl named Joan Taylor, who was under age and who had been left 'divers lands' and other properties, was beguiled into marrying Wayte, who is described, together with his contribution to Gardiner's aggrandizement, in a bill of complaint as 'a certain loose person of no reckoning or value, being wholly under the rule and commandment of the said Gardyner; after which marriage being performed, the said Gardyner (having the said Wayte at his commandment) procured the said William Wayte, and the said Johane his wife by the hard dealing of the said Wayte, for small or no consideration to convey the lands of the said Johane unto the children of the said Gardyner; whereupon the said Johane Tayler, seeing her goods and lands to be gotten from her, consumed and wasted, not long after died.'

Such was Justice Gardiner, and such his stepson, William Wayte, who sought securities of the peace against William Shakespeare, Francis Langley, and two women; and against whom Langley, owner of the Swan, had done the same.

## 2.

How did a Queen's officer, a justice of the peace and of the quorum, become involved in a brawl with a theater owner which necessitated sureties of the peace on either side? I have used the word 'brawl,' for if these petitions mean anything, they mean a personal encounter, with blows given or offered, or, at the least, an exchange of language intended to exasperate and harass.

In the spring of 1596, Justice Gardiner had brought a suit for damages of one thousand pounds against Langley, alleging slander —to wit, that Langley had falsely, maliciously and publicly said that the justice was 'a false knave and a false perjured knave, and I will prove him so,' and likewise, that he was 'a false knave, a false forsworn knave and a perjured knave.'

Francis Langley was forty-six years old. His memory of Gardiner peccadilloes went back a long time. In court, to answer Gardiner's suit, he went back to 1580 to a complicated case in which Gardiner had attempted, by his usual methods, to aggrandize his possessions. A certain Anthony Walker had bought some houses in Barmesey Street, Southwark, which belonged to one Edward Welsh. It happened that, before this purchase, Welsh had become bound to Gardiner for five hundred pounds, giving the justice his recognizance to pay. Welsh paid, and received an acquittance from Gardiner, but not the original bond. In 1585, Gardiner attempted to procure an execution of the recognizance against Walker's son Thomas, who had fallen heir to some of the houses purchased by his father from Welsh. In court, Gardiner swore that he was assured in his conscience that he had never made a release to Welsh. He was thereupon shown the acquittance, and denied that it was his. Quoth Langley in court: 'the said Gardyner had wilfully perjured himself.'

It appears that Justice Gardiner did not press his suit against

Langley any further. His opponent was not to be browbeaten; he could read and write, and was not afraid to talk—it was all rather awkward. And it rankled. I think that the Justice, with a body-guard which included Wayte, appeared at the Swan to threaten Langley, which made Langley crave sureties of the peace against them; and that subsequently Wayte may have come alone to abuse the theater owner. He found Langley with rather distinguished company. There was probably an exchange of words, in which Shakespeare may have taken part, and in which the two women very likely took part. Wayte ran, with the threat of a thrashing or worse ringing in his ears.

### 3.

We have seen Master Abraham Slender, in the opening lines of *The Merry Wives of Windsor,* as an echo to his puffed-up kins-man, picking up the tail end of the justice's titles as a complacent lackey might pick up the train of his master's robe. A few lines farther on, we meet a parallel to the notorious marriage of William Wayte and Joan Taylor in the marriage negotiations between Slender and Mistress Anne Page:

> *Evans.* There is Anne Page, which is daughter to Master Thomas Page, which is pretty virginity.
> *Slender.* Mistress Anne Page? She has brown hair, and speaks small like a woman.
> *Evans.* It is that fery person for all the orld, as just as you will desire; and seven hundred pounds of moneys, and gold and silver, is her grandsire, upon his death's-bed,—Got deliver to a joyful resurrections!—give, when she is able to overtake seven-teen years old. It were a goot motion if we leave our pribbles and prabbles, and desire a marriage between Master Abraham and Mistress Anne Page.
> *Shallow.* Did her grandsire leave her seven hundred pound?
> *Evans.* Ay, and her father is make her a petter penny.
> *Shallow.* I know the young gentlewoman; she has good gifts.
> *Evans.* Seven hundred pounds and possibilities is goot gifts.
> *Shallow.* Well, let us see honest Master Page.

Within doors, the negotiations proceed; Slender is willing:

*Slender.* I will do as my cousin Shallow says. I pray you pardon me; he's a justice of peace in his country, simple though I stand here.

Shakespeare with his human heart has managed to transmogrify those selfish men of Southwark into caricatures at whom we may laugh, but not excoriate.

# CHAPTER V

## *The End of the* Swan

### 1.

LANGLEY'S real troubles were yet to come.
The fact that Shakespeare was named with him in a writ may mean that the Lord Chamberlain's Men were acting at the Swan in 1596, but there is no proof of this. On February 21, 1597, eight actors, among them Gabriel Spencer and Robert Shaw, all of them 'servants to the right honorable the Earl of Pembroke,' hired the Swan, each of them binding himself in the sum of one hundred pounds to play there for a year.

The chief dramatic author for Pembroke's Men had been Christopher Marlowe. Now writing for the company was Marlowe's old colleague, Thomas Nashe, and a newcomer named Ben Jonson. In July the company produced a play entitled *The Isle of Dogs,* partly Nashe's, partly Jonson's, with the latter also acting in it.

*The Isle of Dogs* is one of the many lost plays of the Elizabethan era. The script may have been destroyed by the authorities, for on July 28 the Privy Council informed the justices of the peace in Middlesex and Surrey that the Queen, greatly offended by this 'seditious and slanderous' play, had ordered all performances within three miles of the city to cease forthwith until November 1. This must have been an agreeable assignment for Justice Gardiner, all things considered.

Warrants for the arrest of authors and chief actors were also issued. Nashe fled to Norfolk; Jonson, Spencer and Shaw were thrown into Marshalsea jail, Southwark. The rest of the company took to the road.

The incident marked the end of the famous company long known to Londoners and the provinces as the Earl of Pembroke's Servants. By August, members of this troupe, despite their bonds with Langley, were drifting over to the Rose, where they bound themselves to perform for Henslowe. Jonson, Spencer and Shaw did likewise on their release from the Marshalsea in October.

The storm blew over; the Rose was permitted to open on October 11. But not the Swan, even when the original inhibition expired on November 1. Instead, the Privy Council, probably as a compromise with the London corporation, decreed that only two companies were to be licensed: the Lord Admiral's Men, at the Rose, and the Lord Chamberlain's Men at the Curtain—there is a hint here of trouble at the Theatre, the usual playhouse of the Lord Chamberlain's Men.

The decree marked the end of the Swan. The building stood empty; an occasional mountebank harangued from its stage; a contest in extempore versification was held there; a juggler exhibited his skill. The rest was silence.

As for Ben Jonson, it was not to be the last time he was to be immured, for he afterwards killed his fellow actor and jail companion Spencer in a duel, and escaped hanging by pleading benefit of clergy—i.e., he read a 'neck verse' in Latin from the Bible—and was branded on the hand with a 'T' (for Tyburn).

### 2.

Rowe recounts a tradition that Shakespeare helped Jonson get his start with the Lord Chamberlain's Men, which may have occurred during this unquiet period for the players and playhouses: 'His Acquaintance with *Ben Johnson* began with a remarkable piece of Humanity and good Nature; M^r *Johnson*, who was at that Time altogether unknown to the World, had offer'd one of his Plays to the Players, in order to have it Acted; and the Persons into whose Hands it was put, after having turn'd it carelessly and superciliously over, were just upon returning it to him with an ill-natur'd Answer, when *Shakespear* luckily cast his Eye upon it, and found something so well in it as to engage him first to read it through, and afterwards to recommend M^r *Johnson* and his Writings to the Publick.'

The play, judging from the notice in the folio of Jonson's *Works*, was probably *Every Man in His Humour*, 'first Acted, in the yeere 1598. By the then L. Chamberlayne his Seruants. The principall Comoedians were:

WILL. SHAKESPEARE.                    RIC. BURBADGE.
AUG. PHILIPS.                         IOH. HEMINGS.
HEN. CONDEL.                          THO. POPE.
WILL. SLYE.                           CHR. BEESTON.
WILL. KEMPE.                          IOH. DUKE.'

To the foregoing account of the meeting between Shakespeare and
Jonson, Rowe adds: 'After this they were profess'd Friends; tho'
I don't know whether the other ever made him an equal return
of Gentleness and Sincerity.' This is odd in view of the poems in
the folio of Shakespeare's plays. Yet Jonson did make some slight-
ing remarks about his illustrious friend, perhaps out of envy, or
perversity, when he found everyone praising him. He also took a
humorous swipe at Shakespeare's coat of arms, particularly the
motto; perhaps at the opening scene of *The Merry Wives* as well,
which would have been amusing to audiences that had seen the
earlier play.

In 1599, John Shakespeare attempted to impale the Arden arms
with his own. Jonson's learned friend, William Camden, was now
Clarenceux king-at-arms in the College of Heralds, and Ben may
have received first-hand tidings from him. The scene is the meeting of Sogliardo, Carlo and Puntarvolo in *Every Man Out of His
Humour*, before Jonson had made Englishmen out of them:

I thank God I can write myself 'Gentleman' now; here's my
Patent. It cost me thirty pounds, by this breath.

A very fair Coat, well charg'd and full of Armory.

Nay, it has as much variety of colours in it as you have seen
a Coat have. How like you the Crest, sir?

I understand it not well; what is't?

Marry, sir, it is your Bore without a head Rampant.

A Bore without a head—that's very rare.

I, and Rampant, too; troth, I commend the Herald's wit.

The motto of this 'vile, foolish, absurd, palpable and ridiculous
Escutcheon' is: '*Not without mustard.*'

# CHAPTER VI

## *Shakespeare Buys a House*

### 1.

IT IS PROBABLY only a coincidence that William Shakespeare set about purchasing a house in Stratford shortly after the grant of a coat of arms to his father. Perhaps the world had already begun to pall. A gentlemanly notion that he desired to establish his family in the line of the landed gentry, following that grant, is not borne out by any evidence not the product of fancy. A man who wishes his name and his line to be continued must do something about it—he must beget heirs male; yet it appears that Shakespeare continued to refrain from cohabiting with his wife after the death of their son. The probability is therefore great that establishing his family in the landed gentry through heirs male did not bulk so large in his mind as in the minds of his idolators.

It is not necessary to look beyond the ordinary reasons when a man buys a house, be he Shakespeare or someone else. All that can be deduced from his purchase at this time is that, at thirty-three, he was beginning to think of living elsewhere than in London. Perhaps the Henley Street establishment had become too crowded or too uncomfortable for his wife and remaining children. What is interesting is that he bought the largest house in Stratford, right in the center of the town. This tells us something.

### 2.

The house he bought was New Place, the 'grete house' of the Clopton family, described in 1543 as 'a praty howse of brike and tymbar.' It stood at the corner of Chapel Street, across the street from the Guild Chapel, which had also been built by Sir Hugh Clopton, benefactor of Stratford and Lord Mayor of London. It stands no longer. Intensive study of the site indicates the house had a frontage of sixty feet. There were at least ten rooms with fireplaces. With the house went two gardens and two barns. One garden entrance faced the chapel, and there was a brick wall next to the street.

The house was 'in great ruyne and decay and vnrepayred,' after a succession of tenants. We need consider only two of them. A Clopton descendant had sold New Place to William Bott, erst of Snitterfield, afterwards an alderman of Stratford, whose place in the corporation, following his expulsion, was taken by John Shakespeare. Bott, apparently, not only used 'obprobryous woordes' about his fellow aldermen—he 'oppressed divers poor men, and took away their cattle; whereupon they went to one Master Underhill, a man of law, a very good man dwelling near by, and did desire help for God's sake as they were utterly undone: who did take the matter in hand.' By a surprise denouement, Bott conveyed New Place to him for forty pounds—the sum mentioned in the 'foot of fine,' however, may not be the entire sum paid—and retired to Snitterfield, where he died. The house passed to Underhill's son, William.

### 3.

William Shakespeare seems to have been acquainted with William Underhill in London as well as in Stratford. In Easter Term, 1597, before the justices of the Queen's Bench in Westminster, Master Underhill, of the Inner Temple, London, conveyed New Place to William Shakespeare for the sum of sixty pounds. The following is the court's 'exemplification' recording the transaction [original in Latin]: 'Between William Shakespeare complainant and William Underhill gentleman defendant in regard to one messuage, two granaries, & two gardens with appurtenances in Stratford-upon-Avon, whence a plea of meeting between them has been summoned in the same Court: To wit that the aforesaid William Underhill has recognized the aforesaid tenement with appurtenances to be the right of William Shakespeare himself; that those which the same William holds by gift of the aforesaid William Underhill, he remised & quitclaimed them for himself & his heirs to the aforesaid William Shakespeare & his heirs forever . . .'

By this action, Shakespeare established his legal residence in Stratford. For a time he disappeared from London, which was natural, for he had to attend to the business of putting New Place in order, moving and taking possession. He returned to the bosom of his family to find his father involved in old litigation.

## 4.

Nine years had gone by since, in Michaelmas Term, 1588, John Shakespeare had brought suit against his kinsman, John Lambert, in order to regain forty-eight acres in Wilmcote which had belonged to his wife and which he mortgaged to Lambert's father and apparently forfeited.

In Michaelmas Term, 1597, in the Court of Chancery, London, Sir Thomas Egerton, Lord Keeper of the Great Seal of England, presiding, John Shakespeare again brought suit against John Lambert. This time the bill of complaint was in the name of himself and his wife Mary, but not his son. Perhaps William Shakespeare was too busy to become involved in an action which would necessitate his being present in court. But if John and Mary Shakespeare went down to London at this time, they may have lodged with their son, perhaps in his chambers in St. Helen's, Bishopsgate.

## 5.

The bill of complaint rehearses the background of the suit: the orators, John and Mary Shakespeare, first offered the mortgage money of forty pounds to Edmund Lambert, who refused it; and upon his death, to his son John, who also refused it, 'and did withstande them for entringe into the premisses, and as yet doeth so contynewe still.'

They allege that John Lambert 'hathe of late made sondrie secreate estates of the premisses to dyvers persones to your said oratours unknowen, whereby your saide oratours cannot tell againste whome to bringe their accions att the comen lawe for the recovery of the premisses.'

And forgetful of the fact that he had recently acquired a coat of arms, for which both friends and money were necessary, John Shakespeare says: 'the sayde John Lamberte ys of greate wealthe and abilitie, and well frended and alied amongest gentlemen and freeholders of the countrey in the saide countie of Warwicke, where he dwelleth, and your said oratours are of small wealthe and verey fewe frendes and alyance in the saide countie.'

## 6.

The same day, November 24, 1597, in the same court, John Lambert made answer to the bill of complaint. He, too, rehearsed the background of the mortgage and subsequent litigation, complaining in turn that he had been made to appear before the court once before, at which time he had made full answer. The chief points made by Lambert were as follows:

'John Shakspeere, by his Deede Pole and Liverie theruppon made, did infeoffe the said Edmunde Lamberte and his heires for ever.'

John Shakespeare had not tendered the mortgage money to his father 'accordinge to the said provisoe in the said indenture expressed.' As a result, the property came into the full possession of the defendant's father, and afterwards descended to him 'as sonne and nexte heire of the said Edmunde.' And, John Lambert charged: 'They, the said complainantes, doe now trowble and moleste this defendante by unjuste sutes in lawe, thinkinge therby, as yt shoulde seme, to wringe from him this defendante some further recompence for the said premisses then they have alreddy received.'

## 7.

The old year went out, and a new one came in; and still the suit dragged on. Chancery procedure required a replication, or answer, to the defendant's answer, and this John Shakespeare now submitted.

He makes no mention of the manner in which the Wilmcote estate was conveyed, and no reference to a deed poll delivered to Edmund Lambert. He, or his counsel, was shrewd, as well as persevering: he acknowledges the mortgage, and insists that he attempted to pay it off, with no success: 'he this complaynant, John Shakspere, did come to the dwellinge-house of the said Edmunde Lambert, in Barton-uppon-the-Heathe, uppon the feaste daie of St. Michaell tharcheangell, which was in the yeare of our Lorde God one thousand fyve hundred and eightie, and then and there tendered to paie unto him the said Edmunde Lambert the said fortie poundes, which he was to paie for the redempcion of the said premisses; which somme the said Edmunde did refuse to receyve, sayinge that he owed him other money, and unles that he, the said

John, would paie him altogether, as well the said fortie poundes as the other money, which he owed him over and above, he would not receave the said fortie poundes, and imediatlie after he, the said Edmunde, dyed, and by reason thereof, he, the said defendant, entered into the saide premisses, and wrongfullie kepeth and detayneth the said premisses from him the said complaynant.'

## 8.

The next court record is dated July 5, 1598: 'John Shackspere and Mary, his wief, plaintiffes, John Lamberte, defendant. A commission ys awarded to examyne witnesses on bothe partes, directed to Richard Lane, John Combes, Thomas Underhill and Fraunces Woodward, gentlemen, iij. or ij. of them, returnable octavis Michaelis, by assente of the attorneyes, Powle and Hubard, and the plaintiefes to geve xiiij. daies warninge.'

Almost a year later, on May 18, 1599, the court acknowledged a complaint by John Lambert that John Shakespeare had exhibited two bills—one in his own and his wife's name, and a second only in his own—and 'ordered that, yf Mr. D. Hunt, one of the Masters of this Cowrt, shall, upon consideracion of the said bills, fynde and report that bothe the said billes doe in substaunce conteyne one matter, then the defendant ys to be dismissed from one of the said billes, with such costes as the said Mr. D. Hunt shall tax and asseasse; and the plaintiff ys to proceede to the hearinge thereof withe effect, and the defendant shal be at lyberty to chaunge his commissyones, yf he will, and the plaintiffes attorney is to be warned hereof.'

On June 27, a new commission was awarded, consisting of 'Richard Lane, John Combes, William Berry and John Warne, gentlemen, iij. or ij. of them,' etc.

## 9.

The final record occurs on October 23, 1599, and indicates that the case was, at long last, to be heard and judged: 'John Shakespere and Mary, his wief, plaintiffes; John Lamberte, defendant.— Yf the defendant shewe no cawse for stay of publicacion by this day sevenight, then publicacion ys graunted.'

With this record, the case disappears from view. Perhaps John Shakespeare saw the hopelessness of his suit, and dropped it; perhaps he and John Lambert came to a private agreement, with the same result.

### 10.

John Shakespeare was not unique as a litigious Elizabethan. What is interesting about him is his ambition and perseverance— plus the fact that he was the poet's father. John Shakespeare's perseverance is a corollary to his brother Henry's stubbornness, two family traits sometimes apparent in William.

Also, it should now be apparent, all the law that appears in the plays of William Shakespeare could have been picked up as a result of his own and his father's suits.

# CHAPTER VII

## *A Preview of the 'Second-Best Bed'*

### 1.

WILLIAM SHAKESPEARE'S preoccupation with the purchase and refurbishing of his house in Stratford may explain why, when tax collectors turned up at his residence in St. Helen's, Bishopsgate, to collect a subsidy payment of five shillings from him, he was not to be found. He was set down as a defaulter, with others in his parish. The tax represented an assessment against goods—probably furnishings, clothes and books in his chambers—valued at five pounds. It was payable in February, 1597; on November 15 of that year the collectors charged with the gathering of subsidy payments in Bishopsgate Ward appeared before the Queen's commissioners 'assigned within the sayde Cytye for the taxacon leveying and gathering of the second payment of the last Subsydye,' and deposed as follows: 'vpon their corporall othes vpon the holye Evangeliste of Allmightye God':

'The persons herevnder named are all ether dead departed and gone out of the sayde warde or their goodes soe eloigned or conveyed out of the same or in such pryvate or Coverte manner kepte whereby the seuerall Somes of money on them severally taxed and assessed towarde the sayde second payment of the sayde laste subsydye neither might nor could by anye meanes by them the sayde petty collecto<sup>urs</sup> or either of them be leveyed of them or anye of them to her ma<sup>ties</sup> vse.' Listed as defaulters were the following residents of St. Helen's, together with the value of their goods and the assessments against them:

| | | |
|---|---|---|
| Peter Dallila | 1<sup>li</sup> | 1<sup>s</sup> |
| William Shackspere | V<sup>li</sup> | V<sup>s</sup> |
| Thomas Stythe | XXX<sup>li</sup> | XXX<sup>s</sup> |
| William Boyese | XXX<sup>li</sup> | XXX<sup>s</sup> |

### 2.

By Act of Parliament, 39 and 40 Elizabeth, that is, 1597-1598, a new subsidy was granted the Queen, and Shakespeare, as a supposed resident of St. Helen's parish, was again assessed on his five pounds of goods, this time at thirteen shillings, four pence. Again, on October 1, 1598, his name was put into the list of defaulters:

William Shakespeare  $V^{li}$  $xiij^s$  $iiij^d$

His name appears in the lists of defaulters three more times until, word having been brought to her Majesty's commissioners that he had removed to the Bankside, his name and the amount he owed, together with the names of other defaulters now reported living across the Thames, were forwarded to the sheriff of Surrey. The sheriff not having jurisdiction in the Liberty of the Clink, Southwark, the item was passed on to the Bishop of Winchester, who had; and that ecclesiastic, whose temporal splendor was in part maintained by fees from houses of prostitution, seems to have collected: for the sum afterwards submitted by him to the Exchequer is within four pence of the amount he was charged with collecting.

### 3.

Just where Shakespeare lived at this time is exasperatingly impossible to determine. A letter to him from a fellow townsman all but gives his address. He seems to have been in Stratford on several occasions; but, despite his possession of New Place, his business and residence were still in London. At the beginning of 1598, a survey of Stratford hoarders of 'corne & malte' lists the following neighbors in 'Chapple Street Warde':

> $m^r$ Aspinall aboute xj quart$^{ers}$.
> $w^m$ Shackespere  .  x quart$^s$.
> Juliyvs Shawe  .  vij quart$^s$.

A quarter was eight bushels. The town's charter had expressly forbidden forestalling, that is, buying direct from farmers instead of in the open market; to judge by the lengthy list of hoarders, everyone who could afford to divert wheat and barley for the profitable manufacture of malt was doing so, the poet included. A gossipy letter from Abraham Sturley to his brother-in-law, Richard Quiney, in London on Stratford business, speaks of the general discontent against the maltsters: 'I hope, saith Jho. Grannams, if God send mi Lord of Essex downe shortli, to se them hanged on gibbettes att their owne dores.' Essex was Earl Marshal of England.

## 4.

Richard Quiney was the son of Adrian Quiney, thrice high bailiff of Stratford, and himself an ex-bailiff. Richard's son Thomas afterwards married Judith Shakespeare. In his letter to Richard Quiney, Abraham Sturley gives a Stratford view of Shakespeare as a man of substance: 'This is one speciall remembrance from ur fathers motion. Itt semeth bi him that our countriman, M$^r$. Shaksper, is willinge to disburse some monei upon some od yarde land or other at Shotterie or neare about us; he thinketh it a veri fitt patterne to move him to deale in the matter of our tithes. Bi the instruccions u can geve him theareof, and bi the frendes he can make therefore, we thinke it a faire marke for him to shoote att, and not unpossible to hitt. It obtained would advance him in deede, and would do us much good.' Several years later, Shakespeare began a series of local purchases which included land and a 'moiety' of the Stratford tithes. It appears from Sturley's letter that Shakespeare had already discussed these matters with Stratford worthies, and was encouraged.

## 5.

Richard Quiney was in London from October, 1598, to February, 1599, to petition her Majesty's government for relief from additional Stratford subsidies. Several things had contributed to the town's economic crisis: disastrous fires, which had left hundreds homeless (in one of them, the west house of John Shakespeare's trio on Henley Street was pulled down to save the rest); enclosure of land for grazing, which increased England's wool trade but decreased the number of farmers; hoarding of grain, which sent bread prices up. Quiney himself was an impecunious representative, as a letter addressed to William Shakespeare shows: 'Loveinge Contreyman I am bolde of yo$^w$ as of a ffrende, craveinge yo$^{wr}$ helpe w$^t$h xxx$^{ll}$ vppon m$^r$ Bushells & my securytee or m$^r$ myttons w$^t$h me m$^r$ Rosswell is nott come to London as yeate & I have especiall cawse, yo$^w$ shall ffrende me muche in helpeing me out of all the debett I owe in London I thancke god & muche quiet my minde w$^c$h wolde nott be indebted I am nowe toward the Cowrte in hope of answer for the dispatche of my Busyenes.' The letter was sent 'ffrom the Bell in Carter Lane the 25 octobr 1598,' and was addressed:

> To my Loveinge good ffrend
> & contreymann m$^r$ w$^m$
> Shackespere.

Carter Lane was in the purlieus of St. Paul's, a convenient location for business in Westminster. Shakespeare was apparently in London when Quiney wrote—would that he had added his address! Quiney wrote the same day to Sturley; this letter is now lost, but a reference to it in a letter from Sturley indicates that Quiney got his thirty pounds' loan. He also got seventy-five pounds of relief for Stratford from the Privy Council.

### 6.

Once more we get a fleeting glimpse of Shakespeare—this time in Stratford. While London was having difficulty collecting taxes from him, he managed to receive some remuneration from his native town for a load of stone, presumably left over from repairs to New Place. An entry in the chamberlain's accounts reads:

> Pd to m$^r$ shaxpere for on lod of ston....x$^d$.

The probability is that he now brought his wife and daughters, Susanna and Judith, to New Place. With them, when they removed thither, came old and new furnishings for its many rooms, including a bed which Anne Hathaway Shakespeare had shared with her husband on Henley Street, and which she had occupied alone for many years.

A second probability is that she continued to occupy it alone.

# BOOK FIVE

# SHAKE-SPEARES

# SONNETS.

### Neuer before Imprinted.

AT LONDON
By *G. Eld* for *T. T.* and are
to be folde by *Iohn Wright*, dwelling
at Chriſt Church gate.
1 6 0 9.

# CHAPTER I

## *'Mellifluous & Hony-Tongued* Shakespeare'

### 1.

THE year that saw the republication of Francis Bacon's *Essays* was also remarkable for the appearance of a book in which William Shakespeare was named among the greatest poets and dramatists of his own and ancient times; or, as a wag has remarked, if it was not William Shakespeare, it was at least someone by the same name. The year was 1598, the book, *Palladis Tamia, Wits Treasury*, a religious, moral and literary miscellany remarkable for its profusion of contemporary names. *Wits Treasury* is, in effect, an encyclopedic commonplace book. Its author was Francis Meres, *theologus et poeta*, 'Maister of Arts in both Universities and Student in Divinity,' as he described himself on the title page of a printed sermon. In a section of *Wits Treasury* entitled 'A comparatiue discourse of our English Poets, with the *Greeke, Latine,* and *Italian* Poets,' he first names Shakespeare thus:

'As the Greeke tongue is made famous and eloquent by *Homer, Hesiod, Euripedes, Aeschilus, Sophocles, Pindarus, Phocylides* and *Aristophanes;* and the Latine tongue by *Virgill, Ouid, Horace, Silius Italicus, Lucanus, Lucretius, Ausonius* and *Claudianus:* so the English tongue is mightily enriched, and gorgeouslie inuested in rare ornaments and resplendent abiliments by Sir *Philip Sidney, Spencer, Daniel, Drayton, Warner, Shakespeare, Marlow* and *Chapman.'*

### 2.

Shakespeare is in good company—the best. This is general praise, however, and applies equally to all who are named. But then follow three paragraphs, one after another, which sound down the years like trumpet calls on the battlements of fame.

Item: 'As the soule of *Euphorbus* was thought to liue in

*Pythagoras;* so the sweete wittie soule of *Ouid* liues in mellif-luous & hony-tongued *Shakespeare,* witnes his *Venus* and *Adonis,* his *Lucrece,* his sugred Sonnets among his priuate friends, &c.'

Item: 'As *Plautus* and *Seneca* are accounted the best for Comedy and Tragedy among the Latines: so *Shakespeare* among ỹ English is the most excellent in both kinds for the stage; for Comedy, witnes his *Gentlemen* of *Verona,* his *Errors,* his *Loue labors lost,* his *Loue labours wonne,* his *Mid-summers night dreame,* & his *Merchant of Venice:* for Trag-edy his *Richard the 2. Richard the 3. Henry the 4, King Iohn, Titus Andronicus* and his *Romeo* and *Iuliet.'*

Item: 'As *Epius Stolo* said, that the Muses would speake with *Plautus* tongue, if they would speak Latin: so I say that the Muses would speak with *Shakespeares* fine filed phrase, if they would speake English.'

### 3.

Meres names the two narrative poems to which Shakespeare had put his name and which he had dedicated to the Earl of Southamp-ton, and lists twelve plays, one of them not easy to identify—*Loue labours wonne,* which may or may not be *The Taming of the Shrew.* The list is of the greatest importance in determining Shake-speare's early work. It is perhaps significant that the three parts of *Henry VI* are not listed; they were popular enough—had Shake-speare's hand in them been greater, Meres might have named them. But *Titus Andronicus* is here—it cannot, for all the polite regrets of professors of literature, be pried loose from the canon of Shakespeare's work.

Meres also refers to Shakespeare's 'sugred Sonnets among his priuate friends'; and with this mention of the *Sonnets,* certain aspects of Shakespeare's life, difficult to reconstruct, difficult to com-prehend, must now be considered.

# CHAPTER II

## *The Strands of the* Sonnets

### 1.

IN THE thirty-fourth year of his age, William Shakespeare stood in the forefront of his profession, a grave, quiet man not yet become posterity's fabulous figure, monumental and remote, inspired and unhuman. His swept-back auburn hair was beginning to thin out and recede, the sheer and serene brow was becoming higher. His hazel eyes were thoughtful and piercing, his voice pleasantly modulated, professional and cadenced to his thought. He must have been then, as it was afterwards reported of him, 'of great sweetness in his Manners, and a most agreeable Companion.' Yet he was often uncertain, inclined to melancholy, wearied with life; pressed down by care as by a cloud, and suddenly soaring like a lark above the cloud; but always generous in his praise, constant in friendship, and, later, bitter in his love.

These things the *Sonnets* reveal; and by internal evidence, the parallels with the language of certain plays, by certain events, and by the testimony of Meres, an important portion of the sequence as we know it belongs to the early period of his friendship with Southampton and other noblemen. The poems passed from hand to hand, and finally into the hands of a printer, who arranged them as well as he could; but not well enough.

### 2.

The question whether Shakespeare unlocked his heart in the *Sonnets,* and if so, that he was the less Shakespeare he, is not impossible of decision; but the inquiry, it must be admitted, is fraught with difficulties, not a few of them due to the ponderous exegesis of scholars on a frail text.

The Elizabethan era was remarkable for a sonnet vogue without parallel in the history of English literature. This sonnet vogue utilized the conceits of Continental sonneteers, as a result of which the ladies of the Continental and Elizabethan sonnets bear a remarkable resemblance to each other for heavenly attributes and unexcelled, diaphanous charms. But those who believe that Shakespeare was merely another Elizabethan sonneteer following the rules of flattery and pretense, using conceits common to all, must be mistaken—not only because his sonnets bear little resemblance to other men's, not only because he has himself satirized the other sonneteers, but because he was Shakespeare.

The bulk of his sonnet cycle, if it can be called such, is addressed not to a woman, but to several men; and the woman to whom some of the sonnets are addressed, or whom they concern, met one of the men, and the two of them betrayed the friend and lover. These are not matters which a poet draws from his imagination; nor is there another sonnet cycle of the Renaissance—Continental or Elizabethan—or any other era—which deals with similar subjects.

### 3.

The *Sonnets* number one hundred and fifty-four, one of them (126) not a sonnet at all, but consisting of six rhymed couplets. They were not all written at one time; indeed, their composition extends from the early 1590's to at least 1603, the year Queen Elizabeth died. It is not only probable that several men were recipients of Shakespeare's friendship and praise, instead of one, as has been supposed, but possible that more than one woman is addressed, besides his dark affinity; for while Shakespeare himself wrote,

> Let me not to the marriage of true minds
> Admit impediments. Love is not love
> Which alters when it alteration finds,

it is apparent from the tale told by the *Sonnets* that, so far as the dark woman was concerned, there was no such marriage, and a decade is, in any case, a long time for fidelity, especially the remorseful kind.

The *Sonnets* may be divided as follows: a group about a paragon of young manhood, perhaps a noble friend, perhaps a patron, perhaps one who was both, whom Shakespeare not only praises for his beauty, but whom he urges to marry and beget offspring as fair as himself; a group indicating a protective and possessive attachment for a second youth; a group of sonnets addressed to a person whose sex cannot be determined by anyone living, including the present writer, for the poems might have been addressed, with equal propriety, to a man or a woman; a group of poems about a dark woman in whose power Shakespeare found himself; and mixed in with these a group of sonnets relating his discovery of a betrayal by woman and friend, the latter being unmistakably designated as a man named Will. One other sequence should be noted: Sonnets 76-86, which introduce a writer who is known in literary history as the 'rival poet.'

Reviewing the subjects of the sequences within the framework of Shakespeare's *Sonnets*, it is impossible to believe that these poems represent his contribution to the artificial sonnet vogue of his time. We must believe, instead, that in many places Shakespeare unlocked his heart, even if the personages of the sonnets remain shadowy for all that.

### 4.

The *Sonnets* were registered with the Stationers' Company by a printer named Thomas Thorpe (who also published a posthumous work by Marlowe). His spelling of Shakespeare's name—thus—in the Stationers' register may indicate personal acquaintance—the more so, since he was a friend of Edward Blount, an important member of the publishing syndicate which years later brought out Shakespeare's works; but the fact that he, and not Shakespeare, wrote and signed the dedication; the many inaccuracies in the text, and the absence of a reprint in Shakespeare's lifetime, all indicate that the publication was not sanctioned by the poet—indeed, that he stopped further publication. This not only explains the absence of other editions of the *Sonnets*, in contrast to the numerous editions of *Venus and Adonis* and *Lucrece*, but explains why the emotional chronology of the poems was not followed—for the simple reason that Thorpe did not know what it was. If he had known, it would not now be possible to reshuffle many of them for the sake of a more proper continuity.

The book containing them appeared as a quarto of forty-one leaves. It apparently sold for five pence—the actor, Edward Alleyn, owned a copy, which was thus designated in an account of his 'howshould stuff':

'a book, Shaksper sonnettes, 5$^d$.'

## *The Bright Youth (W. H.)*

### 1.

THE *Sonnets* appeared with the following enigmatic dedication, the most controversial in English literature:

TO.THE.ONLIE.BEGETTER.OF
THESE.INSVING.SONNETS.
Mʳ.W.H. ALL.HAPPINESSE.
AND.THAT.ETERNITIE.
PROMISED.

BY.

OVR.EVER-LIVING.POET.

WISHETH.

THE.WELL-WISHING.
ADVENTVRER.IN.
SETTING.
FORTH.

**T. T.**

Can anyone not a scholar believe that the word 'begetter' refers to a person who procured the manuscript for Thorpe to print, and was thus assured of an eternity of fame for this commercial deed? Yet this is a notion which has been advanced under very renowned and very erudite auspices. No; whoever 'Mr. W.H.' was, he was not a dealer in manuscripts; he may not have been 'the onlie begetter,' but he was assuredly one of the important personages depicted in the *Sonnets*. As a matter of fact, the entire phrase, 'To the onlie begetter of these insuing sonnets,' sounds, not like a printer at all, but like a poet, and I believe that somewhere on the sheets of one of the sequences which make up the *Sonnets*, Shakespeare wrote this inscription, and that Thorpe saw it in the copy that fell into his hands.

The rest of the dedication is less clear. Perhaps a line is missing. It certainly sounds that way. The usual interpretation is that the well-wishing adventurer is Thorpe, setting forth with the publication of this book; but this was not his first book, and it may mean the purchaser of the *Sonnets* setting forth on the adventure of reading them.

But whatever the problems of grammar regarding the dedication, they are as nothing to the mystery posed by the designation 'Mr. W.H.' The difficulties involved in identifying this shadowy and portentous figure are sufficiently great without going to the trouble of switching the initials around, as some commentators insist on doing, to make them fit Henry Wriothesley, Earl of Southampton. Even at the time the *Sonnets* appeared in print, the secretive initials must have proved puzzling to all not intimately acquainted with Shakespeare's circle, and so served their purpose of anonymity as far as the public was concerned.

The provocative initials could stand for William Herbert, Earl of Pembroke. It has been asserted that if 'Mr. W.H.' were really William Herbert, no printer of the period would have dared to refer to him without his title, a prerogative of the nobility which was jealously guarded by her Majesty's government. 'Mr.' is not 'Mister,' of course, for such a word simply did not exist in Elizabethan English. The word is 'Master.' 'Master W.H.'—that could mean the young William Herbert, whose title during the time most of the sonnets were written was still a courtesy one (he became Earl of Pembroke in 1601, on the death of his father). It is therefore possible that the first half of Thorpe's dedication came entirely from the pen of William Shakespeare, including the initials.

## 2.

William Herbert was in his early teens when the first sonnets were written. The language of many of these poems has a filial

as well as platonic tone, in keeping with the disparity in the ages
of writer and subject; although it should be borne in mind that
boys were men in those days, matriculating at Oxford and Cambridge at twelve and thirteen, and being considered ripe for
marriage at fifteen. At year's end, 1595, when William Herbert
was only fifteen, negotiations were already afoot for his marriage
with Elizabeth Carey, granddaughter of Lord Hunsdon, the Lord
Chamberlain. The negotiations came to naught, and Mistress Carey
eventually married Sir Thomas Berkeley. Perhaps it was the Lord
Chamberlain himself who asked Shakespeare to use his powers of
persuasion to further this alliance, although it could have been
the ailing Earl of Pembroke, patron and protector of Marlowe's
company, for whom Shakespeare had also written.

The theme of the first score of sonnets is marriage and fatherhood. It is simply stated in the opening lines:

> From fairest creatures we desire increase,
> That thereby beauty's rose might never die.

The sonnets are addressed to a youth who is termed

> the world's fresh ornament
> And only herald to the gaudy spring.

He is comely:

> Look in thy glass, and tell the face thou viewest
> Now is the time that face should form another;
> Whose fresh repair if now thou not renewest,
> Thou dost beguile the world, unbless some mother,
> For where is she so fair whose unear'd womb
> Disdains the tillage of thy husbandry?
> Or who is he so fond will be the tomb
> Of his self-love, to stop posterity?
> Thou art thy mother's glass, and she in thee
> Calls back the lovely April of her prime;
> So thou through windows of thine age shalt see,
> Despite of wrinkles, this thy golden time.
> > But if thou live, remember'd not to be,
> > Die single, and thine image dies with thee.

Sonnet by sonnet the characterization grows: he is fair, he is very young, he is self-willed, he is single (and apparently averse to marriage). He is also moody:

> Music to hear, why hear'st thou music sadly?
> Sweets with sweets war not, joy delights in joy:
> Why lov'st thou that which thou receiv'st not gladly,
> Or else receiv'st with pleasure thine annoy?
> If the true concord of well-tuned sounds,
> By unions married, do offend thine ear,
> They do but sweetly chide thee, who confounds
> In singleness the parts that thou shouldst bear.
> Mark how one string, sweet husband to another,
> Strikes each in each by mutual ordering;
> Resembling sire and child and happy mother,
> Who, all in one, one pleasing note do sing:
>> Whose speechless song, being many, seeming one,
>> Sings this to thee: 'Thou single wilt prove none.'

The youth is the scion of a noble house, and Shakespeare chides him that

> 'gainst thyself thou stick'st not to conspire,
> Seeking that beauteous roof to ruinate
> Which to repair should be thy chief desire—

all because he will not marry, and marrying, beget children and so continue his line:

> You had a father: let your son say so.

### 3.

Like Ovid before him, Shakespeare, certain of his own powers, boasts that his verse will make the youth immortal, promising him that eternity which Thorpe refers to in the dedication of the *Sonnets*—never, however, losing track of the chief theme:

> But wherefore do not you a mightier way
> Make war upon this bloody tyrant, Time?
> And fortify yourself in your decay
> With means more blessed than my barren rime?

The sonnets follow one another in solemn and majestic reiteration of the theme; as quickly as one argument is exhausted, another takes its place, and in the execution of the task of persuasion which he has set himself, Shakespeare lets his smooth iambics flow forth in mounting beauty and eloquence:

> Who will believe my verse in time to come,
> If it were fill'd with your most high deserts?
> Though yet, heaven knows, it is but as a tomb
> Which hides your life and shows not half your parts.
> If I could write the beauty of your eyes
> And in fresh numbers, number all your graces,
> The age to come would say, 'This poet lies;
> Such heavenly touches ne'er touch'd earthly faces.'
> So should my papers, yellow'd with their age,
> Be scorn'd, like old men of less truth than tongue,
> And your true rights be term'd a poet's rage
> And stretchèd metre of an antique song:
> But were some child of yours alive that time,
> You should live twice,—in it and in my rime.

Bright, bright and beautiful, the sonnets flow, bearing the reader into the dark backward and abysm of Shakespeare's life.

# CHAPTER IV

## *The Bright Youth (H. W.)*

### 1.

IT MAY appear surprising that Shakespeare, who left Stratford
as quickly as possible after his union with Anne Hathaway,
and who, with the reopening of the London theaters after the
plague years of 1592-1594, promptly absented himself from con-
nubial bliss once more, should write in praise of marriage. It would
not be his wedding. . . .

One thing is certain, and with this certainty the identification of
the bright youth of the early *Sonnets* becomes confused: the series
urging fatherhood belong to a period before the death of Hamnet
Shakespeare in the summer of 1596. It is impossible to believe that
William Shakespeare would have written, as though forgetful of
his own loss:

> You had a father: let your son say so

(or the lines:

> But were some child of yours alive that time,
> You should live twice,—in it and in my rime).

He would have chosen other images.

### 2.

If Shakespeare wrote these sonnets before 1596, we are back in
the period of his greatest association with Southampton, and it is
at least possible that the blue-eyed, golden-haired Earl is the noble
personage addressed in this particular sequence. He was fair, young,
willful, and still a bachelor when he came of age in 1594, the year
*Lucrece* appeared bearing a dedication to him. More, it is possible
to see a reference to his coming of age, and to the portrait of him
painted that year—

> Now stand you on the top of happy hours,
> And many maiden gardens, yet unset,

With virtuous wish would bear you living flowers
Much liker than your painted counterfeit.

There is also to be found, in some of these early sonnets, the suggestion of a personal relationship, something which cannot be made to fit the teen-aged William Herbert. Indeed, Shakespeare's devotion is such that it leads him into an almost unmasculine praise of his friend, and of his friend's physical attributes. Even allowing for the conceits and exaggerations of the best of poets—allowing, as well, for the almost unimaginable differences which separated the worshipful commoner from the nobleman in the Elizabethan hierarchy—Shakespeare's praise sometimes makes exasperating reading (the beauty of the verse notwithstanding):

Devouring Time, blunt thou the lion's paws,
And make the earth devour her own sweet brood;
Pluck the keen teeth from the fierce tiger's jaws,
And burn the long-liv'd phoenix in her blood;
Make glad and sorry seasons as thou fleets,
And do whate'er thou wilt, swift-footed Time,
To the wide world and all her fading sweets;
But I forbid thee one most heinous crime:
O! carve not with thy hours my love's fair brow,
Nor draw no lines there with thine antique pen;
Him in thy course untainted do allow
For beauty's pattern to succeeding men.
        Yet, do thy worst, old Time: despite thy wrong,
        My love shall in my verse ever live young.

His thoughts have been set in motion by this favorite of fortune whom it was his good fortune to know, and he has returned to the Ovidian boast of promised eternity for his illustrious friend, whom he terms 'my love.' The dedication of *Lucrece* begins: 'The loue I dedicate to your Lordship is without end' (and concludes, incidentally, with a phrase which recurs in the dedication of the *Sonnets:* Shakespeare's wish for Southampton of 'all happiness.')

## 3.

How have these simple, affectionate terms, addressed by an older man to a young one in the sixteenth century, confused and

confounded generations of commentators! Yet the oft-heard belief
that Shakespeare was homosexual, or at the least bisexual, finds no
corroboration where one ought to find it: in his plays. Taking only
the canonical works, here are thirty-seven dramas—historical,
comic, tragic and tragicomic—peopled by men and women the most
diverse ever created, who utter the most diverse views upon every
conceivable subject, without a single instance, either in characterization or in commentary, of a homosexual bias in their creator. Nor is
the belief compatible with the tale told in *Willobie his Avisa,* with
similar stories which we will hear told, and with the sonnets dealing with the dark woman, to whom Shakespeare addresses images
of love and desire.

As a matter of fact, a moment's thought will show the improb-
ability of a homosexual urging his particular male friend to marry
and beget children; but if this is not enough, Sonnet 20 is a
complete refutation of such an idea by Shakespeare himself:

> A woman's face with Nature's own hand painted
> Hast thou, the master-mistress of my passion;
> A woman's gentle heart, but not acquainted
> With shifting change, as is false women's fashion;
> An eye more bright than theirs, less false in rolling,
> Gilding the object whereupon it gazeth;
> A man in hue all hues in his controlling,
> Which steals men's hearts and women's souls amazeth.
> And for a woman wert thou first created;
> Till Nature, as she wrought thee, fell a-doting,
> And by addition me of thee defeated,
> By adding one thing to my purpose nothing.
>> But since she prick'd thee out for women's pleasure,
>> Mine be thy love, and thy love's use their treasure.

'Master-mistress,' to be sure, is a startling compound; but had
the words been prodded apart, and only one used—it matters not
which—it would be more startling still. The combined form is a
grotesquerie which indicates the writer's doubt over what term to
use at all. The crux of the matter lies in the sestet, and it does not
seem as though any argument can argue away the plain statement
that occurs there:

Nature, as she wrought thee, fell a-doting,
And by addition me of thee defeated,
By adding one thing to my purpose nothing.

As for the pun in the penultimate line, it is a sophistication which Shakespeare might express to a mature man, such as Southampton, not to a boy like William Herbert. It had the same meaning then as now; if any doubt remains, this passage in *Romeo and Juliet* should dispel it:

*Mercutio.* 'Tis no less, I tell you; for the bawdy hand of the dial is now upon the prick of noon.
*Nurse.* Out upon you! what a man are you!

### 4.

From the foregoing, I have concluded that the first youth of the *Sonnets* was the Earl of Southampton, and that the next, and the most considerable figure in the entire sequence, was William Herbert. The emotional attachment apparent in the sonnets which follow the marriage-and-fatherhood sequence can be sufficiently explained, without drawing upon a perverse exegesis, if we accept William Herbert as one of the personages. He was sixteen when Hamnet Shakespeare died. The poet may have met him when he was even younger, seeing in him all that his own son might become, except for differences of birth. With the death of Hamnet, a transference of affection may have taken place.

My conclusion is helped by the language of the sequence dealing with the dark woman and a youth named Will; by the subsequent and apparently continuous relationship of Shakespeare and William Herbert; by Thorpe's dedication of the *Sonnets* to 'Mr. W. H.,' and by the dedication of the folio, by Heminge and Condell, to William Earl of Pembroke.

# CHAPTER V

## *The Dark Woman*

### 1.

RUFFED and jeweled, caped and cloaked, the gentlefolk of Elizabeth's court flowed like a bright stream into the suburbs of London to beguile their beautiful idleness with a play. Now, from the opposite pole of the theater, William Shakespeare observed the inhabitants of that high world, first glimpsed with patron and protector; mingling with them after performances, he singled out, in that dazzling throng, his fatal affinity, the dark woman of the *Sonnets*. She is Rosaline of *Love's Labour's Lost*, that

> wanton with a velvet brow,
> With two pitch balls stuck in her face for eyes,

a dark and perhaps imperious beauty who was to fulfill the earlier Rosalind's catalogue of female humors: 'changeable, longing and liking; proud, fantastical, apish, shallow, inconstant.' Her name may even have been Rosaline or Rosalind—

> For nothing this wide universe I call,
> Save thou, my Rose; in it thou art my all.

The evidence of the *Sonnets* aside, Shakespeare has been writing like a man in love—witness Romeo's first appearance, lovesick over a girl named Rosaline, who does not appear in the play. Benvolio tells him:

> At this same ancient feast of Capulet's,
> Sups the fair Rosaline, whom thou so lov'st,
> With all the admired beauties of Verona:
> Go thither; and, with unattainted eye
> Compare her face with some that I shall show,
> And I will make thee think thy swan a crow.

To which Romeo replies:

When the devout religion of mine eye
Maintains such falsehood, then turn tears to fires!

But Benvolio expostulates further:

Tut! you saw her fair, none else being by.

It sounds like a conversation from life. Perhaps it was; it also
turns up in the *Sonnets:*

Thou art as tyrannous, so as thou art,
As those whose beauties proudly make them cruel;
For well thou know'st to my dear doting heart
Thou art the fairest and most precious jewel.
Yet, in good faith, some say that thee behold,
Thy face hath not the power to make love groan;
To say they err I dare not be so bold,
Although I swear it to myself alone.

## 2.

Rosaline or Rosalind, or known to him by some other sweet
English name forever lost, she dwells in the *Sonnets*, a dark spirit
forever imprisoned in the bars of Shakespeare's verse—dark-eyed,
dark in her beauty, and dark in the mystery of her life and being:

What is your substance, whereof are you made,
That millions of strange shadows on you tend?

She is an enigma, the greatest in the literature of love, for she
was Shakespeare's beloved:

Being your slave, what should I do but tend
Upon the hours and times of your desire?
I have no precious time at all to spend,
Nor services to do, till you require.
Nor dare I chide the world-without-end hour
Whilst I, my sovereign, watch the clock for you,
Nor think the bitterness of absence sour
When you have bid your servant once adieu;
Nor dare I question with my jealous thought
Where you may be, or your affairs suppose,
But, like a sad slave, stay and think of nought,

Save, where you are how happy you make those.
So true a fool is love that in your will,
Though you do anything, he thinks no ill.

How deep in love he was, all lovers may judge who read this.
It was not enough; nor was it enough that he was Shakespeare
when other men were by, for her glance went out to them:

O! call me not to justify the wrong
That thy unkindness lays upon my heart;
Wound me not with thine eye, but with thy tongue:
Use power with power, and slay me not by art.
Tell me thou lovest elsewhere; but in my sight,
Dear heart, forbear to glance thine eye aside—

but she did not forbear, and it was noted again:

Bear thine eyes straight, though thy proud heart go wide.

Only once in this melancholy sequence of sonnets does he seem
lighthearted when writing about her, when his praise of her becomes a device to make fun of the sonneteers of his time:

My mistress' eyes are nothing like the sun;
Coral is far more red than her lips' red:
If snow be white, why then her breasts are dun;
If hairs be wires, black wires grow on her head.
I have seen roses damask'd, red and white,
But no such roses see I in her cheeks;
And in some perfumes is there more delight
Than in the breath that from my mistress reeks.
I love to hear her speak, yet well I know
That music hath a far more pleasing sound:
I grant I never saw a goddess go,—
My mistress, when she walks, treads on the ground:
   And yet, by heaven, I think my love as rare
   As any she belied with false compare.

Perhaps she was literate enough to be amused by this.
Only once is he happy, when he pictures her at the virginals as
she played for him, the lover of music; out of the chamber framed
by his sonnet the high, sweet concord of those strings sounds down

the years (telling us, incidentally, that there is no sonnet of his
which can be said with certainty to have been addressed to a man
which expresses the images and desire of physical love, as does
the following):

> How oft, when thou, my music, music play'st,
> Upon that blessed wood whose motion sounds
> With thy sweet fingers, when thou gently sway'st
> The wiry concord that mine ear confounds,
> Do I envy those jacks that nimble leap
> To kiss the tender inward of thy hand,
> Whilst my poor lips, which should that harvest reap,
> At the wood's boldness by thee blushing stand!
> To be so tickl'd, they would change their state
> And situation with those dancing chips,
> O'er whom thy fingers walk with gentle gait,
> Making dead wood more bless'd than living lips.
>     Since saucy jacks so happy are in this,
>     Give them thy fingers, me thy lips to kiss.

### 3.

But usually it was otherwise; he records the degradation of his
position, warring against himself to excuse her and save himself

> For, if I should despair, I should grow mad,
> And in my madness might speak ill of thee—

but at length he speaks out plain:

> My love is as a fever, longing still
> For that which longer nurseth the disease;
> Feeding on that which doth preserve the ill,
> The uncertain sickly appetite to please.
> My reason, the physician to my love,
> Angry that his prescriptions are not kept,
> Hath left me, and I desperate now approve
> Desire is death, which physic did except.
> Past cure I am, now Reason is past care,
> And frantic-mad with evermore unrest;
> My thoughts and my discourse as madmen's are,
> At random from the truth vainly express'd;

> For I have sworn thee fair, and thought thee bright,
> Who art as black as hell, as dark as night.

The *Sonnets*, moving toward a climax, are about to turn back to their beginnings in a complicated yet ineffectual denouement. The dark woman and the youth of the triangle have met; the attraction is immediate, the betrayal merely deferred. Shakespeare, a participant of the friendship of one and the love of the other, is also a helpless observer:

> Two loves I have of comfort and despair,
> Which like two spirits do suggest me still:
> The better angel is a man right fair,
> The worser spirit a woman, colour'd ill.
> To win me soon to hell, my female evil
> Tempteth my better angel from my side,
> And would corrupt my saint to be a devil,
> Wooing his purity with her foul pride.

It seems unlikely that 'the better angel' of this octave could apply to Southampton, now a notorious gallant carrying on an intrigue with at least one of Elizabeth's ladies in waiting, getting her with child, and bringing down on both the Queen's wrath over their secret marriage.

# CHAPTER VI

## *The Youth of the Triangle*

### 1.

I HAVE said that, the *Sonnets* aside, Shakespeare has been writing like a man in love—witness the duet between Lorenzo and Jessica in *The Merchant of Venice:*

> The moon shines bright: in such a night as this,
> When the sweet wind did gently kiss the trees
> And they did make no noise, in such a night
> Troilus methinks mounted the Troyan walls,
> And sigh'd his soul toward the Grecian tents,
> Where Cressid lay that night.

>                  In such a night
> Did Thisbe fearfully o'ertrip the dew,
> And saw the lion's shadow ere himself,
> And ran dismay'd away.

>                In such a night
> Stood Dido with a willow in her hand
> Upon the wild sea-banks, and waft her love
> To come again to Carthage.

In *Much Ado About Nothing*, the climax of the *Sonnets* receives a commentary:

> Friendship is constant in all other things
> Save in the office and affairs of love:
> Therefore all hearts in love use their own tongues;
> Let every eye negotiate for itself
> And trust no agent; for beauty is a witch
> Against whose charms faith melteth into blood.
> This is an accident of hourly proof,
> Which I mistrusted not.

The betrayal has taken place.

## 2.

The sonnets which tell of the betrayal underscore the extreme youthfulness and innocence of the friend. Shakespeare's attitude toward him, as well as the language used, recalls the emotional attachment for William Herbert which was noted earlier:

> Take all my loves, my love, yea, take them all;
> What hast thou then more than thou hadst before?
> No love, my love, that thou mayst true love call;
> All mine was thine before thou hadst this more.

Men have turned on mistress or friend, and sometimes on both; but never in the history of affection has the injured party to a triangle glossed over the ill done him, or sought to belittle it, as Shakespeare is about to do.

Only an unusual relationship, such as that projected earlier between William Shakespeare and the young William Herbert, can account for the poet's ambivalence:

> Gentle thou art, and therefore to be won,
> Beauteous thou art, and therefore to be assail'd;
> And when a woman woos, what woman's son
> Will sourly leave her till she have prevail'd?
>
> That thou hast her, it is not all my grief,
> And yet it may be said I lov'd her dearly;
> That she hath thee, is of my wailing chief,
> A loss in love that touches me more nearly.
>
> But here's the joy; my friend and I are one;
> Sweet flattery! then she loves but me alone.

## 3.

Love's fever, longing in his blood, has turned him back to his erstwhile sovereign. They appear to have parted, to have become reconciled, to have pledged new vows, even; but all to no avail. There is no longer any evidence of the love that shook him before his young friend became involved. His involvement changed Shakespeare's attitude toward the dark woman:

> In loving thee thou know'st I am forsworn,
> But thou art twice forsworn, to me love swearing;
> In act thy bed-vow broke, and new faith torn,
> In vowing new hate after new love bearing.

A cynical detachment becomes evident—

> When my love swears that she is made of truth,
> I do believe her, though I know she lies—

and with it the end, glossed over with a sardonic humor:

> Beshrew that heart that makes my heart to groan
> For that deep wound it gives my friend and me!
> Is't not enough to torture me alone,
> But slave to slavery my sweet'st friend must be?

His real concern is his friend:

> So, now I have confess'd that he is thine,
> And I myself am mortgag'd to thy will,
> Myself I'll forfeit, so that other mine
> Thou wilt restore, to be my comfort still:
> But that thou wilt not, nor he will not be free,
> For thou art covetous, and he is kind.

He has ceased to love, and he has begun to pun on the names of her two lovers:

> Whoever hath her wish, thou hast thy *Will*,
> And *Will* to boot, and *Will* in over-plus;

and again:

> Make but my name thy love, and love that still,
> And then thou lov'st me,—for my name is *Will*—

a last feeble flutter of affection. The net had dissolved.

Such was the experience of the man who, of all men who ever lived and wrote, wrote not only the greatest praise of love, but love's law:

> Let me not to the marriage of true minds
> Admit impediments. Love is not love
> Which alters when it alteration finds . . .

# CHAPTER VII

## The 'Rival Poet'

### 1.

THE enigmas of the *Sonnets* grow, rather than diminish, with study.

It might be supposed that if the 'rival poet' of the sequence numbered 76-86 could be identified, identification of the nobleman whose friendship Shakespeare wished to keep or feared to lose would be easier (I say 'friendship,' not 'patronage,' for the sonnets indicate true affection):

> O! how I faint when I of you do write,
> Knowing a better spirit doth use your name,
> And in the praise thereof spends all his might,
> To make me tongue-tied, speaking of your fame!
>
> Who is it that says most? which can say more
> Than this rich praise,—that you alone are you?
>
> I think good thoughts, while others write good words
> And, like unletter'd clerk, still cry 'Amen'
> To every hymn that able spirit affords,
> In polish'd form of well-refined pen.

The word 'spirit' and the word 'hymn' point to George Chapman, the first because he was the great spirit-invoker of his time, calling on 'assistful spirits' to help him in his writing, and second because he not only translated the *Iliad* and *Odyssey* (calling on Homer's spirit while doing so), but Homer's *Hymns* as well. But the mystery of the nobleman remains, for Chapman addressed commendatory verses to both Southampton and Pembroke.

### 2.

Perhaps it was neither. A man's style does not change with each new subject. The similarities of thought and expression throughout the *Sonnets* may be due to a perfected medium. The possibility exists of a third nobleman striding silently, anonymously, through these poems; and if we can be reasonably certain that Chapman was indeed the poet of the sequence under discussion, it may be possible to name him. I think that Sonnet 86 contains the evidence that is needed for the identification of Chapman:

> Was it the proud full sail of his great verse,
> Bound for the prize of all too precious you,
> That did my ripe thoughts in my brain inhearse,
> Making their tomb the womb wherein they grew?
> Was it his spirit, by spirits taught to write
> Above a mortal pitch, that struck me dead?
> No, neither he, nor his compeers by night
> Giving him aid, my verse astonished.
> He, nor that affable familiar ghost
> Which nightly gulls him with intelligence,
> As victors of my silence cannot boast;
> I was not sick of any fear from thence:
> > But when your countenance fill'd up his line,
> > Then lack'd I matter; that enfeebled mine.

This not only depicts a writer who invoked spirits—no poet's work published in the decade during which Shakespeare wrote his sonnets is more aptly described by 'the proud full sail of his great verse' than Chapman's 'fourteener' or seven-foot-line translation of *Seauen Bookes of the Iliades of Homere,* and *Achilles Shield, Translated as the other seuen Bookes of Homer,* both of which appeared in 1598.

## 3.

There is yet a further clue to the identification of Chapman as the 'rival poet,' and that has to do with the ghost which Shakespeare brought in for good measure in Sonnet 86. Even without the adjectives 'affable' and 'familiar' it must be apparent that the ghost which rises from the ninth line is something quite different from the earlier spirits. It is not a spirit at all, but the characterization of someone formerly known to Shakespeare, and perhaps to the 'rival poet' as well, who had been 'affable' and 'familiar' in life, and who was now dead. Which of his 'precious friends hid in death's dateless night' did Shakespeare mean?

Chapman himself supplies the answer, for in his continuation of *Hero and Leander,* which likewise appeared in 1598, there is a passage which parallels the spirit-and-ghost imagery of Sonnet 86 —his invocation to slain Christopher Marlowe:

> Then thou most strangely-intellectual fire,
> That proper to my soul hast power t'inspire
> Her burning faculties, and with the wings
> Of thy unsphered flame visit'st the springs
> Of spirits immortal; now (as swift as Time
> Doth follow Motion) find th'eternal Clime
> Of his free soul, whose living subject stood
> Up to the chin in the Pierean flood,
> And drunk to me half this Musean story,
> Inscribing it to deathless Memory.
> Confer with it, and make my pledge as deep,
> That neither's draught be consecrate to sleep;
> Tell it how much his late desires I tender,
> (If yet it know not) and to light surrender
> My soul's dark offspring. . . .

### 4.

It is impossible to approach Chapman from any point without encountering spirits. . . .

His *Seauen Bookes of the Iliades of Homere* was dedicated 'TO THE MOST HONORED *now liuing Instance of the Achilleian vertues eternized by diuine* HOMERE, *the Earle of* ESSEXE, *Earle Marshall* &c.'—with a significant device at the top of the first page of the dedication embodying the arms of the Kings of England. The dedication is a paean: 'To you then (most abundant President of true Noblesse) in whose manifest actions all these sacred obiects are diuinely pursude, I most humblie and affectionatlie consecrate this President of all learning, vertue, valour, honor & societie: who (with his owne soule) hath eternizde Armies of Kings and Princes.' Essex is the 'Most true *Achilles* (whom by sacred prophecie *Homere* did but prefigure).' His 'honord countenance' and attributes fill up Chapman's line: 'And thus wishing for the worthy expence of my future life to follow by al oportunitie your honord attempts, & admirde disposition, I doubt not my zeale to the truth of your rare vertues wil enable me (inferior to none) to turne my paper to Christall, from whence no time shall race the engrauen figures of your graces.'

'Inferior to none'—is it a hint of rivalry? The dedication contains two words in extraordinary combination which reappear in Shakespeare: 'standing Lakes'—

> Ye elves of hills, brooks, standing lakes, and groves.

The long and learned preface to *Achilles Shield* is likewise addressed to Essex. 'Onely kings & princes haue been *Homers* Patrones,' says Chapman flatteringly; and if Essex was already nursing dreams of the crown, the phrase must have made him catch his breath. Chapman concludes: 'Thus confidently affirming your name and dignities shall neuer bee more honored in a poore booke then in English *Homer*, I cease to afflict your Lordshippe with my tedious dedicatories, and to [dis] still sacred *Homers* spirit through a language so fitte and so fauourles; humbly presenting your Achilleian vertues with *Achilles* Shield.'

Flattering, too, was the comparison with Achilles. Two years before, Spenser had sung the Earl's martial prowess in *Prothalamion*, naming Leicester House in his poetic tour of the Thames, where his first patron, the Earl of Leicester and favorite of Elizabeth, had lived, and where the Queen's latest favorite was now ensconced (it being called Essex House in his honor):

> Yet therein now doth lodge a noble Peer,
> Great *Englands* glory and the Worlds wide wonder,
> Whose dreadful name, late through all *Spaine* did thunder.

What but martial fame can Shakespeare have meant by the opening of Sonnet 80( quoted at the beginning of this chapter)? He was to praise Essex himself in the role of warrior, in *Henry V*.

# CHAPTER VIII

## *The* Sonnets *as Autobiography*

### 1.

THE *Sonnets*, which some erudite commentators hold to be non-autobiographical, and which some prurient ones wish had never been written, perhaps because they make Shakespeare human, tell more than the poet's friendships and the poet's love. They offer his own commentary on his life as a member of a wandering company of players which moved with its trunkloads of costumes and other gear from suburban theater to theater, and occasionally from London itself to produce plays in the incorporated towns of the hinterland. He was not always happy to leave:

> How heavy do I journey on the way,
> When what I seek, my weary travel's end,
> Doth teach that ease and that repose to say,
> 'Thus far the miles are measur'd from thy friend!'
> The beast that bears me, tired with my woe,
> Plods dully on, to bear that weight in me,
> As if by some instinct the wretch did know
> His rider lov'd not speed, being made from thee:
> The bloody spur cannot provoke him on
> That sometimes anger thrusts into his hide,
> Which heavily he answers with a groan
> More sharp to me than spurring to his side;
>     For that same groan doth put this in my mind:
>     My grief lies onward, and my joy behind.

He had not foreseen this when, at the age of five, he heard the trumpets of the Queen's Men in the streets of Stratford.

### 2.

Was it the dark woman, herself already faithless, or to become so, whose reproaches over his absences wrung forth this reply?

O! never say that I was false of heart,
Though absence seem'd my flame to qualify.
As easy might I from myself depart
As from my soul, which in thy breast doth lie:
That is my home of love: if I have rang'd,
Like him that travels, I return again;
Just to the time, not with the time exchang'd,
So that myself bring water for my stain.
Never believe, though in my nature reign'd
All frailties that besiege all kinds of blood,
That it could so preposterously be stain'd,
To leave for nothing all thy sum of good;
    For nothing this wide universe I call
    Save thou, my Rose; in it thou art my all.

A time had come when his position as a member of a wandering troupe facing the vicissitudes of the road was all but intolerable to his proud spirit; and in one of the most revealing of his utterances it found expression:

Alas! 'tis true I have gone here and there,
And made myself a motley to the view,
Gor'd mine own thoughts, sold cheap what is most dear.

Again and again does he set down what his role in life is, and his growing repugnance for that role:

O! for my sake do you with Fortune chide,
The guilty goddess of my harmful deeds,
That did not better for my life provide
Than public means which public manners breeds.

### 3.

The mystery of the personages of the *Sonnets* persists to the end. Was this addressed to one of his noble friends—or to the dark woman?

When in disgrace with fortune and men's eyes
I all alone beweep my outcast state,
And trouble deaf heaven with my bootless cries,
And look upon myself, and curse my fate,

Wishing me like to one more rich in hope,
Featur'd like him, like him with friends possess'd,
Desiring this man's art, and that man's scope,
With what I most enjoy contented least;
Yet in these thoughts myself almost despising,
Haply I think on thee,—and then my state,
Like to the lark at break of day arising
From sullen earth, sings hymns at heaven's gate;
    For thy sweet love remember'd such wealth brings
    That then I scorn to change my state with kings.

Was this one addressed to the dark woman or to a noble friend, and to what depths did Shakespeare have to descend in order to rise to such heights?

Then hate me when thou wilt; if ever, now;
Now, while the world is bent my deeds to cross,
Join with the spite of fortune, make me bow,
And do not drop in for an after-loss:
Ah! do not, when my heart hath 'scaped this sorrow,
Come in the rearward of a conquer'd woe;
Give not a windy night a rainy morrow,
To linger out a purpos'd overthrow.
If thou wilt leave me, do not leave me last,
When other petty griefs have done their spite,
But in the onset come: so shall I taste
At first the very worst of fortune's might;
    And other strains of woe, which now seem woe,
    Compar'd with loss of thee will not seem so.

So much for the renowned commentators who see nothing topical in Shakespeare's plays, and nothing autobiographical in the *Sonnets.*

# BOOK SIX

# CHAPTER I

## *The End of the* Theatre

### 1.

THE Privy Council and the London Corporation were not the only dangers confronting theater owners. There were landlords then, as now.

James Burbage had built his Theatre east of Finsbury Field, on land of the dissolved Priory of Holywell. This land he had leased of one Gyles Alleyn in the year 1576 for twenty-one years, the annual rent to be fourteen pounds, with the proviso that before the expiration of ten years, a new lease for an additional twenty-one years would be drawn up. Nine years went by, and Burbage did in fact draw up such a new lease; but Alleyn procrastinated and did not sign. He never signed. In jeopardy was the Theatre itself and a house near it inhabited by the Burbages, and several other houses probably inhabited by some members of the Lord Chamberlain's company.

James Burbage was a stubborn and sometimes irascible man. But first and foremost he was a businessman. In negotiating with Alleyn he had effectively sized him up and had managed to insert a clause in the lease which offered a form of protection if things turned out as they eventually did. This clause stipulated that if Burbage, in the first ten years of the term of the original lease spent the sum of two hundred pounds in improving Alleyn's land, he would be entitled 'to take downe and carrie awaie to his and their owne proper use all such buildinges and other thinges as should be builded, erected, or sett up, in or uppon the gardeines and voide grounde by the said indentures graunted, or anie parte thereof, by the said Jeames, his executors or assignes, either for a theatre or playinge place or for anie other lawefull vse.'

### 2.

Blackfriars had advantages similar to Shoreditch and Southwark: its residents were subject to none but the sovereign, which meant that neither Lord Mayor nor sheriffs had jurisdiction there. It was an aristocratic district, near St. Paul's, and easily accessible. When the troubles with his landlord were at their height, James Burbage purchased the Frater Building of the dissolved Blackfriars Monastery, and threw the hall and parlor—'a great room, paved'—together to make a playhouse. Chambers over the parlor provided lodgings. It was in this building that one Rocho Bonetti had long maintained a fencing school; and it is perhaps at him that Shakespeare makes a 'passado' in *Romeo and Juliet*, for Bonetti had boasted that he could 'hit anie Englishman with a thrust vpon anie button':

> *Benvolio.* Why, what is Tybalt?
> *Mercutio.* More than prince of cats, I can tell you. O! he is the courageous captain of compliments. He fights as you sing prick-song, keeps time, distance, and proportion; rests me his minim rest, one, two, and the third in your bosom; the very butcher of a silk button.

Burbage no sooner got under way with his alterations than the aristocratic residents of Blackfriars drew up a petition to the Privy Council to bar a 'common' playhouse in their midst, and it was so ordered. Shortly after, James Burbage died.

### 3.

James Burbage had two sons, Richard and Cuthbert, who had inherited not only their father's histrionic ability, and likewise his short temper, but a good deal of his acumen.

In 1597 the lease of the Theatre ran out. A playhouse was needed if they were not to perish utterly, and they considered how to obtain one. The Lord Chamberlain's Servants included another man not altogether without business sense, and they now conferred with William Shakespeare. A plan was drawn up for the organization of a theatrical company which would be safe from the ordinary vicissitudes, including time, leases, and landlords. Other participants were the actors John Heminge, Augustine Phillips, Thomas Pope and William Kemp, the last not only a renowned comedian, but occasionally the Queen's jester.

The original members of the organization were to be known as 'housekeepers,' on whom would fall the expenses of a site and building, as well as the operation of the new playhouse. For this, ten shares were devised, Richard and Cuthbert Burbage retaining five between them, and the men named above one each. The company itself, as distinct from the housekeepers, also was organized on a share basis. The housekeepers were to receive one-half the income from the galleries, the company the other half plus entrance fees at the doors (theatergoers paid at the door, and if they wished to sit in one of the galleries, paid to go up the stairs to get to them, and possibly a third time for a seat or a place to stand). Thus, actors who were also housekeepers shared double. It was an arrangement which brought out the best in all concerned, for new members of the troupe, if they were loyal as well as talented, could own shares in the company and even rise to the position of a housekeeper. To safeguard individual interests, a joint tenancy was devised, so that the share of a member who withdrew would go back into the control of the organization; but the shares of a deceased member went to his heirs or assigns.

### 4.

The Burbages and other members of this organization, after scouting the suburbs for the site of a new theater, now decided to try their fortunes on the Bankside. In Maiden Lane, near the ancient church of St. Mary Overies, and closer to London Bridge than the Rose or the Bear Garden, there was a parcel of ground which could be leased. A lease was accordingly drawn up to run thirty-one years; and for the mutual protection of all concerned, one-half the property was leased to the Burbages at a yearly rental of seven pounds five shillings, while the other half was leased to William Shakespeare and the other actor-housekeepers on the same terms.

The Burbages now consulted Peter Street, a carpenter and builder, who looked over the old Theatre, as well as the new site, with a practiced eye, and submitted certain plans, which the new organization found agreeable for their enterprise.

As a result, as Gyles Alleyn afterwards complained in her Majesty's courts, on December 28, 1598, Richard and Cuthbert Burbage; Peter Street, William Smyth 'and divers other persons, to the number of twelve,' came together in the neighborhood of the Theatre, 'and then and there armed themselves with dyvers and manye unlawfull and offensive weapons, as, namelye, swordes, daggers, billes, axes and such like, and soe armed, did then repayre unto the said Theater, and then and there, armed as aforesayd, in very ryotous, outragious and forcyble manner, and contrarye to the lawes of your highnes realme, attempted to pull downe the sayd Theater; whereuppon divers of your subjectes, servauntes and farmers, then goinge aboute in peaceable manner to procure them to desist from that their unlawfull enterpryse, they the sayd ryotous persons aforesayd notwithstanding procured then therein with great vyolence, not onlye then and there forcyblye and ryotouslye resisting your subjectes, servauntes and farmers, but allso then and there pulling, breaking and throwing downe the sayd Theater in verye outragious, violent and riotous sort, to the great disturbance and terrefyeing not onlye of your subjectes sayd servauntes and farmers, but of divers others of your Majesties loving subjectes there neere inhabitinge; and having so done, did then alsoe in most forcible and ryotous manner take and carrye awaye from thence all the wood and timber therof unto the Banckyside in the parishe of St. Marye Overyes, and there erected a newe playehowse with the sayd timber and woode.'

Perhaps William Shakespeare was one of the twelve.

### 5.

The playhouse thus spectacularly erected was given the appellation of *The Globe,* and became, virtually at once, the most important theater ever to be erected in England—'the glory of the Bank,' in Ben Jonson's noble phrase. Built of timber, and with a thatched roof open to the sky, it was polygonal outside, probably circular within, to judge by its name and certain other allusions, the most important of which was made by Shakespeare himself.

Although a number of representations of the exterior of the Globe exist, there is no description of the interior. It is possible, however, to visualize its fittings and proportions from the details presented in a contract drawn up a year later between Philip Henslowe and Edward Alleyn, the great star of Marlowe's plays at the Rose, and Peter Street, carpenter and builder, for the erection of *The Fortune* playhouse 'near Goldinge Lane in the parish of Saint Giles withoute Cripplegate of London.' Street, as we have seen, was instrumental in the pulling down of the Theatre and the

London by Visscher

The Globe *at left*

erection of the Globe; and it is evident from the contract that
Henslowe wanted the same kind of building as the new home of
the Chamberlain's Men, that is: 'the saide fframe to conteine three
Stories in heighth, the first or lower Storie to conteine Twelue
foote of lawfvll assize in heighth, the second Storie Eleaven foote
of lawfvll assize in heigth, and the third or vpper Storie to conteine Nyne foote of lawfull assize in height; All which Stories
shall conteine twelue foote and a halfe of lawfull assize in breadth
throgheoute, besides a juttey forwardes in either of the saide two
vpper Stories of Tenne ynches of lawfull assize, with fflower convenient divisions for gentlemens roomes, and other sufficient and
convenient divisions for Twoe pennie roomes; with necessarie
seates to be placed and sett aswell in those roomes as throgheoute
all the rest of the galleries of the saide howse, and with suchelike
steares, conveyances & divisions withoute & within, as are made &
contryved in and to the late erected Plaihowse on the Banck, in
the saide parishe of Ste. Saviours called the Globe; With a Stadge
and Tyreinge howse to be made, erected & settupp within the saide
fframe, with a shadowe or cover ouer the saide Stadge, which
Stadge shalbe placed & sett, as alsoe the stearecases of the said
fframe, in suche sorte as is prefigured in a plott thereof drawen, and
which Stadge shall conteine in length Fortie and Three foote of
lawfull assize and in breadth to extende to the middle of the yarde
of the said howse; The same Stadge to be paled in belowe with
good, stronge and sufficyent new oken bourdes, and likewise the
lower Storie of the saide fframe withinside, and the same lower
storie to be alsoe laide over and fenced with stronge yron pykes;
And the said Stadge to be in all other proporcions contryved and
fashioned like vnto the Stadge of the saide Plaiehowse called the
Globe.'

# CHAPTER II

## *Portrait of an Ideal Man*

### 1.

THUS it was that the prince who was crowned 'Passion sundaie, which was a sore, ruggie, and tempestuous day,' on the stage of the Theatre in Shoreditch, sometime in 1599 crossed the Thames with his retinue to appear, in the new trappings of his royalty, on the stage of the new-built Globe. Shakespeare had promised to continue the story of Prince Hal, 'and make you merry with fair Katharine of France.' In *Henry V* he kept his promise, even to the death of banished Falstaff. Again the anonymous *Famous Victories* helped; but Shakespeare turned also to Holinshed for firsthand information.

### 2.

There is something about Prince Hal in Shakespeare's characterization of him that sets him apart from every other male personage in the plays. Holinshed, to be sure, describes him in admiring terms —even allowing for the natural pride of an English historian writing of the victor of Agincourt, his tribute is exceptional: 'In strength and nimblenesse of bodie from his youth few to him comparable; for in wrestling, leaping, and running, no man well able to compare. In casting of great iron barres and heauie stones he excelled commonlie all men; neuer shrinking at cold, nor slothfull for heat; and, when he most laboured, his head commonlie vncouered; no more wearie of harnesse than a light cloake; verie valiantlie abiding at needs both hunger and thirst; so manfull of mind as neuer seene to quinch at a wound, or to smart at the paine; to turne his nose from euil sauour, or to close his eies from smoke or dust; no man more moderate in eating and drinking, with diet not delicate, but rather more meet for men of warre, than for princes or tender stomachs.' Holinshed's admiration rises to a paean: 'Knowen be it therefore, of person and forme was this prince rightlie representing his heroicall affects; of stature and proportion tall and manlie, rather leane than grose, somewhat long necked, and blacke haired, of countenance amiable; eloquent and graue was his speech, and of great grace and power to persuade: for conclusion, a maiestie was he that both liued & died a paterne in princehood, a lode-starre in honour, and mirrour of magnificence.'

Perhaps any dramatist of Shakespeare's day could have taken this portrait, together with the incidents of Henry's reign, and made a play which could charm Elizabethan playgoers, ever in a mood for patriotic fare. Yet Shakespeare's predecessors, trying to do so, had managed badly; Prince Hal himself appeared profligate without charm, and King Henry victorious without stirring the heart.

### 3.

What is it that makes Shakespeare's Hal so admirable and so winning? It is not only that he was a more skillful dramatist than his predecessors, one whose blank verse rang vibrantly in the round hollow of his playhouse. He brought to his characterization a knowledge of men who were closely akin to Holinshed's paragon—noble personages who, but a step below the throne, led similar lives of action, profligacy and charm; who were renowned for their wit, their bounty, and their exploits by sea and land, under Mars or Venus. Shakespeare was able to visualize Henry whole because of his acquaintance with Southampton and Essex. The bright youths of the *Sonnets* must have been in his thoughts as he began to write.

The verse aside, there are two things in *Henry V* which are not in Holinshed and not in *The Famous Victories:* the scene where fair Katharine of France learns English—'de hand, de fingre, de nails, d'arm, d'elbow, de nick, de sin, de foot'—and the wooing of Katharine which ends the play:

> Fair Katharine, and most fair!
> Will you vouchsafe to teach a soldier terms,
> Such as will enter at a lady's ear,
> And plead his love-suit to her gentle heart?

Your majesty sall mock at me; I cannot speak your England.

O fair Katharine! if you will love me soundly with your

French heart, I will be glad to hear you confess it brokenly with your English tongue. Do you like me, Kate?

*Pardonnez moy,* I cannot tell vat is 'like me.'

An angel is like you, Kate; and you are like an angel.

*Que dit-il? que je suis semblable à les anges?*

The whole scene is a triumph of Shakespeare's art. He drew not only from stores of wisdom, but from life; for in St. Helen's, Bishopsgate, he had dwelt among the French and Flemings of 'Petty France,' situated there, and had heard their broken speech, their accents ludicrous and charming. As a matter of fact, he actually lived in a French household at about this time, and the wooing of Katharine is a contrast to the strange wooing of his host's daughter, in which he played the role of matchmaker.

### 4.

In St. Olave's parish, in a house at the corner of Monkwell and Silver streets, near St. Olave's Church, lived Christopher Mountjoy, maker of women's headdresses. His daughter, Mary, was his only child. He taught her his trade, foreseeing that she would need one to support herself—perhaps spinsterhood was written on her plain face. Then came an apprentice, one Stephen Belott, like Mountjoy a French Huguenot refugee. It was not unusual for apprentices to marry into the families of their employers, but Belott was very reluctant, or Mary was very plain, and certainly Mountjoy was very anxious. He promised Belott a number of things as inducements: a marriage portion of sixty pounds, household stuffs, and two hundred pounds in his will. Belott remained obdurate and adamant.

In this pass, Mountjoy turned to 'one Mr Shakespeare that laye in the house to perswade the plaintiff to the same Marriadge'—so a witness testified when the case came to court. Another deposed: 'Mr: William Shakespeare tould him this deponent that the defendant sent him the said Mr Shakespeare to the plaintiff about suche a marriadge to be hadd betweene them, And Shakespeare tould this deponent that the defendant tould him that yf the plaintiff would marrye the said Marye his daughter he would geue hime the plaintiff A some of monney with her for A porcion in Marriadge with her. And that yf he the plaintiff did not marry with her the said Marye and shee with the plaintiff shee should neuer coste him the defendant her ffather A groat. Wherevppon, and in regard M^r Shakespeare hadd tould them that they should haue A some of money for a porcion from the father, they weare made suer by M^r Shakespeare by geuinge there Consent, and agreed to marrye, and did marrye.'

Mountjoy, however, kept none of his promises—he did not even die. Belott and Mary Mountjoy were married in St. Olave's and continued to live under Mountjoy's roof until quarreling broke out. The Belotts moved away and set up their own headdress establishment. Nobody could say that Belott rushed into court— more than ten years went by before he brought suit.

# CHAPTER III

## *The Portrait Enlarged*

### 1.

THE *Life of King Henry the Fifth,* as Shakespeare entitled it, was introduced to audiences at the Globe by an opening Chorus which, considering the splendor of its scenes and lines, rather modestly cried:

> *O! for a Muse of fire that would ascend*
> *The brightest heaven of invention;*
> *A kingdom for a stage, princes to act*
> *And monarchs to behold the swelling scene.*
> *Then should the war-like Harry, like himself,*
> *Assume the port of Mars; and at his heels,*
> *Leash'd in like hounds, should famine, sword, and fire*
> *Crouch for employment. But pardon, gentles all,*
> *The flat unraised spirits that hath dar'd*
> *On this unworthy scaffold to bring forth*
> *So great an object: can this cockpit hold*
> *The vasty fields of France? or may we cram*
> *Within this wooden O the very casques*
> *That did affright the air at Agincourt?*

More than the excitement of a stage spectacle charged the air, for once more an English army was in the field.

### 2.

The Earl of Essex, rushing in where older and more experienced commanders had failed, had persuaded Queen Elizabeth that he was the right man to subdue Ireland. He had received a box on the ear for turning his back on her during discussions, but he had received his appointment. On March 27, 1599, he had set forth, commander of an army numbering 1,300 horse and 16,000 foot soldiers. He left London on horseback, making his exit to the wars a triumphal tour all the way to Islington—he left, his ill-wishers noted, in the manner of Bolingbroke in *Richard II*, idolized by the people. With him went a gallant company of earls and knights and captains-at-arms, Southampton and Rutland among them, and many a youth of noble and gentle birth, presented in allegory in the Chorus to Act Two of *Henry V*:

> *Now all the youth of England are on fire,*
> *And silken dalliance in the wardrobe lies;*
> *Now thrive the armourers, and honour's thought*
> *Reigns solely in the breast of every man:*
> *They sell the pasture now to buy the horse,*
> *Following the mirror of all Christian kings,*
> *With winged heels, as English Mercuries.*
> *For now sits Expectation in the air.*

### 3.

The allegory was continued in the Choruses preluding Act Three and Act Four; before Act Five, allegory turned to reality as the Chorus invoked the great figure of Essex, presumed victorious in Ireland:

> *But now behold,*
> *In the quick forge and working-house of thought,*
> *How London doth pour out her citizens.*
> *The mayor and all his brethren in best sort,*
> *Like to the senators of the antique Rome,*
> *With the plebeians swarming at their heels,*
> *Go forth and fetch their conquering Caesar in:*
> *As, by a lower but loving likelihood,*
> *Were now the general of our gracious empress,—*
> *As in good time he may,—from Ireland coming,*
> *Bringing rebellion broached on his sword,*
> *How many would the peaceful city quit*
> *To welcome him!*

What his welcome would have been, and with it his aspirations, had he proved victorious in Ireland and truly brought 'rebellion broached on his sword,' may be considered in the light of subsequent events. He could not change his fate.

4.

Essex returned in the fall of the year 1599 not only a failure as a pacifier of the Irish, but charged with an ignominious truce with the leaders of the Irish rebels. Galloping furiously to reach Elizabeth at Nonesuch before his ill-wishers could, booted and spurred and splashed with mud, he dashed as one demented through palace halls and into the Queen's bedchamber, and flung himself at her feet. It was ten in the morning. The way to royalty was familiar to him. It proved Elizabeth's peril and his undoing.

Although she had received him graciously enough, she remembered her position and his, and ordered him to report to the Privy Council. His friends quickly perceived which way the wind was blowing. The Earl of Southampton needed no further reminder of Elizabeth's temper; he had not forgotten his treatment at her hands when his secret marriage to Essex's cousin became public scandal. A letter to Sir Robert Sidney told the news: 'My Lord *Southampton*, and Lord *Rutland* come not to the court; the one doth but very seldome; they pass away the Tyme in *London* merely in going to Plaies euery day.'

5.

Their Lordships of the Privy Council were not pleased by Essex's account of the campaign in Ireland. For years the riches of the nobility and commonwealth had been drained away by armies invading that stubborn isle. Little had come of them—from Essex, less than ever. He had disobeyed orders in treating with the Earl of Tyrone. Their Lordships' displeasure was conveyed to Elizabeth. The way to the royal presence was closed to him, and he was restricted to York House, to sulk in its vast rooms and gardens in the custody of the Lord Keeper.

Although he was thirty-three, and a veteran if not actually a hardened campaigner, his reactions were those of a courtier instead of a warrior. By year's end he was reported dangerously ill. Elizabeth softened and sent eight physicians. Her Majesty was gracious to her erstwhile favorite; it was not until he was well enough, the following June, that he was brought to the Star Chamber to stand trial for disobeying orders. Something weak and theatrical in his nature appeared in the course of his interrogation. He knelt by the

*Robert Devereux,*
*Earl of Essex*

Lords' table, submissive, penitent and pathetic. He admitted his guilt in parleying with the Earl of Tyrone instead of seeking to crush him. Some were for the Tower, some for a fine, some for both. His sole punishment was on the whole a light one, considering what some of his predecessors as Lord Deputy in Ireland had been made to suffer: he was deprived of his offices and ordered to remain in Essex House until it pleased her Majesty to express her pleasure otherwise. It proved galling to one who had, times without number, scornfully brushed her guards aside when he wished to see her, including the Captain of her Guard, Sir Walter Raleigh.

## 6.

It was not so easy to topple the Queen's erstwhile warrior-favorite from the popular imagination. For all his failure in Ireland, and subsequent disgrace at court, he retained the admiration and affection of the common people. The parallels between Bolingbroke and Essex were more than ever noticed in Westminster, where his followers were being termed 'Richard men.' He remained under surveillance even after the Queen allowed him full liberty; but his way to her remained barred.

Whatever his aspirations were, something immediate, something closer to earth, affected his reason as much as his loss of offices and access to the Queen: Elizabeth, long before, had awarded him the monopoly from 'the farm of sweet wines'; the renewal was due, and it was not forthcoming. It represented his chief source of revenue.

A man who is pressed down by cares arising from loss of position and a lack of money is an easy prey to uneasy thoughts. His mind is a stage on which malevolent beings plot and encompass his destruction. Those whom he merely disliked, his fantasy makes hateful. The Earl of Essex began to imagine himself the unhappy victim of the highest personages in the realm, particularly the Cecils. In a fantasy of this kind, where there is no interruption to one's own thoughts, extraordinary ideas take shape; and actions which the realities of life would make impossible appear not only feasible but inevitable. In such a fantasy the individual is both protagonist and antagonist, and he accepts the persuasions of self-interest.

Thus it was that Essex, unable to bear the brunts of his misfortune, and unable to bide his time; unable to withdraw himself to let the winds of ill-will blow over, and unable to remain idle while the ill winds blew, allowed his sick mind to enlarge upon an idea which was born of desperation and was to be buried by disaster.

# CHAPTER IV

## *Preludes to* Hamlet

### 1.

TO FORECAST trends after events have transpired is a
specialty of the historian. The biographer must be more
wary. And yet, as one reads the plays that belong to this
crucial period, and seeks an explanation for the choice of subject
matter, and puzzles over the meaning of certain passages, it is
necessary to conclude that Shakespeare watched with concern the
disintegration of Essex's character and sought to help him, in any
case to warn him. It would have been strange if it had not been so.

Was it rumors of conspiracy in the Essex camp? The Earl had
gone forth to invade and conquer as ambitious Caesar had. He had
not returned like Caesar; there, to be sure, the comparison stopped.
But that may have been the very reason why it was necessary to
guide him in his future course, and to seek that guidance in history.
The Rome of the emperors offered parallels.

Shakespeare turned to Plutarch's *Lives of the Noble Grecians
and Romans*. He must have known North's famous translation
long before. What was the catalyst, if not the tragedy of Essex?
Shakespeare was looking for parallels. He looked hard. He gathered up the materials of three lives in North's Plutarch—Julius
Caesar, Marcus Brutus, and Marcus Antonius—to find them (and
in the process, like an imagined encounter, he suddenly saw
Antony's dark woman of Egypt; 'a wonderfull passing sweete
sauour of perfumes' was wafted from the Cydnus to the Thames).

### 2.

*The Tragedy of Julius Caesar* was at the Globe a week before
Essex rushed unannounced into the Queen's presence. It was thus
recorded by Thomas Platter, traveler from Germany: 'After dinner on the 21st September, at about two o'clock, I went with my
companions over the water, and in the strewn roof-house saw the
tragedy of the first Emperor Julius with at least fifteen characters

very well acted.' The performance was followed by a jig: 'danced according to their custom with extreme elegance. Two in men's clothes and two in women's gave this performance, in wonderful combination with each other.'

Those who, like Platter and his companions, saw *Julius Caesar* acted that day—on a stage thrust deep into the 'wooden O,' under the lightfall from the thatched roof open to the sky—relaxed from the horrors of assassination and suicide to dancing and music at the close. What did they make of Brutus's soliloquy near the opening —what did Essex's friends make of it—

> Between the acting of a dreadful thing
> And the first motion, all the interim is
> Like a phantasma, or a hideous dream:
> The genius and the mortal instruments
> Are then in council; and the state of man,
> Like to a little kingdom, suffers then
> The nature of an insurrection—?

Brutus, the leader and the most honorable of the conspirators, was depicted as a sick man; at the beginning of *Julius Caesar*, he is Hamlet in embryo. His wife tells him:

>                          yesternight at supper
> You suddenly arose, and walk'd about,
> Musing and sighing, with your arms across,
> And when I ask'd you what the matter was,
> You star'd upon me with ungentle looks.
> I urg'd you further; then you scratch'd your head,
> And too impatiently stamp'd with your foot;
> Yet I insisted, yet you answer'd not,

and he replies:

> I am not well in health, and that is all.

> Brutus is wise, and were he not in health,
> He would embrace the means to come by it.

> Why, so I do. Good Portia, go to bed.

> Is Brutus sick, and is it physical
> To walk unbraced and suck up the humours

Of the dank morning? What! Is Brutus sick,
And will he steal out of his wholesome bed
To dare the vile contagion of the night,
And tempt the rheumy and unpurged air
To add unto his sickness? No, my Brutus;
You have some sick offence within your mind.

### 3.

Chapman's *Homer*, particularly in the light of the dedications to the Earl Marshal, offered another opportunity for dramatic reconstruction and precept. How else explain *Troilus and Cressida*, that subtle and enigmatic play, the most enigmatic in the entire canon? It appears, at first glance, like a late and final mockery of the sonnet-woman's infidelities; at second glance, the 'rival poet' is there, too, for Shakespeare appears to be holding up to ridicule the Homeric heroes, particularly Achilles, to whom Chapman had compared Essex; further study brings into focus a warning to Essex and his faction not to proceed in their dangerous course (the lesson of *Julius Caesar* had been lost on them: civil strife, and the harsh and lonely deaths of the conspirators).

A trumpet sounds; the Grecian leaders enter; Agamemnon speaks, offering fresh courage from the old failure to topple Troy after seven years' siege:

> you princes,
> Do you with cheeks abash'd behold our works,
> And call them shames? which are indeed nought else
> But the protractive trials of great Jove,
> To find persistive constancy in men:
> The fineness of which metal is not found
> In Fortune's love.

Is it an apology for Essex's failure in Ireland addressed to those who ruled in Westminster—and with the apology, fair words to comfort the disconsolate Earl himself? The theme is underscored by Nestor:

> In the reproof of chance
> Lies the true proof of men.

And then Ulysses speaks—it is a final admonition:

> when degree is shak'd,
> Which is the ladder to all high designs,
> The enterprise is sick. How could communities,
> Degrees in schools, and brotherhoods in cities,
> Peaceful commerce from dividable shores,
> The primogenitive and due of birth,
> Prerogative of age, crowns, sceptres, laurels,
> But by degree, stand in authentic place?
> Take but degree away, untune that string,
> And, hark! what discord follows.

After the disaster, there was yet another play which was both commentary and memorial of Essex's madness.

# CHAPTER V

## The Tragedy of Essex

### 1.

IT IS difficult to be certain of Essex's intentions, since it appears that he was uncertain of them himself. Everything he did was contradictory, but all led to shameful death. He communicated with James; he plotted to storm Whitehall and the Tower with his followers, imprison his enemies on the Privy Council, and take the Queen herself into his custody. Did he aspire to the throne? At his trial, the Attorney General, Sir Edward Coke, taunted him for wishing to be 'of his earldom *Robert* the last, that of a kingdom *Robert* the first.' Perhaps he had not thought any of these matters out very carefully. He was a man distraught. Perhaps what he most wished was to dash once more into the presence of his sovereign, to throw himself at her feet, abject yet spectacular, and in the tumult and danger of rebellion reveal his desperation, hoping somehow that things would take a proper turn at such a juncture.

### 2.

On February 6, 1601, a number of his malcontent followers, including Lord Mounteagle, Sir Christopher Blunt, Sir Charles Percy and Sir Gilly Merrick, 'went all together to the Globe over the water wher the L. Chamberlens men vse to play and were ther somewhat before the play began, Sʳ Charles tellyng them that the play wold be of harry the iiijᵗʰ.' How these gentlemen spent their time 'before the play began' may be seen from the deposition of Augustine Phillips: 'He sayeth that on Fryday last was sennyght or Thursday Sʳ Charles percy Sʳ Josclyne percy and the L. montegle with some thre more spak to some of the players in the presans of thys examinate to have the play of the deposyng and kyllyng of Kyng Rychard the second to be played the Saterday next promysyng to gete them xls. more then their ordynary to play yt. Wher thys Examinate and hys fellowes were determyned to have played some other play, holdyng that play of Kyng Richard to be so old & so long out of vse as that they shold have small or no Company at yt. But at their request this Examinate and his fellowes were Content to play yt the Saterday and had their xl*s.* more then their ordynary for yt and so played yt accordyngly.'

### 3.

*Richard II* was indeed 'so old & so long out of vse' that the players had let it go to a printer as far back as 1597. It had been reprinted twice in 1598—all three times significantly without the deposing scene. Merely reading it could not give Essex and his followers the satisfaction they looked for. It was not only the deposition of Richard—they would take heart from the account of Bolingbroke's return and triumph:

> You would have thought the very windows spake,
> So many greedy looks of young and old
> Through casements darted their desiring eyes
> Upon his visage, and that all the walls
> With painted imagery had said at once
> 'Jesu preserve thee! welcome, Bolingbroke!'
> Whilst he, from one side to the other turning,
> Bare-headed, lower than his proud steed's neck,
> Bespake them thus, 'I thank thee, countrymen.'

It must have been an extraordinary feat to distribute parts, memorize them and perform the play—all within twenty-four hours. On Saturday, February 7, as Phillips testified, *The Tragedie of King Richard the Second* was performed at the Globe by the Lord Chamberlain's Servants, before an audience which included a group of cloaked and armed men who had paid forty shillings above their admission price. That night at Essex House the ill-fated Earl heard the familiar tale of the deposing of a king. Perhaps his sick mind exulted. It was so simple—audacity was all. Richard had his Bolingbroke, and Elizabeth would have her Essex. He apparently did not know her as well as he thought he did. He did not even know that he lacked audacity.

### 4.

His sickness or madness reached its height the following day.

Essex House swarmed with armed men to the number of three hundred. It had been converted into a fortress and an arsenal.

This, the government had noted. It dispatched, by warrant from Queen Elizabeth, the Earl of Worcester, Lord Keeper of the Great Seal of England, in whose house Essex had been detained, and three other noblemen, to inquire into the reasons for this warlike display; to order Essex to disperse his followers, and to take his grievances, if he had any, to the Queen. Essex permitted them to enter, but barred their escort. He behaved like one distracted—his life had been threatened, he said.

The presence of the Queen's emissaries acted as a goad on the adventurers assembled in Essex House. The Lord Keeper was threatened with death, and Essex himself was taunted for his vacillations and interminable parleying. Desperate and distracted, he rushed forth, followed by his friends, and the cry rose: 'To Court! To Court! A plot is laid for my life!' Pressing forward with Southampton, Rutland, Blunt and others, he sought the way to Whitehall, but the way was barred by barricades and armed men. Did he expect the city to rise in his behalf? The spectacle of his pell-mell expedition merely aroused curiosity. At the very moment that his tumultuous and disorderly column poured forth, heralds proclaimed him a traitor throughout London. His followers melted away; he retreated with only his closest friends to Essex House to withstand a siege. By ten o'clock at night he capitulated, and was taken to the Tower, together with Southampton.

## 5.

On February 19, Lord Buckhurst, the Lord Treasurer, preceded by seven sergeants-at-arms bearing aloft their maces, entered Westminster Hall in his judicial capacity of High Steward of England and took his place under a canopy of state. When he was seated, the earls, barons and judges of the land took their places, according to their degrees. There were nine judges, and twenty-five peers, among them Lord Hunsdon, the Lord Chamberlain. Also present was Sir Walter Raleigh, Captain of the Queen's Guard, and forty guardsmen. Essex and Southampton were then brought in by the Lord High Constable of the Tower, the Lieutenant of the Tower, and the gentleman porter, who carried an ax before the prisoners, with the edge turned away from them.

The ax was toward them when they departed.

Two points of law undid both: *That in case where a subject attempteth to put himself into such strength, as the king shall not be able to resist him, and to force and compel the king to govern otherwise than according to his own royal authority and direction it is manifest rebellion;* and: *That in every rebellion the law intendeth as a consequent the compassing the death and deprivation of the king, foreseeing that the rebel will never suffer that king to live or reign, who might punish or take revenge of his treason and rebellion.*

One by one the twenty-five peers of the realm were asked whether the prisoners were guilty, and one by one each rose and replied: 'Guilty, my lord.' The sentence was: to be taken back to the Tower, thence to be drawn on a hurdle through London, and so to the place of execution, there to be hanged, boweled and quartered, head and quarters to be disposed at her Majesty's pleasure.

### 6.

Southampton pleaded ignorance of the law and his long service to the Queen, and besought her mercy; Essex disdained to plead for his life. The royal mercy was thus expressed: Southampton's sentence was changed to life imprisonment in the Tower; Essex was spared the suffering and degradation of a felon's death, and was executed on Tower Hill on the morning of February 25, after Elizabeth had blocked the first warrant for his death, and then signed a second.

Thus perished, in the thirty-fourth year of his life, Robert Devereux, Earl of Essex, her Majesty's Master of the Horse, afterwards General of the Horse; Knight of the Garter, Earl Marshal of England, and Lord Deputy of Ireland. He had not sought the Queen's pardon, and she had withheld it. Tall, well proportioned, of an amiable and mercurial disposition, courtly and bold, a poet and patron of literature, he had come into her life, like so many other beautiful young men of noble birth; and like them, had gone down to death—while she lingered, lingered, knowing that young James waited for her to die.

# CHAPTER VI

## *'William the Conquerer'*

### 1.

THE year 1601 marked a turning point in the life of Shakespeare. The melancholy events which shattered the noble fellowship he had known were followed, in the early fall, by the death of his father, ripe in years, with a prefix in the Stratford parish register burial notice to mark his late-won gentry-hood:

> Septemb 8    M$^r$ Johañes Shakspear.

John Shakespeare's will has not been found. Whatever money and property he left passed, presumably, to his son William. He had lived long enough to see William renowned among the renowned, and he bequeathed to him the coat of arms and the honorable appellation of 'gentleman.'

### 2.

A single incident provides comic relief from the somber events previously narrated.

On March 13, 1602, John Manningham, law student of the Middle Temple, London, wrote in his diary: 'Vpon a tyme when Burbidge played Rich 3. there was a citizen grewe soe farr in liking w$^{th}$ him that before shee went from the play shee appointed him to come that night vnto hir by the name of Ri: the 3. Shakespeare ouerhearing their conclusion went before, was intertained, and at his game ere Burbidge came. Then message being brought that Rich. the 3$^{d.}$ was at the dore Shakespeare caused returne to be made that William the Conqueror was before Rich. the 3. Shakespeares name was wllm.'

### 3.

Manningham's diary is in the British Museum. His opening phrase, 'Vpon a tyme,' leaves the period of the incident uncertain.

*Richard III* is a very early play; although not published until 1597, it must have been off the boards for several years.

The account of Shakespeare's forestalling bears out Aubrey's description of him as 'very good company, and of a very readie and pleasant smooth Witt.' But it is not relished by his idolators. Yet it is of a piece with the seduction in the meadows of Shottery; with the tale told in *Willobie his Avisa;* with the strange story of the *Sonnets,* and one more tale which, the scholars are agreed, is the most scandalous of all, and which will shortly be told.

# BOOK SEVEN

# CHAPTER I

## *The Tragicall Historie of* Hamlet

### 1.

WE HAVE had sufficient examples of Shakespeare's allusions to current events—amorous, political and literary—to prepare us to accept the probability that passages in his plays which have an appearance of personal expression, which are not based on source books like Holinshed and Plutarch, or the work of a predecessor, and which have an existence apart from the necessities of plot and characterization, are in fact an expression of his own feelings.

The death of Essex, the imprisonment of Southampton in the Tower in the full tide of his manhood, could not but bring oppressive thoughts to one who had stood in relationship to both. He had lost his only son, and his father. The *Sonnets* reveal a crisis of his spirit, aside from the dismal tale of the dark woman. He had observed the world and its inhabitants for a good many years, and it is difficult, even with the best intentions, for one who does so, not to become bitter and misanthropic.

These things are reflected in his work. The commentators who would have preferred to have him continue hewing to the line of their liking have not grasped the simple fact that he was a man who, as his work took shape and grew, was growing himself. Unless we accept the unacceptable thesis, that all men may feel, but not Shakespeare, it is foolish or idle to ask why the great tragedies which are the product of Shakespeare's maturity are steeped in melancholy, a dusk of the spirit in which his mind glows like filament.

### 2.

The story of Hamlet, Prince of Denmark, exists in several forms: in Latin (the *Historia Danica* of Saxo Grammaticus); in Italian, in a French translation from the Italian, and in an English translation from the French entitled *The Hystorie of Hamblet.*

Shakespeare's drama has some things in common with *The Hys-torie:* the murder of Hamlet's father (but slain by his brother at a banquet); the marriage of his mother and uncle; Hamlet's pretended madness, his interview with his mother and the death of a councilor behind the arras; the voyage to England. *The Hystorie,* however, contains much more, which Shakespeare did not use; and there is hardly anything which he did which remains the same in his treatment. He may have got the material for his play from this anonymous prose tract, but I do not think so. It is more likely that he used as his source material an earlier *Hamlet,* in the possession of his company.

This earlier *Hamlet* has disappeared, but there are contemporary allusions to it, viz., 'English *Seneca* read by Candle-light yeelds many good sentences, as *Blood is a beggar,* and so forth; and if you intreate him faire in a frostie morning, hee will affoord you whole *Hamlets,* I should say handfuls of Tragicall speeches'— Thomas Nashe lambasting Thomas Kyd in 1589. It is the usual fate of the innovator. Kyd, profoundly influenced by *Seneca his tenne Tragedies translated into English,* had given the stage one of its most popular dramas, *The Spanish Tragedie,* which Shake-speare collaborating with Marlowe had imitated, and had followed it up with another drama of revenge with a play about Hamlet, in which Shakespeare himself was probably an actor, for his company gave it at the playhouse in Newington Butts in the summer of 1594 (when the Rose was under repair). Henslowe has recorded it in his account book thus: 'In the name of god Amen begininge at newington my Lord Admeralle men & my Lorde chamberlen men As ffolowethe 1594 . . . . yᵉ 9 of June R[eceived] at hamlet viijˢ.' This would account for the way in which the 'booke,' or script, of the play passed into the possession of the Lord Chamberlain's Men.

### 3.

There is nothing in Kyd, nothing in *The Hystorie of Hamblet,* to prepare one for the melancholy which cloaks Shakespeare's pro-tagonist. Passage after passage—the great and usually quoted ones —is steeped in a grief and despair deeper and greater than are required by dramatic necessity. Hamlet not only feigns madness, like his prototype; he is mad, and undergoing a disintegration like Essex. He grows out of Shakespeare's lines in the usual manner

of a Shakespearean hero; but superimposed on his character is
another who appears to be Shakespeare himself. Like a dark
affinity, dark and full of grief, this other projection of Hamlet
speaks for himself:

> O! that this too too solid flesh would melt,
> Thaw and resolve itself into a dew;
> Or that the Everlasting had not fix'd
> His canon 'gainst self-slaughter! O God! O God!
> How weary, stale, flat, and unprofitable
> Seem to me all the uses of this world.

It is not the speech of a man resolved to avenge his murdered
father; but rather of one grown weary with the workaday world:

> For who would bear the whips and scorns of time,
> The oppressor's wrong, the proud man's contumely,
> The pangs of dispriz'd love, the law's delay,
> The insolence of office, and the spurns
> That patient merit of the unworthy takes,
> When he himself might his quietus make
> With a bare bodkin? who would fardels bear,
> To grunt and sweat under a weary life,
> But that the dread of something after death,
> The undiscover'd country from whose bourn
> No traveller returns, puzzles the will,
> And makes us rather bear those ills we have
> Than fly to others that we know not of?

It is not the language of a prince confirmed in his faith, but of a
man oppressed and full of doubt.

### 4.

Marlowe's *Edward II* is strangely in Shakespeare's mind:

> Farewell, fair Queen, weep not for *Mortimer*,
> That scorns the world, and as a traveller,
> Goes to discover countries yet unknown.

A second echo from *Edward II* occurs in Hamlet's quibble with
his mother—

Seems, madam! Nay, it is; I know not 'seems.'
'Tis not alone my inky cloak, good mother,
Nor customary suits of solemn black,
Nor windy suspiration of forc'd breath,
No, nor the fruitful river in the eye,
Nor the dejected haviour of the visage,
Together with all forms, modes, shows of grief,
That can denote me truly; these indeed seem,
For they are actions that a man can play:
But I have that within which passeth show.

Thus Marlowe a decade before:

'Tis not a black coat and a little band,
A Velvet cap'd cloak, faced before with Serge,
And smelling to a Nosegay all the day,
Or holding of a napkin in your hand,
Or saying a long grace at a table's end,
Or making low legs to a nobleman,
Or looking downward, with your eyelids close,
And saying, 'truly an't may please your honor,'
Can get you any favour with great men;
You must be proud, bold, pleasant, resolute,
And now and then, stab as occasion serves.

I can only assume that Shakespeare, with his prodigious memory, remembered the play which had so influenced his *Richard II*; and thinking of his own play, he remembered the role it had played in the life and death of Essex.

### 5.

Again and again the memory of 'precious friends hid in death's dateless night' troubled his thoughts. It will be found that not only the Dane's father strides ghostly and portentous through the pages of his *Hamlet*, but the spirit of Essex and the ghost of Marlowe. To take Marlowe first: were there but one paraphrase of him in this play, it could be passed over in silence; if there were only the two just given, they might be set down as coincidences; but when we come to a third, and then to a fourth, both of them integrated to the plot, a different explanation is required. The link is Essex, for he also is here; once more we have the distracted nobleman disintegrating before our eyes:

> his doublet all unbrac'd;
> No hat upon his head; his stockings foul'd,
> Ungarter'd, and down-gyved to his ancle;
> Pale as his shirt; his knees knocking each other—

as in the colloquy between Brutus and Portia. (At the very opening of *Hamlet* there is a direct reference to *Julius Caesar:*

> In the most high and palmy state of Rome,
> A little ere the mightiest Julius fell,
> The graves stood tenantless and the sheeted dead
> Did squeak and gibber in the Roman streets.)

Is not this more appropriate to the fall of Essex than to the disintegration of Hamlet:

> O! what a noble mind is here o'erthrown:
> The courtier's, soldier's, scholar's, eye, tongue, sword;
> The expectancy and rose of the fair state,
> The glass of fashion and the mould of form,
> The observ'd of all observers, quite, quite down!

Hamlet's last speech recalls Essex's bid to James:

> I cannot live to hear the news from England,
> But I do prophesy the election lights
> On Fortinbras: he has my dying voice.

# CHAPTER II

## Hamlet *Continued: Homage to Marlowe*

### 1.

THE undercurrent of autobiography already apparent in *Hamlet* receives its greatest expression in the passages dealing with the play within the play. The first relates to James Burbage's venture in Blackfriars, which turned out even more disastrously for his troupe than it had for him.

Shortly after the elder Burbage's death, his son Richard leased the Blackfriars property to one Henry Evans, who apparently was able to put on plays in the 'great room, paved,' with the assistance of the Master of the Children of the Royal Chapel. This worthy, Nathaniel Giles, held a patent from Elizabeth to provide singing boys for Windsor and St. Paul's. It was no new thing for the chapel children to act as well as sing, for their predecessors in the choir had put on plays by John Lily. Giles obtained Elizabeth's approval to recruit boy actors as well as singers, and under the guise of private rehearsals for her Majesty's entertainment, gave public performances. One method of recruiting for the Blackfriars playhouse created a scandal. boys on their way to grammar school, if they looked likely, were waylaid and carried off to the chambers over the stage, given parts to learn, and were threatened with whipping, and whipped, if they didn't memorize their lines quickly enough.

Skilled in music, richly appareled for their roles, more convincing than their elders in feminine parts with their girlish faces, high voices and slim figures, the boys of the Chapel Royal drew crowds away from the Bankside to Blackfriars. How delightful an evening there could be is seen in the testimony of the visiting Duke of Stettin-Pomerania: 'For a whole hour before the play begins, one listens to charming instrumental music played on organs, lutes, pandoras, mandolins, violins, and flutes.' The playhouse itself, being roofed, was lighted by great chandeliers stuck with candles.

Such was the first fruit borne by James Burbage's investment in Blackfriars. The following dialogue, which introduces the subject of players in *Hamlet*, reflects the feelings of the adult actors:

*Hamlet.* What players are they?

*Rosencrantz.* Even those you were wont to take delight in, the tragedians of the city.

*Hamlet.* How chances it they travel? their residence, both in reputation and profit, was better both ways.

*Rosencrantz.* I think their inhibition comes by the late innovation.

*Hamlet.* Do they hold the same estimation they did when I was in the city? Are they so followed?

*Rosencrantz.* No, indeed they are not.

*Hamlet.* How comes it? Do they grow rusty?

*Rosencrantz.* Nay, their endeavour keeps in the wonted pace: but there is, sir, an aery of children, little eyases, that cry out on the top of the question, and are most tyrannically clapped for't: these are now the fashion.

## 2.

Now, with a flourish of trumpets, as once, long ago, when his father was high bailiff of Stratford, and afterwards in so many towns and boroughs of the hinterland whither his company had traveled, Shakespeare marks the arrival of the players discussed above.

*Hamlet.* I heard thee speak me a speech once, but it was never acted; or, if it was, not above once; for the play, I remember, pleased not the million; 'twas caviare to the general: but it was —as I received it, and others, whose judgments in such matters cried in the top of mine—an excellent play, well digested in the scenes, set down with as much modesty as cunning. I remember one said there were no sallets in the lines to make the matter savoury, nor no matter in the phrase that might indict the author of affectation; but called it an honest method, as wholesome as sweet, and by very much more handsome than fine. One speech in it I chiefly loved; 'twas Aeneas' tale to Dido; and thereabout of it especially, where he speaks of Priam's slaughter. If it live in your memory, begin at this line: let me see, let me see:—

*The rugged Pyrrhus, like the Hyrcanian beast,* etc.

The tiger of Hyrcania springs from the *Aeneid* into dramatic blank verse via Marlowe. In his *Tragedie of Dido Queene of Carthage* there occurs a memorable account of the sack of Troy, narrated by Aeneas:

> At last came Pyrrhus, fell and full of ire,
> His harness dropping blood, and on his spear
> The mangled head of Priam's youngest son,
> And after him his band of Myrmidons,
> With balls of wild-fire in their murdering paws,
> Which made the funeral flame that burnt fair *Troy*.

The players take up the speech where Hamlet leaves off:

> *the hellish Pyrrhus*
> *Old grandsire Priam seeks.*

> *Anon, he finds him*
> *Striking too short at Greeks; his antique sword,*
> *Rebellious to his arm, lies where it falls,*
> *Repugnant to command. Unequal match'd,*
> *Pyrrhus at Priam drives; in rage strikes wide;*
> *But with the whiff and wind of his fell sword*
> *The unnerved father falls.*

This appears to be a recollection of Marlowe's:

> Whereat he lifted up his bed-rid limbs,
> And would have grappled with *Achilles'* son,
> Forgetting both his want of strength and hands,
> Which he disdaining whiskt his sword about,
> And with the wind thereof the King fell down;
> Then from the navel to the throat at once,
> He rip't old *Priam:* at whose latter gasp
> *Jove's* marble statue 'gan to bend the brow,
> As loathing *Pyrrhus* for this wicked act.

Thus did Shakespeare, by the light of burning Troy, pay homage once again to his dead but never-forgotten friend.

3.

It is apparent from Shakespeare's advice to the players that he had become impatient with the manner in which dramatic compositions, his own included, were sometimes projected on the stage. He took the opportunity afforded by the play within the play to insert a series of strictures on contemporary acting, with emphasis on the speaking of lines. To this he added a coaching primer which still has point as regards the acting of his own plays, particularly *Hamlet*. The whole has an air of oft-repeated conversation—his own:

*Hamlet*. Speak the speech, I pray you, as I pronounced it to you, trippingly on the tongue; but if you mouth it, as many of your players do, I had as lief the town-crier spoke my lines. Nor do not saw the air too much with your hand, thus; but use all gently: for in the very torrent, tempest, and—as I may say— whirlwind of passion, you must acquire and beget a temperance, that may give it smoothness. O! it offends me to the soul to hear a robustious periwig-pated fellow tear a passion to tatters, to very rags, to split the ears of the groundlings, who for the most part are capable of nothing but inexplicable dumb-shows and noise: I would have such a fellow whipped for o'er-doing Termagant; it out-herods Herod: pray you, avoid it.

*First Player*. I warrant your honour.

*Hamlet*. Be not too tame neither, but let your own discretion be your tutor: suit the action to the word, the word to the action; with this special observance, that you o'erstep not the modesty of nature; for anything so overdone is from the purpose of playing, whose end, both at the first and now, was and is, to hold, as 'twere, the mirror up to nature; to show virtue her own feature, scorn her own image, and the very age and body of the time his form and pressure. Now, this overdone, or come tardy off, though it make the unskilful laugh, cannot but make the judicious grieve; the censure of which one must in your allowance o'erweigh a whole theatre of others. O! there be players that I have seen play, and heard others praise, and that highly, not to speak it profanely, that, neither having the accent of Christians nor the gait of Christian, pagan, nor man, have so strutted and bellowed that I have thought some of nature's journeymen had made men and not made them well, they imitated humanity so abominably.

*First Player.* I hope we have reformed that indifferently with us.

*Hamlet.* O! reform it altogether.

To complete his acting manual, Shakespeare added a few remarks for the benefit of the clowns, who apparently were not content to buzz the words given or, as was sometimes the case in a hasty script, merely indicated; but took it on themselves to engage a buffoon on the other side of the stage to attract attention to themselves: 'Let those that play your clowns speak no more than is set down for them; for there be of them that will themselves laugh, to set on some quantity of barren spectators to laugh too, though in the mean time some necessary question of the play be then to be considered; that's villanous, and shows a most pitiful ambition in the fool that uses it.'

Such were the thoughts about acting set down at the height of his fame and powers by the greatest dramatic poet of his time, in the full consciousness of his art, and in his own accents.

4.

*The Hystorie of Hamblet* depicts the death of Hamlet's father at a banquet. We do not know how Kyd projected it. When Hamlet decides

> the play's the thing
> Wherein I'll catch the conscience of the king,

the murder is accomplished by poison poured into the sleeping monarch's ear, while the prince gives a running commentary, with an eye on his uncle: 'He poisons him i' the garden for's estate. His name's Gonzago; the story is extant, and writ in very choice Italian.'

It was writ in very choice English by Marlowe, in *Edward II:*

> 'Tis not the first time I have killed a man;
> I learned in Naples how to poison flowers,

To strangle with a lawn thrust through the throat,
To pierce the wind-pipe with a needle's point,
Or whilst one is asleep, to take a quill
And blow a little powder in his ears.

Thus did the tragedy of revenge, launched long ago by Kyd, receive its highest expression at the hands of Shakespeare. In writing it, he took a backward glance at the men with whom he had begun his career as a dramatist. Of the two most important, and most spectacular, Marlowe was dead, slain in 1593; Kyd disappeared at the end of 1594 after torture in Bridewell because a manuscript religious tract had been found in his chambers, supposedly heretical and 'which he affirmethe that he had had ffrom Marlowe.' Lodge, too, was in his thoughts; and before the end he was to turn to Lodge's friend, Robert Greene, whose romance, *The History of Pandosto,* became *The Winter's Tale.*

## Shakespeare in Stratford Again

### 1.

IF *ALL'S WELL THAT ENDS WELL* belongs to this period, and it seems to do so, and yet seems not, it is an astonishing performance. Its plot is like the clown's device in this play: 'a barber's chair that fits all buttocks; the pin-buttock, the quatch-buttock, the brawn-buttock, or any buttock.' A' had him a maid once that was a lawyer; here's one that's a doctor and can cure a king. It is like the plays he was writing fifteen years before; and full of rhyme, too. The plot's in Boccaccio's *Decameron,* the ninth story of the third day, Englished by Paynter in his *Palace of Pleasure.* Shakespeare, as usual, added characters of his own, and developed the others as only he could do—'tis a strange play for all that, for this period of his life.

Perhaps it had lain unfinished in a trunk, and he fished it out to beguile his time during a sojourn in Stratford. Here is the dying father's advice from Lodge's *Rosalynde,* already used once in *Hamlet:*

> Love all, trust a few,
> Do wrong to none: be able for thine enemy
> Rather in power than use, and keep thy friend
> Under thy own life's key: be check'd for silence,
> But never tax'd for speech.

Here's Rosalind's thought (Shakespeare's, rather) in *As You Like It,*

> I see no more in you
> Than without candle may go dark to bed,

in Bertram's running from Helena:

> War is no strife
> To the dark house and the detested wife.

It smacks of Stratford; and other signs point to his being there about this time.

## 2.

On May 1, 1602, William Shakespeare purchased 107 acres of arable land from John Combe of Old Stratford and his kinsman, William Combe, two members of a local family which had grown powerful by usury. He paid the rather considerable sum of three hundred and twenty pounds, probably in cash, since there is nothing in the indenture about a mortgage. The indenture has the following endorsement: 'Sealed and deliued to Gilbert Shakespeare to the vse of the wthin named William Shakespeare,' which indicates that the poet had left Stratford after concluding his negotiations, probably to go on the road with *Hamlet*. Since some of the land was rented out to tenant farmers, the purchase made Shakespeare a landlord. He was rising faster than his father.

On September 28 of the same year he purchased a cottage and garden on Walkers' Street across the street from New Place. The cottage belonged to the Manor of Rowington, and in order to complete the transaction it was necessary for him to pledge fealty to the lady of the manor, Anne, Countess of Warwick, widow of the Earl of Warwick. The document transferring the copyhold of the cottage with its appurtenances 'to the behoof and use of William Shakespeare and his heirs forever,' ends as follows: 'And so it remains in the hands of the Lady of the Manor aforesaid until such time as the aforesaid William Shakespeare shall come to receive the premises aforesaid' (original in Latin). It meant a trip to Warwick. If the ceremony of fealty was carried out, he knelt before the lady of the manor, holding his hands together between hers, and pledged life and limb and all earthly worship save that due to the sovereign.

His motive in purchasing a cottage in the heart of Stratford, when he had a house there, remains obscure. It was probably a good investment, and he obviously had money to invest. Perhaps he used it himself as a place in which to work, and as a retreat from his spouse.

# CHAPTER IV

## *Shakespeare a King's Man*

### 1.

THE title pages of Shakespeare's plays are a repository of information about the companies that produced them and the places where they were produced. The title page of the first quarto of *Hamlet*, 1603, has more than the usual amount of such information: 'The Tragicall Historie of HAMLET *Prince of Denmarke* by William Shake-speare. As it hath beene diuerse times acted by his Highnesse seruants in the Cittie of London: as also in the two Vniuersities of Cambridge and Oxford, and else-where.'

His company was no longer the Lord Chamberlain's Men, but the King's.

### 2.

The many faults of James I have been set down by many writers; his virtues, so far as they pertain to Shakespeare, will be set forth here. To begin with, he was a poet, though not to be compared with his illustrious ancestor, James I of Scotland. He was also a patron of the drama, first in Scotland, afterwards in England. He could converse in Latin, and he was the author of *Ane schort Treatise, conteining some revlis and cautelis to be obseruit and eschewit in Scottis Poesie.*

James kept his Scots burr to the end of his days.

The Venetian ambassador has described him: 'of moderate height, of a very good complexion, of an agreeable presence, and of a very robust constitution, which he endeavours to preserve in its vigour. He ardently loves hunting, and makes use of it not only for his diversion, but also for his health; so thoroughly does he devote himself to it, that he has abandoned and thrown under foot all other business, which he has resigned to his Council and Ministers, so that one may truly say that he is merely a Prince by name, and rather in appearance than in fact. This proceeds purely

246

from inclination, seeing that he is endowed with an excellent understanding and extraordinary learning.' His Majesty's dislike of crowds was noted down: 'He does not make much of his subjects, and does not receive them with the same cordiality by which Queen Elizabeth used to gain the hearts of this people, who love their prince so much, that if he passed a hundred times a day through a street, they would always run to see him, feeling pleased that royalty should be gratified with this mark of affection.' The English haven't changed very much.

### 3.

Queen Elizabeth died in the fullness of years on March 24, 1603, having reigned forty-five. James might have become a philosopher while waiting for her to die; he became, instead, a poet and patron of the drama. On May 17 he commanded the Lord Keeper of the Great Seal of England to issue a patent whereby the famous company of the Lord Chamberlain's Men became the King's own actors: 'To all Iustices Maiors Sheriffes Constables hedborrowes and other our Officers and louinge Subiectes greetinge. Knowe yee that Wee of our speciall grace, certeine knowledge, & mere motion haue licenced and aucthorized and by theise presentes doe licence and aucthorize theise our Servauntes Laurence ffletcher, William Shakespeare, Richard Burbage Augustyne Phillippes Iohn Heminges Henrie Condell William Sly Robert Armyn Richard Cowly and the rest of theire Assosiates freely to vse and exercise the Arte and faculty of playinge Comedies Tragedies histories Enterludes moralls pastoralls Stageplaies and Suche others like as theie haue alreadie studied or hereafter shall vse or studie aswell for the recreation of our lovinge Subiectes as for our Solace and pleasure when wee shall thincke good to see them duringe our pleasure. And the said Commedies tragedies histories Enterludes Moralles Pastoralls Stageplayes and suche like to shewe and exercise publiquely to theire best Commoditie when the infection of the plague shall decrease aswell within theire nowe vsual howse called the Globe within our County of Surrey, as alsoe within anie towne halls or Moute halls or other conveniente places within the liberties and freedome of anie other Cittie vniversitie towne or Boroughe whatsoever within our said Realmes and domynions. Willinge and Commaundinge

you and everie of you as you tender our pleasure not onelie to per-
mitt and suffer them herein without anie your lettes hindranc or
molestacions during our said pleasure but alsoe to be aidinge and
assistinge to them yf anie wronge be to them offered. And to allowe
them such former Courtesies as hath bene giuen to men of theire
place and quallitie and alsoe what further favour you shall shewe
to theise our Servauntes for our sake wee shall take kindlie at your
hand.'

Such was the letter patent, issued two days after his Majesty's
commandment, by which Shakespeare's company became the King's
Men, with the rank of Grooms of the Royal Chamber. Two of the
first plays produced by the newly created royal troupe were
Shakespeare's *Hamlet*, and *Sejanus* by Ben Jonson, who afterwards proudly announced that fact in his *Workes:* 'This Tragoedie
was first acted, in the yeere 1603. By the Kings Maiesties Seruants
The principall Tragoedians were

| | |
|---|---|
| Ric. Burbadge. | Will. Shake-Speare. |
| Aug. Philips. | Ioh. Hemings. |
| Will. Sly. | Hen. Condel. |
| Ioh. Lowin. | Alex. Cooke.' |

### 4.

The poets who had flattered Elizabeth living, as Cynthia the
chaste goddess of the moon, mourned her dead. Alone of all the
renowned men then writing Shakespeare failed to mark her passing
with an elegy. He could not flatter her dead who living had let
Essex die and Southampton languish in prison. His expecta-
tions were keyed up to the arrival of James—whatever the Scottish
monarch might bring in his train, he would bring release for the
Earl, for he had long known who his English friends were. And
so it turned out, for Southampton, sequestered by a queen, was
released by a king; and Shakespeare noted queen's death, king's
arrival and friend's freedom in a powerful sonnet which nevertheless has mystified the scholars:

Not mine own fears, nor the prophetic soul
Of the wide world dreaming on things to come,
Can yet the lease of my true love control,
Suppos'd as forfeit to a confin'd doom.

The mortal moon hath her eclipse endur'd,
And the sad augurs mock their own presage;
Incertainties now crown themselves assur'd,
And peace proclaims olives of endless age.
Now with the drops of this most balmy time
My love looks fresh, and Death to me subscribes,
Since, spite of him, I'll live in this poor rime,
While he insults o'er dull and speechless tribes:
 And thou in this shalt find thy monument,
 When tyrants' crests and tombs of brass are spent.

The scholars date this sonnet 1596 or 1598, yet the second quatrain shows the year to have been 1603. 'The mortal moon hath her eclipse endur'd' has no meaning if it does not mean the death of Elizabeth; 'the sad augurs mock their own presage' is a reference to fears and prophesies of civil war or invasion at her death, for which the next two lines offer their own commentary:

Incertainties now crown themselves assur'd,
And peace proclaims olives of endless age.

The word 'crown' can hardly be an accident; and Count Villamediana, the Spanish ambassador, came over in great pomp in 1603, 'bearing the olive-branch of peace.' Together with Shakespeare's comments on affairs of state, we have once more the very language of the sonnet sequence earlier applied to Southampton:

My love looks fresh, and Death to me subscribes.

It was not long before the Earl resumed his place and his possessions to bask in the favor of the new monarch and a new queen. A letter from Sir Walter Cope to Robert Cecil, Lord Cranborne, who was instrumental in having the Earl's sentence commuted, terming him 'the poor young Earl' to soften Elizabeth's heart, shows that his passion for plays was unabated, and that performances were given in his London residence: 'I have sent and bene all thys morning huntyng for players Juglers & Such kinde of Creaturs, but fynde them harde to finde, wherfore Leavinge notes for them to seeke me, Burbage ys come, & Sayes ther ys no new playe that the quene hath not seene, but they hav Revyved an olde one, Cawled *Loves Labore lost*, which for wytt & mirthe he sayes will please her excedingly. And Thys ys apointed to be playd to

Morowe night at my Lord of Sowthamptons, unless yow send a wrytt to Remove the Corpus Cum Causa to your howse in Strande. Burbage ys my messenger.'

## 5.

Because of a recurrence of plague, and perhaps James's dislike of crowds, the royal entry and progress from the Tower to White-hall did not take place until March 15, 1604. James, meanwhile, permitted his new lieges the happy but expensive privilege of enter-taining him and his court until London became a fit habitation once more. In September, 1603, he was at Winchester, from which place he sent an embassy to the Duke of Württemberg, Elizabeth's 'Cousin Mumpellgart,' charged with the investment of that 'high and mighty Prince' with the order and ornaments of the Garter, which Elizabeth, in the six years since the Duke's election, had somehow neglected to send him, although he importuned her with letters and private ambassadors. At length he began to importune James. . . . James was a peacemaker. Stow's *Annals* recounts how 'Lord Spencer of Wormleyton, and Sir William Dethicke, Garter Knight, principall King at Armes, was sent to the sayd Duke in that behalfe,' and how joyous the said Duke was when he heard the reason of their coming to him in Stuttgart: 'Uppon the sixt of November (which was the day appointed for that action), the Duke was invested, the robes, Garter and other ornaments of the sayd Order, and other ceremonies were performed in the Cathe-drall Church of that citie, in as religious and solemne manner as in like cases hath beene used, and all the residue of that day was spent in great feasts, and triumpes, fower dayes after were spent in hunting the wild Bore, and other pastimes, the evening before they departed, were made very admirable and costly fire-workes, and nothing was omitted.' The Duke's subjects were no doubt delighted.

For two months in the fall of 1603, James and his court were at Wilton, being sumptuously entertained by the Earl of Pembroke. The King's Men performed there on December 2.

## 6.

Because Shakespeare's troupe was now a royal entity, and as such entitled to wear the King's livery of scarlet, the members of his company were included in the list of the Master of the Wardrobe, Sir George Home, to receive four and a half yards of scarlet-red cloth each with which to make garments to wear in the royal procession of March 15. Whether they marched or not, clad in the royal colors, is not known; the company is not named in any of the accounts of the King's progress through London. Yet the names of the King's Men are set down for this occasion in the account book of Sir George, which tells of 'all manner of furnitures and prouisions whatsoeuer by him bought and prouided for his Majesties use and seruice against his royall entry and proceeding through his honorable Citie of London together w^th our Souereign Lady Queen Anne his wife and the noble Prince Henry his son,' including 'Red Cloth bought of sondrie persons and giuen by his Majestie to diuerse persons against his Maiesties sayd royall proceeding through the Citie of London viz.

|  | Scarlet-Red Cloth |
|---|---|
| William Shakespeare | iiij yard di |
| Augustine Phillipps | iiij yard di |
| Lawrence ffletcher | iiij yard di |
| Iohn Hemming | iiij yard di |
| Richard Burbidge | iiij yard di |
| William Slye | iiij yard di |
| Robert Armyn | iiij yard di |
| Henry Cundell | iiij yard di |
| Richard Cowley | iiij yard di.' |

## 7.

James continued his peacemaking. On his invitation, King Philip III of Spain sent as ambassador the Constable of Castile, Juan Fernandez de Velasco, Duke of Frias, who was royally entertained, with his entourage, at Somerset House, the dower-house of James's consort, Queen Anne of Denmark. This palace by the river had immense gardens with hedges of rosemary; two acres were under cultivation by John Gerard, the herbalist, who supplied the Queen with flowers, fruits and herbs.

In the summer of 1604, twelve new Grooms of the Chamber, all of them members of the royal troupe, helped to make the ambassador's stay a delightful one, and were rewarded by Sir

John Stanhope, Treasurer of the King's Majesty's Chamber: 'To Augustine Phillipes and John Hemyng for thallowance of themselves and tenne of theire ffellowes his Ma$^t$ groomes of the chamber, and Players for waytinge and attendinge on his Ma$^t$ service by comaundmente vppon the spanishe Embassador at Som'sette House the space of xviij dayes viz$^d$ from the ix$^{th}$ day of Auguste 1604 vntill the xxvij$^{th}$ day of the same as appeareth by a bill therof signed by the Lord chamblayne xxj$^{li}$ xij$^s$.'

Whether Shakespeare was one of the 'tenne' cannot now be determined. It seems unlikely, in view of his usual precedence. Augustine Phillips died in 1605. On May 4 of that year he made his will, in which he remembered the obscure workers as well as the greatest member of his illustrious troupe: 'Item I geve and bequeathe unto and amongste the hyred men of the Company which I am of, which shalbe at the tyme of my decease, the some of fyve pounds of lawfull money of England to be equally distributed amongeste them. Item I geve and bequeathe to my Fellowe William Shakespeare a thirty shillings peece in gould.'

The money was for a memorial ring.

### 8.

Shakespeare's preoccupation with death, which gives *Hamlet* and the other great tragedies of this period their supererogatory somber cast, was earlier projected in the *Sonnets:*

> That time of year thou mayst in me behold
> When yellow leaves, or none, or few, do hang
> Upon those boughs which shake against the cold,
> Bare ruin'd choirs, where late the sweet birds sang—

the very mood of Macbeth. It is introduced in an unexpected place, a play which is neither tragedy nor comedy, but as it were, partaking of both—*Measure for Measure:*

> Ay, but to die, and go we know not where;
> To lie in cold obstruction and to rot;
> This sensible warm motion to become
> A kneaded clod; and the delighted spirit
> To bathe in fiery floods, or to reside
> In thrilling region of thick-ribbed ice;

To be imprison'd in the viewless winds,
And blown with restless violence round about
The pendant world—

still the accent of the Dane. The play is a dark corridor leading to
the vast glooms and madness, the perfection of language and art,
of *Othello* and *Lear;* and also to the golden world of Shakespeare's desire.

# CHAPTER V

## *Mistress Davenant of the* Crown

### 1.

I HAVE said that the title-page of *Hamlet* shows that it was acted 'in the two Vniuersities of Cambridge and Oxford.' In Cambridge, Spenser's 'singular good frend' Gabriel Harvey, Fellow of Pembroke Hall, saw a performance, and in his chambers afterwards, added to the marginalia in his folio Chaucer: 'The younger sort takes much delight in Shakespeares Venus & Adonis: but his Lucrece, & his tragedie of Hamlet, Prince of Denmarke, haue it in them, to please the wiser sort,' of whom, no doubt, he was pleased to consider himself one.

The visit of the King's Men to Oxford brings us to an interesting chapter in Shakespeare's life. Their performance of *Hamlet* definitely places him there; and he is afterwards, by tradition, a frequent visitor.

### 2.

Midway between London and Stratford-upon-Avon, Oxford was a convenient stopping place for the journey to and from the metropolis. The Crown Inn, according to seventeenth century tradition, was the usual place where Shakespeare lodged: 'Mr William Shakespeare was wont to goe into Warwickshire once a yeare, and did commonly in his journey lye at this house in Oxon: where he was exceedingly respected' (Aubrey).

The host of the Crown was one John Davenant, who had a son, William, christened March 3, 1606, in St. Martin's Church, Oxford, being named, if the tradition is to be trusted, for William Shakespeare. William Davenant's mother 'was a very beautiful woman, of a good wit and conversation, in which she was imitated by none of her children but by this William. The father, who was a very grave and discreet citizen (yet an admirer and lover of plays and play-makers, especially Shakespeare, who frequented his house in his journies between Warwickshire and London) was of a

254

melancholic disposition, and was seldom or never seen to laugh'
(Anthony à Wood).

It is already all there. A man with a beautiful and witty wife
usually has need of a grave face; and if the rest of this story is to be
believed, John Davenant quite properly was 'seldom or never seen
to laugh,' particularly when he looked at his son: 'M^r. Shakespear
was his God-father & gave him his name. (In all probability he
got him.) 'Tis further said that one day going from school a grave
Doctor in Divinity met him, and ask'd him, *Child whither art thou
going in such hast?* to w^ch the child reply'd, *O Sir my Godfather
is come to Town, & I am going to ask his blessing.* To w^ch the D^r.
said, *Hold Child, you must not take the name of God in vaine*'
(Thomas Hearne).

There are at least half a dozen printed versions of the tale, with
only slight variations.

### 3.

John Davenant's will gives no hint of a scandal—on the contrary, it appears that he continued to love his wife, whom he out-
lived, to his last gasp: 'my body I committ to the earth to be buryed
in the parish of St. Martins in Oxford as nere my wife as the
place will give leave where shee lyeth.' The item relating to
William is inconclusive: 'my will is also that my sonne William,
being now arrived to sixteen yeares of age, shall be put to prentice
to some good marchant of London or other tradesman by the consent and advise of my overseers.' William followed the Muses
instead of a trade, became poet laureate, was knighted, wrote plays,
and is thought to have been the first man to introduce women on
the English stage, after the Restoration.

Perhaps the most curious part of the whole story is that William
Davenant was not averse to being thought Shakespeare's son—in
Aubrey's account: 'Sr. W^m would sometimes when he was pleasant
over a glasse of wine with his most intimate friends e.g. Sam:
Butler (author of Hudibras) &c. say, that it seemed to him that
he writt with the very spirit that Shakespeare, and seemed contented enough to be thought his Son: he would tell them the story
as above (in which way his mother had a very light report).'

Shakespeare's will does not mention him.

## 4.

One may deprecate the tale told by Aubrey and company, and shut one's mind to it, as some eminent scholars indicate they would like to do—as though it were an affront to their morality; but this seems ludicrous as well as unscholarly. It is part of Shakespeare's story—a stubborn fact.

Anthony à Wood lived in Oxford. He is known to have taken great liberties with Aubrey's texts, as Aubrey himself complained; but there is some significance in the fact that he did not destroy Aubrey's account of Shakespeare at the Crown, and even more in the fact that he wrote one himself. It is better, therefore, to pursue the tale. Here is a mature woman, beautiful and witty, linked to Shakespeare: did she evoke memories of the dark woman of the *Sonnets?* In *Antony and Cleopatra* the two women seemed to be merged.

# CHAPTER VI

## *Portrait of a Dark Woman*

### 1.

*A*NTONY AND CLEOPATRA opens dramatically on a landscape of sunlight and sand, and on a woman glimpsed years before in the pages of North's *Plutarch:* 'Caesar and Pompey knew her when she was but a yong thing, & knew not then what the world meant: but now she went to Antonius at the age when a womans beauty is at the prime, and she also of best iudgment.'

Shakespeare, too, was no longer young. He had known a world of women, and had created a world of women: paragons, in their way; witty and learned, masters of law and medicine; orators, adventurers; charming in men's clothes, companions of youths as charming as themselves, full of peeves and passions, primpers before mirrors, young, sweet, a field of flowers—here and there, a sad one, a deep one, among them. But a woman such as one might wish to know in this world? He returned to her, the dweller in two worlds, Plutarch's, and his own thoughts. She was there as he would have desired her, as she is to Antony, one

> Whom every thing becomes, to chide, to laugh,
> To weep; whose every passion fully strives
> To make itself, in thee, fair and admir'd.

So true is this that when Antony appears, having been sent for, and she says she won't look at him, and leaves, we begin to see her consistency, and with it her charm; she is characterized by her whims:

> See where he is, who's with him, what he does;
> I did not send you: if you find him sad,
> Say I am dancing; if in mirth, report
> That I am sudden sick.

257

## 2.

He comes to say good-bye; she upbraids him before he can speak. Yet he is never out of her thoughts. The day is a pageant of Antonies:

> Where think'st thou he is now? Stands he, or sits he?
> Or does he walk? or is he on his horse?
> O happy horse, to bear the weight of Antony!

Emperors have been her paramours; what was her substance, whereof was she made?

> *Cleopatra.*                Did I, Charmian,
> Ever love Caesar so?
> *Charmian.*            O! that brave Caesar.
> *Cleopatra.* Be chok'd with such another emphasis!
> Say the brave Antony.
> *Charmian.*            The valiant Caesar!
> *Cleopatra.* By Isis, I will give thee bloody teeth,
> If thou with Caesar paragon again
> My man of men.

She reigns as the queen of Shakespeare's women by being a woman. He brought to her characterization something which sprang from the deeps of memory and being. It is frank and tender at once. Plutarch has praised her: 'so sweet was her companie and conuersation, that a man could not possibly but be taken'; but what is this to the tribute Shakespeare wrought?

> Age cannot wither her, nor custom stale
> Her infinite variety; other women cloy
> The appetites they feed, but she makes hungry
> Where most she satisfies.

## 3.

She is all woman; she does not offend even when she is coarse.

> *Cleopatra.* Give me some music; music, moody food
> Of us that trade in love.
> *Attendant.*            The music, ho!
> *Cleopatra.* Let it alone; let's to billiards: come, Charmian.

*Charmian.* My arm is sore; best play with Mardian.
*Cleopatra.* As well a woman with a eunuch play'd
As with a woman. Come, you'll play with me, sir?
*Mardian.* As well as I can, madam.
*Cleopatra.* And when good will is show'd, though't come too
    short,
The actor may plead pardon.

A messenger comes from Italy with the news of Antony's marriage to Octavia. She strikes him down; she strikes him again; she hales him up and down by the hair; she draws a knife. He runs away. She sends for him.

*Cleopatra.*                Is he married?
I cannot hate thee worser than I do
If thou again say 'Yes.'
*Messenger.*          He's married, madam.
*Cleopatra.* The gods confound thee! dost thou hold there still?

Her violence dies in her grief; her stature returns to her:

    Let him for ever go:—let him not—Charmian!—
    Though he be painted one way like a Gorgon,
    The other way's a Mars. Bid you Alexas
    Bring me word how tall she is. Pity me, Charmian,
    But do not speak to me.

### 4.

Her stature is greatest in adversity:

    I dream'd there was an Emperor Antony:
    O! such another sleep, that I might see
    But such another man.

Antony being dead, death's the sleep to give her such a dream:

    Give me my robe, put on my crown; I have
    Immortal longings in me.

She sets forth forever, perverse but regal, 'to take her barge in the riuer of Cydnus, the poope whereof was of gold, the sailes of purple, and the oares of siluer, which kept stroke in rowing after the sound of the musicke of flutes, howboyes, cithernes, vials, and such other instruments as they played vpon.' She drifts upon the Cydnus of the mind, wafting to aftertimes 'a wonderfull passing sweete sauour of perfumes'—Antony's dark woman, and Shakespeare's.

# BOOK EIGHT

# CHAPTER I

## Business and Vital Statistics

### 1.

THE pattern of John Shakespeare's life, political office aside, was now to be repeated by his son. For this reason, among the many fatuous ideas put forward by those who prefer to believe that William Shakespeare of Stratford-upon-Avon could not possibly have been the author of the works that bear his name is one dealing with the number of his business records which have come down. Yet this is hardly extraordinary, for business is based on records, which are charily kept. On the other hand, the books and manuscripts of writers have a way of being scattered and lost, particularly by those to whom they have been entrusted.

A poet who has money to invest would not be more of a poet if he invested it unwisely. Perhaps the fatuous prefer their poets poor. . . .

### 2.

One of the most important of Shakespeare's business transactions was his purchase of a portion of the Stratford tithes. Like his purchase of New Place in 1597, which carried with it the right to a pew in the parish church, this was a social as well as a business investment, for it carried with it the privilege of being buried within the church itself. So great was his horror of the bone house in the parish graveyard that it may be that the purchase of the tithes was dictated—in part, in any case—by this very factor.

The possibility of his purchase of a portion of the tithes had been broached as early as 1598, in the Sturley-Quiney correspondence. The Stratford Corporation, which received revenues from these collections, had confidence in his ability to manage the business with prudence. On July 24, 1605, he received an assignment in a moiety of the tithes, which included 'divers messuages landes tenementes and glebe landes, scituate, lyeinge and beinge within the parishe of Stratford uppon Avon aforesaid, and of and in the tythes of corne

263

grayne and haye, and of and in all and all manner of tythes of wooll lambe and all other small and pryvye tythes and oblacions and alterages whatsoever, cominge groweinge aryseinge reneweinge or happeninge within the whole parishe of Stratford uppon Avon.' The sum involved was the considerable one of £440.

### 3.

William Shakespeare's thoughts were already turning toward retirement in his native town when his first-born child, Susanna, in 1607 a spinster of twenty-four, was married. The Stratford parish register records the event:

> Junij 5    John Hall gentlemã & Susanna Shaxpere.

Her husband, a B.A. and M.A. of Oxford, and a 'practitioner of Physicke,' was thirty-two. He took his bride to live in a house called Hall's Croft, Old Town Street, Stratford, near the parish church. Among his patients were Michael Drayton, the poet; the Earl and Countess of Northampton; neighbors and kinfolk like the Quineys, Sadlers, Sturleys and Combes; and John Thornborough, Bishop of Worcester, whose license was necessary for him to practice. He was no quack; his motto is impressive for that period: 'Qui sine via et methodo Medicinam facit est sine clavo et remis navigit' (He who practices medicine without a definite course and method is like one who navigates without rudder or oars). He kept a diary in Latin which lists patients and cures; unfortunately, it was not begun until 1617, and does not mention his illustrious father-in-law.

### 4.

Another parish record, this time in London, tells what became of Shakespeare's brother Edmund. The register of St. Saviour's, Southwark, has the following entry for year's end, 1607:

> Decemb 31    Edmond Shakespeare a player in the Church.

He was twenty-seven and a half years old. It is not known whether he was a player in his brother's company. Beyond the fact that he was born Shakespeare's brother, died a player, and was buried in St. Saviour's, nothing is known. The church was near the Globe, and it may have been William Shakespeare, or members of his company, who defrayed the expenses of his burial. A sexton's note, in the fee book of St. Saviour's, records for the same day a final tribute:

> Edmund Shakespeare a player buried in the Church
> with a forenoone knell of the great bell, xxs.

### 5.

A year and three months after the marriage of John Hall and Susanna Shakespeare, a child was born to them; the parish register records the baptism, February 21, 1608, of

> Elizabeth dawghter to John Hall geñ.

Dr. Hall's diary has an entry concerning her: 'Elizabeth Hall my onely Daughter was vexed with Tortura Oris or the Convulsion of the mouth, and was happily cured as followeth. First I exhibited these pils ℞ pil, Coch. et Aurean. ana 31. f, pil. 10. She took five the first day.' Another time, 'she took cold and fell into the said distemper on the contrary side of her face, before it was on the left side, now on the right, and although she was grievously afflicted with it, yet by the blessing of God she was cured in sixteen dayes.'

She survived these and other complaints, married twice, and died a lady, her second husband being Sir John Bernard.

### 6.

In September, 1608, died William Shakespeare's mother. Her burial was duly noted in the parish register:

> Sept 9   Mayry Shaxpere wydowe.

She had survived her husband, John Shakespeare, seven years. Surviving her were William and two other sons, Gilbert and Richard, and a daughter, Joan Hart. She had lived to see both husband and oldest son attain gentryhood. The acres frittered away by her husband had been replenished by her son.

The bare entry of the parish register cannot be made to yield anything further. It is conjectural whether William Shakespeare was in Stratford during her last illness, or even present when she was buried. Be it sentimental or not, the thought is inescapable that Mary Arden Shakespeare was an important influence in the life of her eternally renowned son. With her death, he became the head of the family she had helped to raise from obscure beginnings.

Just over a month after her burial, on Sunday, October 16, William Shakespeare stood godfather at the baptism of William Walker, son of Henry Walker, mercer, of High Street, Stratford, and afterwards remembered him in his will with a twenty shilling goldpiece.

### 7.

Stratford engrossed him more and more; his preoccupation with borough affairs shows that. Perhaps his health was now not of the best. When Aubrey began to make inquiries about him, he learned, from the son of an actor in the Lord Chamberlain's troupe, that Shakespeare 'was not a company keeper'; that he 'lived in Shoreditch, wouldnt be debauched, & if invited to writ: he was in paine.' The only exegesis possible on this brief but illuminating text is this: that he was not—toward the end, in any case,—a roisterer; and when pressed to go out, excused himself by saying he was unwell.

The reference to Shoreditch must mean his earliest residence in London, rather than his last. By the end of the first decade of the seventeenth century, the King's Men had ousted the 'little eyases' from the Blackfriars theater and had ensconced themselves there. Shakespeare may have lodged in the vicinity; in March, 1613, he actually purchased a house and grounds in Blackfriars, perhaps the one in which he habitually lodged.

# CHAPTER II

## *William Shakespeare Sues*

### 1.

THE Stratford Court of Record, which John Shakespeare, ably assisted by other town worthies, had managed to keep busy, and over which he once presided as high bailiff, was also resorted to by his son William. A series of entries in the court register shows that, between August 17, 1608, and June 7, 1609, William Shakespeare tried to collect a debt of six pounds plus court costs of twenty-four shillings from John Addenbrooke, specified 'gentleman,' but otherwise unknown.

The entries offer a fairly comprehensive, and fairly interesting, picture of proceedings in the borough of Stratford.

The first is the record of the arrest of the defendant: 'John Addenbrooke, gentleman, was ordered by the sergeants at mace, the same which they executed, etc., etc., greetings, etc., thus that they have his body in the presence of the bailiff of the borough aforesaid, to answer to William Shakespeare, gentleman, concerning the payment of a debt.'

The second is the summoning of jurors; the third names all summoned as jurors, and the fourth orders them to report to the Court of Record at its next meeting.

The fifth names the jury and its verdict: 'Philip Greene and James Elliott were ill; Edward Hunt; Robert Wilson, juror; Thomas Kerby; Thomas Bridges; Richard Collins, juror; John Ingraham, juror; Daniel Smyth, juror; William Walker, juror; Thomas Mills, juror; John Tubb, juror; Richard Pincke, juror; John Smyth, pannier, juror; Laurence Holmes; John Boyce; Hugo Piggen, juror; John Samwell; Robert Cawdry, juror; John Castle; Paul Bartlett; John Yeate, juror; Thomas Bradshawe; and John Gunn. Each of the aforesaid jurors, for himself separately, was made bondsman by pledges of John Doe and Richard Roe. And all and each of them having retired, the jurors return verdict for plaintiff.'

The sixth reveals that 'John Addenbrooke was summoned by the sergeants at mace the same which they have executed, whether etc., greetings, etc., thus they have his body in the presence of the bailiff of the aforesaid borough, at the next Court of Record held there, to satisfy William Shakespeare, gentleman, concerning not only a debt of six pounds which said William recovered in said court against him but also twenty-four shillings which were adjudged to him for damages and costs which he sustained on the occasion of withholding said debt.'

### 2.

The seventh and last entry offers an interesting denouement. John Addenbrooke, gentleman, absconded, leaving behind him his bondsman, Thomas Hornby, to face the music: 'There is an order to the sergeants at mace that when a certain William Shakespeare, gentleman, recently in the court of James, now King of England, of the aforesaid borough, the same held by virtue of letters patent from King Edward VI,[1] recently King of England, carried his own certain complaint against a certain John Addenbrooke concerning the payment of a debt; and when a certain Thomas Hornby of the said borough in the same complaint became a pledge and mainpernor[2] for the said John, to wit, that if the said John in the said suit were convicted in a legal manner that the same John would satisfy the said William Shakespeare not only for the debt in the said complaint by the said William against the said John to be recovered in the aforesaid court but also for the loss and cost to the same William in that complaint by the said court that would be adjudged against the said John; or that he would go to prison in the said year of the reign of James, now King in the said borough, to satisfy to William Shakespeare the said debt, loss, and costs; and furthermore, that if the same John does not satisfy the same William the debt, loss, and costs, and does not go to the aforesaid prison in the said year of our king to satisfy the said William in the form aforesaid, then the same Thomas Hornby wishes to satisfy for the recovery of the debt, losses, and costs thus adjudged to the same William. And since also in that complaint such proceeding were had in the same court that the said William

[1] A reference to the charter of incorporation.
[2] Bondsman.

in the said case by the judgment of the said court recovered against the said John not only six pounds for debt but also twenty-four shillings for the payment of losses and costs of the same William, appropriate to his suit and complaint. For which there was the order to the sergeant at mace the same which they executed, etc., etc., the said John, if, etc., greetings, that they have his body in the presence of the bailiff of the said borough at the next Court of Record there held to satisfy the said William concerning the said debt so recovered; namely, to the extent of twenty-four shillings for said damages and costs adjudged. Wherefore Francis Boyle, then and now sergeant at mace on the day for returning the writ, announced that the said John was not found within his bailiwick. Wherefore the said William prays to the said court of the said Lord King that there be provided to him the said suitable remedy against the aforesaid mainpernor in the suit concerning which it was ordered to the sergeants at mace which they make known through upright and legal men of the said borough, whether etc., that the aforesaid Thomas be in the presence of the bailiff of the said borough at the next court of record held in the said district to show either if he has anything to say or whether or not he knows why the aforesaid William ought not have his execution against the said Thomas, concerning the debt, the losses, and the costs, according to the force, form, and effect of the said mainpernor, whether or not he should see how to extricate himself and furthermore, whether or not he would do and would accept what the said court of the said King decrees in this matter, and therefore they have this order.'

There are no further entries. Thomas Hornby probably settled.

# CHAPTER III

## *Shakespeare Puts His House in Order*

### 1.

TRIPS to London were less and less frequent as he became increasingly immersed in Stratford affairs. Rowe says: 'The latter Part of his Life was spent, as all Men of good Sense will wish theirs may be, in Ease, Retirement, and the Conversation of his Friends. He had the good Fortune to gather an Estate equal to his Occasion, and, in that, to his Wish; and is said to have spent some Years before his Death at his native *Stratford*. His pleasurable Wit, and good Nature, engag'd him in the Acquaintance, and entitled him to the Friendship of the Gentlemen of the Neighbourhood.'

No doubt, some of the players came to visit him—Heminge and Condell; writers—Drayton, himself a native of Stratford, and Jonson, who went as far as Scotland to visit William Drummond of Hawthornden. Such, in any case, are the probabilities. If *The Tempest* was, in fact, his last play, he had expressed his hope in it,

> For quiet days, fair issue and long life;

had looked beyond that, even, knowing that

> We are such stuff
> As dreams are made on, and our little life
> Is rounded with a sleep.

But retirement from the theater and the loud metropolis on the Thames did not mean inactivity. He began to put his affairs in order. He had two daughters, and a granddaughter, and houses and lands with innumerable appurtenances to leave them. He would leave them unencumbered.

### 2.

In the spring of 1611, a conveyance of twenty additional acres of pasture land to William Shakespeare from William and John Combe not only added to his holdings but confirmed the purchase of 1602: 'one hundred and seven acres of land and twenty acres in pasture with their appurtenances in Old Stratford and Stratford-upon-Avon,' according to the foot of fine. The price agreed on for the additional land was one hundred pounds sterling.

In the fall of the same year he contributed two shillings, six pence, 'towardes the charge of prosecutyng the Bill in parliam^t for the better Repayre of the highe waies.' Seventy-two townsmen contributed, among them the most prominent citizens of the borough. It was a project to interest a man with vast properties to oversee.

One of the things which troubled him was the investment in the Stratford tithes. Parcels of the tithes had been leased and subleased to others, to the number of fifty. There was confusion as to what part of the annual rent was to be paid by each holder; some of the subleases actually had no provision for rent. To correct this, and protect his investment, sometime in 1611 Shakespeare, in concert with Thomas Greene, town clerk, and a Richard Lane of Aston, addressed a bill of complaint 'To the Right Honorable Thomas Lord Ellesmere Lord Chauncellour of England' to bring the matter into the Court of Chancery and effect an equitable pro-rating. Some of the recalcitrants fell immediately into line. William Combe admitted 'that he holds as executor to his late father Thomas Combe a moiety of the tithes of corn and grain in Old Stratford, Bishopton, and Welcombe and of other tithes, for which he pays £5 annually. Is willing to pay for yet other tithes 6s. 8d. annually.'

### 3.

The mind follows the eye's focus on business and legal documents. It is easy to forget that in addition to ordinary family life, delight in his granddaughter, and visits and visiting, he found time to reacquaint himself with the walks of his boyhood,

Here on this grass-plot, in this very place,

and hail again and again, with an April delight in his soul through all the seasons,

Ye elves of hills, brooks, standing lakes, and groves.

Everything reminded him of the past—and of oncoming death. In February, 1612, his brother Gilbert, born two years and a half after him, and with whom he had grown up, died—once more there was a brief entry in the parish register:

February 3   Gilbertus Shakspere adolescens.

'Adolescens' after his name appears strange. It cannot mean Gilbert's son, for that wasn't the way such things were recorded. A conjecture is that it means bachelor. There is no record to show that he was ever married. He was forty-five years old. The Shakespeare men were not long-lived.

# CHAPTER IV

## *Shakespeare as a Witness*

### 1.

ABOUT two weeks after his forty-eighth birthday, William Shakespeare received an unexpected summons to appear in London. It was issued by the Court of Requests, Westminster, May 7, 1612: 'A compulsory to Wilm Shakespeare gent and others,' and was returnable immediately. He appeared in court on May 11, the key witness in the case of Stephen Belott versus his father-in-law, Christopher Mountjoy.

### 2.

On May 11 the court examined the witnesses it had summoned. The method used was a series of interrogatories put to each. It was all so long ago. Yet Shakespeare's answers are rather cautious than vague:

'Willm Shakespeare of Stratford vpon Aven in the Countye of Warwicke gen of the age of xlviij yeres or thereabout sworne and examined the daye and yere abouesaid deposethe & sayethe

'To the first interrogatory this deponent sayethe he knowethe the partyes plaintiff and deffendant and hathe knowne them bothe as he now remembrethe for the space of tenne yeres or thereabout.

'To the second interrogatory this deponent sayeth he did know the complainant when he was servant with the deffendant, and that duringe the tyme of his the complainantes service with the said deffendant he the said complainant to this deponentes knowledge did well and honestly behaue himselfe, but to this deponentes remembrance he hath not heard the deffendant confesse that he had gott any great profitt and comodytye by the service of the said complainant, but this deponent saithe he verely thinkethe that the said complainant was a very good and industrious servant in the said service And more he canott depose to the said interrogatory.

'To the third interrogatory this deponent sayethe that it did evydentlye appeare that the said deffendant did all the tyme of

273

the said complainantes service with him beare and shew great good will and affeccion toward the said complainant, and that he hath hard the deffendant and his wyefe diuerse and sundry tymes saye and reporte that the said complainant was a very honest fellow: And this deponent sayethe that the said deffendant did make a mocion vnto the complainant of marriadge with the said Mary in the bill mencioned beinge the said deffendantes sole chyld and daughter, and willinglye offered to performe the same yf the said complainant shold seeme to be content and well like thereof: And further this deponent sayeth that the said deffendantes wyeffe did sollicitt and entreat this deponent to move and perswade the said complainant to effect the said marriadge and accordingly this deponent did moue and perswade the complainant thervnto: And more to this interrogatorye he cannot depose.

'To the ffourth interrogatory this deponent sayth that the defendant promissed to geue the said complainant a porcion in marriadge with Marye his daughter, but what certayne porcion he rememberethe not, nor when to be payed nor knoweth that the defendant promissed the plaintiff twoe hundered pound with his daughter Marye at the tyme of his decease. But sayth that the plaintiff was dwellinge with the defendant in his house, and they had amongeste them selues manye conferences about their marriadge which afterwardes was consumated and solempnized. And more he cannott depose.'

Mountjoy had provided the court with a list of household articles which he had given the newlyweds, claiming, apparently, that these amounted in value to whatever sums he may have promised his son-in-law. Out of the fifth interrogatory this 'household stuffe' flows, to muster itself in dark Elizabethan chambers: '(vizt.) one ould ffetherbed, one oulde ffether boulster. A locke boulster, a thin greene Rugg two ordanarie blanckettes woven, two paire sheetes A dozine of napkines of Course Dyaper, twoe short table Clothes, six short Towelles & one longe one, An ould drawinge table, two ould Joyned stooles, one Wainscott Cubberd, one Twistinge wheele of Woode, twoe paire of little Scyssers, one ould Truncke and a like old Truncke One Bobbine box: And what doe youe thincke in yo$^r$ Conscyence all these said parcelles might be woorthe at the tyme when they weare so deliuered by the defendauntes appoyntm$^t$, vnto the plaintiffes declare the truthe hearein at lardge.'

Shakespeare refused to become involved: 'To the v$^{th}$ Interrogatory this deponent sayth he can saye nothinge touchinge any parte or poynte of the same interrogatory, for he knoweth not what implementes and necessaries of houshould stuffe the defendant gaue the plaintiff in marriadge with his daughter Marye.'

The clerk of the court, having written the answers down, handed the sheet of paper to the witness, who thereupon subscribed his name.

### 3.

The English court got nowhere. The case was eventually turned over to the French Consistory Court in Threadneedle Street. Three years later, Belott was awarded twenty nobles, which remained unpaid. Mountjoy died in 1620. His will indicates an inflexible hatred of Belott, which perforce included his daughter. He had married a second time, his first wife having died in 1606. London custom required a division of property into three parts: one to wife, one to children, one to others. Mountjoy's will reads: 'Three third Parts of my goods and chattels (the whole being diuided into fower third partes) I giue and bequeath unto my well-beloued wife Isabel. And one other third parte of the said fower parts I doe hereby giue and bequeath unto my daughter Mary Blott the weif of Stephen Blott.'

Four third parts—only a lawyer could have thought up this mathematical monstrosity; and only a father-in-law would have paid him to do so.

# CHAPTER V

## Shakespeare's Plays at Court

### 1.

TO ENGLAND in the fall of 1612 came Frederick V, Prince Palatine Elector of the Rhine, after a month's intensive instruction in dancing to cut a better figure at the English court. He was sixteen. He was betrothed to Princess Elizabeth of England, also sixteen, and they were married the following February 14, 1613.

For the entertainment of their Royal Highnesses, foreign and domestic, eighteen plays were produced by the King's Men at Whitehall during the winter season of 1612-1613. The accounts of the Treasurer of the Chamber to James I show that Shakespeare continued to be the most popular dramatist of his time: 'Item paid to Iohn Heminges vppon the Cowncells warrant dated att Whitehall xx° die Maij 1613 for presentinge before the Princes Highnes the La: Elizabeth and the Prince Pallatyne Elector fowerteene severall playes viz one play called ffilaster, One other called the knott of ffoules One other Much adoe abowte nothinge, The Mayeds Tragedy The merye dyvell of Edmonton, The Tempest, A kinge and no kinge The Twins Tragedie/The Winters Tale, S$^r$ Iohn ffalstofe, The Moore of Venice, The Nobleman, Caesars Tragedye/And one other called Love Lyes a bleedinge, All w$^{ch}$ Playes weare played w$^{th}$in the tyme of this Accompte, viz p$^d$ the some of iiij$^{xx}$ xiij$^{li}$ vj$^s$ viij$^d$.

'Item paid to the said Iohn Heminges vppon the lyke warrant dated att whitehall xx° die Maij 1613 for presentinge sixe severall playes viz one playe called a badd beginninge makes a good endinge, one other called the Capteyne one other the Alcumist one other Cardenio, one other Hotspur and one other called Benidicte and Betteris all played w$^{th}$in the tyme of this Accompte viz p$^d$ ffortie powndes And by waye of his ma$^{ties}$ rewarde twentie powndes In all lx$^{li}$.'

Some writers hold that *The Tempest* was written for the mar-

276

riage festivities of Frederick and Elizabeth; the marriage song in Act IV, Scene I, gives such a notion plausibility (though it could have been inserted for the occasion):

> Honour, riches, marriage-blessing,
> Long continuance, and increasing,
> Hourly joys be still upon you!

Ferdinand's remark, following this song, may likewise be a compliment for James:

> Let me live here ever:
> So rare a wonder'd father and a wise,
> Makes this place Paradise.

*Much Ado About Nothing* was apparently given twice, the second time as 'Benidicte and Betteris.' 'S<sup>r</sup> Iohn ffalstofe' and 'Hotspur' probably mean the two parts of *Henry IV*. Two new dramatists had begun to make their mark—Beaumont and Fletcher. Jonson also was represented.

The total paid the King's Men for these performances was considerable. The royal household was apparently determined not to let the death of the beloved Prince Henry cast a pall upon the nuptials of his sister.

## 2.

Although Shakespeare was in London in March, 1613, there is no way of knowing whether he was present earlier during the performances of his plays at court. In Stratford, on February 4, was buried his brother Richard, leaving him and his sister Joan the sole survivors of the Shakespeare family. On March 10, a real estate transaction took place 'Betweene Henry Walker citizein and Minstrell of London of th'one partie, And William Shakespeare of Stratford Vpon Avon in the countie of Warwick gentleman, William Iohnson citizein and Vintener of London, Iohn Jackson, and Iohn Hemmyng of London gentleman of th'other partie' by which the dramatist acquired a dwelling house and a plot of ground in Blackfriars 'abutting vpon a streete leading downe to Pudle wharffe on the east part, right against the Kinges Maiesties Wardrobe.' The sale price was £140, with a mortgage of £60. Shakespeare's purpose, other than investment, in buying this property in London is not known. He may have resided there. The joint tenancy of the conveyance of the property barred his wife from any dower right in it. By his will he left it to his daughter Susanna.

### 3.

If William Shakespeare actually named his first-born child Susanna in order to give her a lifelong reminder of chastity, a strange denouement was in the offing.

On July 15, Susanna Shakespeare Hall, aged thirty, wife of Dr. John Hall of Stratford-upon-Avon, appeared before the clerk of the Consistory Court of the diocese of Worcester, and charged that she had been defamed by one John Lane, to wit: 'about 5 weekes past the defendant reported that the plainant had the runninge of the raynes & had bin naught w$^{th}$ Rafe Smith.'

This was a serious slander for a prominent matron to take cognizance of, and it was probably courageous of her to strike back as she did. She brought with her a character witness, one Robert Whatcott, who later witnessed her father's will.

John Lane, the defendant, was a grandson of testy Nicholas Lane, who had sued John Shakespeare to recover a loan to John's brother Henry. Ralph Smith was a haberdasher of Stratford, son of the late Alderman John Smith, and grandson of Master William Smith of Henley Street, who may have been the poet's godfather. Ralph was also a nephew of Hamnet Sadler, who with his wife Judith had stood godparents to Hamnet and Judith Shakepeare.

It does not appear from the register of the Consistory Court that John Lane ever appeared to substantiate, if he could, the charge imputed to him. On July 27 he was excommunicated, the usual punishment in such a case. His first cousin, Thomas Nash, afterwards married Susanna's daughter Elizabeth.

### 4.

While this action stirred the Shakespeare household, an event occurred which once more threatened the fortunes of the poet's fellows in the royal troupe. On the afternoon of June 29, 1613, the thatch-roofed Globe caught fire during the performance of a play called *All Is True*, afterwards known as *Henry VIII*, a collaboration between Shakespeare and John Fletcher. In the audience were Ben Jonson and Sir Henry Wotton.

The play had reached the last scene of Act I. To the roll of a drum and the blare of trumpets, two cannon were discharged.

*Wolsey.*                               What's that?
*Lord Chamberlain.* Look out there, some of ye.
                                    [*Exit* a Servant.
*Wolsey.*                               What war-like voice,
And to what end, is this? Nay, ladies, fear not.

Prophetical words! The cannon were pointed upward; a wad from one reached the roof, and smoldered there. Suddenly a train of fire began to run around the thatched opening, giving the playhouse a flaming halo. Spectators looked up, and saw flames like an arras lowered all around. There was a rush to the doors. All the eyewitness accounts testify to the rapidity with which the Globe was consumed. On July 2, Sir Henry Wotton wrote to his friend Sir Edmund Bacon: 'to let matters of state sleep, I will entertain you at the present with what happened this week at the Bank's side. The King's players had a new play, called *All is True,* representing some principal pieces of the reign of Henry VIII, which was set forth with many extraordinary circumstances of pomp and majesty, even to the matting of the stage; the Knights of the Order with their Georges and garters, the Guards with their embroidered coats, and the like: sufficient in truth within a while to make greatness very familiar, if not ridiculous. Now, King Henry making a masque at the Cardinal Wolsey's house, and certain chambers being shot off at his entry, some of the paper, or other stuff, wherewith one of them was stopped, did light on the thatch, where being thought at first but an idle smoke, and their eyes more attentive to the show, it kindled inwardly, and ran around like a train, consuming within less than an hour the whole house to the very grounds. This was the fatal period of that virtuous fabric, wherein yet nothing did perish but wood and straw, and a few forsaken cloaks; only one man had his breeches set on fire, that would perhaps have broiled him, if he had not by the benefit of a provident wit put it out with bottle ale.'

Later, Ben Jonson, in *An Execration upon Vulcan,* lamented:

The Globe, the glory of the Bank;
Which, though it were the fort of the whole parish,
Flanked with a ditch, and forced out of a marish,
I saw with two poor chambers taken in,
And razed ere thought could urge this might have been!

5.

There was additional excitement in Stratford. The enclosure of
lands, which turned arable acres yielding crops into pasture for
sheep, for the benefit of the wool trade, was a constant threat to
farmers. Their case had been vividly portrayed by Mr. Secretary
Cecil in the House of Commons: 'If we debar Tillage, we give
scope to the Depopulator; And then if the poor being thrust out
of their Houses go to dwell with others, straight we catch them
with the Statute of Inmates; if they wander abroad, they are
within the danger of the Statute of the Poor to be whipt.' It was
enclosures, and not anything romantic, which had sent Robin Hood
and others into the forests of England.

In the fall of 1614 there was talk in Stratford of enclosing some
of the Welcombe fields, which yielded Shakespeare income in the
form of tithes. He naturally opposed it. He hedged his investment
by making a private agreement with one William Replingham
'for all such losse detriment & hinderance as he the said Willm
Shackespeare, his heires & assignes' might sustain as a result of
any enclosure. Associated with him in this deal was Thomas
Greene, town clerk, whose records yield the excitement of those
days.

Greene played a double role, but not from any desire to deal
double. As a tithe owner himself, he had joined Shakespeare in the
agreement with Replingham; as town clerk, he was the spokesman
for the Stratford Corporation, which used tithe money for charitable works, and was unalterably opposed to enclosure. Replingham
came to Greene in a fury: 'I sayd I did it accordyng to the trust in
me reposed by the Baylyff &c & howe I was tyed to them &c. & as
for myne owne particuler interest I would not vary from what I
hadd sayd before & soe wee parted.'

Meanwhile, William and Thomas Combe ordered a ditch dug
in the Welcombe area. Word was brought to them that the corporation would oppose it, and that if the ditch were dug, it would

be filled in; whereupon Thomas Combe called the corporation council 'doggs' and cursed its members, and William Combe went to the high bailiff and said: 'O would they durst in a threatinyng manner with very great passion & anger.'

One Stratfordian durst. On March 2, 1615, 'm$^r$ Chandlers man Richard Ward went to the place where they were dyggyng & Stephen Sly John Terry Thomas Hiccox William Whitehead and Michael Pigeon assalted him soe as he could not proceede with throweing downe the dytches & Sly sayd yf the best in Stratford were there to throwe yt downe he wold bury his head in the bottom of the dytche.'

The battle of the enclosures continued. Thomas Combe offered to buy up corporation tithes; William Combe told the corporation, 'I did especiallie charge my workemen that they should not dige enie parte of the common'; both claimed the right to enclose their own land. The corporation replied firmly: 'You might yf yo$^u$ pleased take notice that whether the place be yo$^r$ owne or noe you may not by digginge of ditches diminishe or hinder other mens Commons.'

The last word was written by the Privy Council, which ordered William Combe to turn the land converted into pasture back to corn and grain: 'yo$^u$ will answeare the contrary at yo$^r$ perrill.'

# CHAPTER VI

## *The Death of William Shakespeare*

### 1.

TOWARD the end of January, 1616, William Shakespeare believed himself not long for this world, and sent for Francis Collins, attorney. The nature of his last illness and the cause of his death are unknown, and cannot even be guessed at. There was a Stratford tradition that he had overreached himself in a drinking bout with old cronies; the Rev. John Ward, after becoming vicar, wrote in his diary: 'Shakespear, Drayton, and Ben Jhonson had a merry meeting, and itt seems drank too hard, for Shakespear died of a feavour there contracted.' Ward wrote this almost half a century after Shakespeare's death, and it can have no great value as evidence one way or the other, particularly as it is the usual tale told of artists and authors.

He had lived a strenuous life, his mind a long blaze of thought and imagery. He had felt deeply. The fact that he lived long enough to revise his will two months later, and then lingered to at least April 23, indicates not a fever but a gradual decline. His baptism in midweek makes it possible to assume that the seeds of his fatal illness were with him from the first.

### 2.

He was three months short of fifty-two when the first draft of the will was made, January 25, 1616. The will consists of three sheets of paper, each a fraction over twelve by fifteen inches. He had managed to accumulate a great deal of property, and it is a lengthy, and in places an involved, document. There are many interlineations and deletions. The first sheet seems to have been entirely rewritten between January 25 and March 25. A marriage entry in the parish register may explain why:

Feabruary 10   Tho. Queeny tow Judith Shakespeare—

i.e., William Shakespeare set about changing his youngest

daughter's dowry to a marriage portion. She was no longer young, being a spinster of thirty-one. Her husband was the son of Richard Quiney, draper and whilom high bailiff of Stratford, son of Adrian Quiney, the friend and corporation colleague of John Shakespeare. It was Richard Quiney who wrote to William Shakespeare in London 'ffrom the Bell in Carter Lane the 25 octobr 1598' requesting a loan of thirty pounds. Thomas was a vintner, and reputed unreliable.

### 3.

Another circumstance also contributed to the revision of the first sheet of the will, and the top of the second, where three lines were crossed out and new matter substituted above them: while Judith Shakespeare got herself a husband at last, Joan Hart, Shakespeare's sister, lost hers. The parish register gives the date of his burial:

Aprill 17    Will Hartt hatter.

A week later, her brother followed her husband to the grave. The Harts lived in the Henley Street property, and Shakespeare devised it to his sister 'for her naturall lief' for a yearly rent of twelve pence. He also left her twenty pounds and all his wearing apparel, a useful bequest because she had three sons to clothe. To her sons he left five pounds apiece.

### 4.

On sheet three occurs the famous interlineation: 'Item I gyve vnto my wief my second best bed with the furniture' (the word 'furniture' meaning, of course, the furnishings of the bed). There is no other mention of her. In other parts of England—in London, York and Wales—local custom decreed a one-third dower right to a widow. There was no such custom in Warwickshire. In the light of Shakespeare's career away from her, and because of the absence of any endearing expression whatsoever, the bequest of the second best bed to Anne Hathaway Shakespeare may mean a final sign of their lifelong estrangement. His 'wief' was an afterthought, as the interlineation shows. The interlineation may have come at the suggestion of Mrs. Shakespeare herself, the bed probably being the one she had used in Henley Street and afterwards at New Place.

It is, of course, possible that Shakespeare's concern with the off-spring and future offspring of his two daughters, and the continu-ance of the family properties in the direct line of descent, despite the fact that his name would not be carried on, dictated his course.

It was probably understood by all concerned that Mrs. Shake-speare would continue to live at New Place, even though her son-in-law Hall and his wife Susanna were to occupy it.

A commentary on the foregoing is the statement in the will that it was 'my Sonne in Lawe John Hall gent & my daughter Susanna his wief whom I ordaine & make executours of this my Last will and testament.' One has a right to suppose that the wife of a dying man, had she been in fact the wife of his bosom, would have been named to see his last wishes carried out.

### 5.

Another interesting interlineation is the following: 'to my ffel-lowes John Hemynge, Richard Burbage & Henry Cundell xxvj$^s$ viij$^d$ A peece to buy them Ringes.' What thoughts of the thronged past were Shakespeare's as he lay dying in New Place, remember-ing his 'ffellowes' who had acted with him in Shoreditch, South-wark, and the court years without number and plays without end!

Also interesting is an item concerning Thomas Russell, a Worcestershire gentleman who was related by marriage to the great Berkeley family of Burton, and to Henry Willoughby, au-thor of *Willobie his Avisa:* 'I doe intreat & Appoint the saied Thomas Russell Esquier & ffrauncis Collins gent to be overseers hereof.' Russell was the friend of Francis Bacon, as well, and of Endymion Porter, patron and friend of poets.

### 6.

The will follows (it is perhaps worth pointing out here that the language of the opening, together with the absence of any reference to the saints and the company of heaven, indicates that Shakespeare died a Protestant):

'In the name of god Amen I William Shackspeare of Strat-ford vpon Avon in the countie of Warr gent in perfect health

& memorie god be praysed doe make & Ordayne this my last will & testament in manner & forme followeing. That is to saye ffirst I Comend my Soule into the handes of god my Creator, hoping & assuredlie beleeving through thonlie merittes of Jesus Christe my Saviour to be made partaker of lyfe everlasting. And my bodye to the Earth whereof yt ys made. Item I Gyve & bequeath vnto my daughter Judyth One Hundred & ffyftie poundes of lawfull English money to be paied vnto her in manner & forme followeing; That ys to saye, One Hundred Poundes in discharge of her marriage porcion within one yeare after my deceas, with consideracion after the Rate of twoe shillinges in the pound for soe long tyme as the same shalbe vnpaied vnto her after my deceas, & the ffyftie poundes Residewe thereof vpon her Surrendring of, or gyving of such sufficient securitie as the overseers of this my will shall like of to Surrender or graunte, All her estate & Right that shall discend or come vnto her after my deceas or that shee nowe hath of in or to one Copiehold tenemente with thappurtenaunces lyeing & being in Stratford vpon Avon aforesaied in the saied countie of Warr, being parcell or holden of the mannour of Rowington, vnto my daughter Susanna Hall & her heires for ever. Item I Gyve & bequeath vnto my saied daughter Judith One Hundred & ffyftie Poundes more if shee or Anie issue of her bodie be Lyvinge att thend of three Yeares next ensueing the daie of the date of this my will, during which tyme my executors to paie her consideracion from my deceas according to the Rate aforesaied. And if she dye within the saied terme without issue of her bodye then my will ys & I doe gyve & bequeath One Hundred Poundes thereof to my Neece[1] Elizabeth Hall & the ffiftie Poundes to be sett fourth by my executours during the lief of my Sister Johane Harte & the vse & profitt thereof Cominge shalbe payed to my saied Sister Jone, & after her deceas the said 1ᵘ shall Remaine Amongst the children of my saied Sister Equallie to be devided Amongst them. But if my saied daughter Judith be lyving att thend of the saied three Yeares or anie yssue of her bodye, then my will ys & soe I devise &

---

[1] Granddaughter; is 'Neece' an endearing term or lawyer's confusion?

bequeath the saied Hundred & ffyftie poundes to be sett out
by my executours and overseers for the best benefitt of her
& her issue & the stock not to be paied vnto her soe long as she
shalbe marryed & covert Baron[1] but my will ys that she shall
have the consideracion yearelie paied vnto her during her lief
& after her deceas the saied stock and consideracion to bee
paied to her children if she have Anie & if not to her executours or assignes she lyving the saied terme after my deceas.
Provided that yf such husbond as she shall att thend of the
saied three Yeares be marryed vnto or attaine after doe suf-
ficientlie Assure vnto her & thissue of her bodie landes
Awnswereable to the porcion by this my will gyven vnto her
& to be adiudged soe by my executours & overseers then my
will ys that the said cl[li] shalbe paied to such husbond as shall
make such assurance to his owne vse. Item I gyve & bequeath
vnto my saied sister Jone xx[li] & all my wearing Apparrell to
be paied & deliuered within one yeare after my deceas, And I
doe will & devise vnto her the house with thappurtenaunces in
Stratford wherein she dwelleth for her naturall lief vnder the
yearelie Rent of xij[d]. Item I gyve and bequeath Vnto her
three sonns Welliam Harte [Thomas][2] Hart & Michaell
Harte ffyve poundes A peece to be payed within one Yeare
after my deceas. Item I gyve & bequeath vnto her the saied
Elizabeth Hall All my Plate (except my brod silver & gilt
bole) that I now have att the date of this my will. Item I
gyve & bequeath vnto the Poore of Stratford aforesaied tenn
poundes, to m[r] Thomas Combe my Sword, to Thomas Russell
Esquier ffyve poundes, & to ffrauncis Collins of the Borough
of Warr in the countie of Warr gent thirteene poundes Sixe
shillinges & Eight pence to be paied within one Yeare after
my deceas. Item I gyve & bequeath to thelder Hamlett Sadler
xxvj[s] viij[d] to buy him A Ringe, to William Raynoldes gent
xxvj[s] viij[d] to buy him A Ringe, to my godson William Walker
xx[s] in gold, to Anthonye Nashe gent xxvj[s] viij[d], & to M[r] John
Nashe xxvj[s] viij[d] in gold, & to my ffellowes John Hemynge
Richard Burbage & Henry Cundell xxvj[s] viij[d] A peece to buy
them Ringes. Item I Gyve Will bequeath & Devise vnto my
daughter Susanna Hall for better enabling of her to performe

[1] Lawfully sojourning with her husband.
[2] Blank in original; he had been so much away, he had forgotten the name.

this my will & towardes the performans thereof All that
Capitall Messuage or tenemente with thappurtenaunces in
Stratford aforesaied Called the newe place wherein I nowe
dwell & twoe[1] messuages or tenementes with thappurtenaunces
scituat lyeing & being in Henley streete within the borough
of Stratford aforesaied, And all my barnes stables Orchardes
gardens landes tenementes & hereditamentes whatsoever
scituat lyeing & being or to be had Receyved perceyved or
taken within the townes Hamlettes villages ffieldes & groundes
of Stratford vpon Avon Oldstratford Bushopton & Welcombe
or in anie of them in the saied countie of Warr, And alsoe All
that Messuage or tenemente with thappurtenaunces wherein
one John Robinson dwelleth, scituat lyeing & being in the
blackfriers in London nere the Wardrobe, & all other my
landes tenementes and hereditamentes whatsoever; To Have
& to hold All & singuler the saied premisses with their Appur-
tenaunces vnto the saied Susanna Hall for & during the terme
of her natural lief, & after her Deceas to the first sonne of her
bodie lawfullie yssueing & to the heires Males of the bodie
of the saied first Sonne lawfullie yssueing, & for defalt of such
issue to the second Sonne of her bodie lawfullie issueing and
to the heires Males of the bodie of the saied Second Sonne
lawfullie yssueinge, & for defalt of such heires to the third
Sonne of the bodie of the saied Susanna Lawfullie yssueing
and of the heires Males of the bodie of the saied third sonne
lawfullie yssueing, And for defalt of such issue the same soe
to be & Remaine to the ffourth sonne ffyfth sixte & Seaventh
sonnes of her bodie lawfullie issueing one after Another & to
the heires Males of the bodies of the said fourth fifth Sixte
& Seaventh sonnes lawfullie yssueing, in such manner as yt ys
before Lymitted to be & Remaine to the first second and third
Sonns of her bodie & to their heires Males; And for defalt of
such issue the said premisses to be & Remaine to my sayed
Neece Hall & the heires males of her bodie Lawfullie yssueing, and for defalt of issue to my daughter Judith & the heires
Males of her bodie lawfullie yssueing, And for defalt of such
issue to the Right heires of me the saied William Shackspere
for ever. Item I gyve vnto my wief my second best bed with

---

[1] One of the trio of buildings was torn down in 1594.

the furniture Item I gyve & bequeath to my saied daughter Judith my broad silver gilt bole. All the Rest of my goodes chattels Leases plate Jewels & householde Stuffe whatsoever, after my dettes and Legasies paied & my funerall expences discharged, I gyve devise & bequeath to my Sonne in Lawe John Hall gent & my daughter Susanna his wief whom I ordaine & make executours of this my Last will and testament. And I doe intreat & Appoint the saied Thomas Russell Esquier & ffrauncis Collins gent to be overseers hereof. And doe Revoke All former wills & publishe this to be my last will and testament. In witnesse whereof I have hereunto put my hand the daie & Yeare first aboue Written.

                          By me William Shakspeare.

witnes to the publishing
hereof. Fra: Collyns
Juliyus Shawe
Iohn Robinson
Hamnet Sadler
Robert Whatcott.'

'By me William Shakspeare' is the clearest of the three signatures on the will; but it is apparent that bodily weakness made his hand waver when he reached the end of his name. His hand was extremely shaky when he signed sheet one and two, probably after signing the third.

## 7.

The will was not the only composition with which William Shakespeare occupied himself in his last weeks on earth. He had never forgotten his terror of the bone house in the Stratford graveyard. To guard against the removal of his bones, he composed a verse which was simple enough to be understood by anyone, particularly ghouls, and it was inscribed in capitals on a slab of stone placed over his grave:

> GOOD FREND FOR IESVS SAKE FORBEARE
> TO DIGG THE DVST ENCLOASED HEARE:
>                   E       T
> BLESTE BE Y MAN Y SPARES THESE STONES
>                   T
> AND CVRST BE HE Y MOVES MY BONES.

*Holy Trinity Church*

*Shakespeare's Will*

The combination, of poetry and a curse, sufficed. He was never disturbed.

8.

The Stratford parish register entry of his burial is brief, but interesting:

April 25    wiłł Shakspere gent.

Present, no doubt, were his widow; his daughters, Susanna and Judith, with their husbands, John Hall and Thomas Quiney; his sister Joan, in mourning for her husband and now the sole survivor of the Shakespeare family, and her three sons; as well as Elizabeth Hall, his only grandchild. Whether anyone came from London is not known; but friends and neighbors from Stratford probably filled the parish church as his coffin was lowered into the grave prepared for it within the chancel rail next to the altar.

So died and was buried this wonderful man, whose life I have told in the outline indicated by the records that remain, by the great works that have come down to us, and by the conjectures which the probabilities of life in this world have suggested. I came to the task with no preconceived notions, but with reverence for his achievements; and I have finished it with reverence for the man himself.

9.

Anne Hathaway Shakespeare, born eight years before her illustrious husband, survived him seven. She died on August 6, 1623, aged sixty-seven, and was buried two days later. The burial entry in the parish register reads:

Aug 8    M$^{rs}$ Shakespeare.

Her grave is to the left of the poet's, within the chancel rail. On it is the following inscription:

HEERE LYETH INTERRED THE BODY OF ANNE WIFE OF WILLIAM SHAKESPEARE WHO DEPTED THIS LIFE THE 6$^{TH}$ DAY OF AVGV̄: 1623 BEING OF THE AGE OF 67 YEARES.

The great folio of her husband's works was already under production when Mrs. Shakespeare died. Perhaps she knew of it, even if she did not live to see a copy. Perhaps she knew, before she died, of the visit to Stratford of the surviving 'ffellowes,' headed by Heminge and Condell, who came, but did not perform—at least, not in the Corporation Hall, for an entry, as ambiguous as any to be found for this period, states:

To the Kinges Players for not playing in the Hall vj$^s$.

Is it a sign of Puritanism in Stratford? But if so, why the payment? Perhaps the hall was under repair, and the corporation marked the arrival of the King's Men with the customary entry in the town records, making a courtesy payment.

### 10.

It is possible, however, that the old and new members of Shakespeare's company came, not to perform his plays, but on a proud and sad mission: to erect a monument in Holy Trinity Church, to keep his memory alive in Stratford as in London and the libraries of the world. A poem prefixed to the First Folio, by Leonard Digges, whose mother became the third wife of Thomas Russell, Esquire, overseer of Shakespeare's will, indicates that the poet's bust was already in place when the book went to press:

> Shakespeare, *at length thy pious fellows give*
> *The world thy Works: thy Works by which, outlive*
> *Thy Tomb thy name must, when that stone is rent,*
> *And Time dissolves thy* Stratford *Monument.*

The monument is on the chancel wall. In an arched niche of white marble with black marble inlays, a black marble pillar on either side, a life-size bust of William Shakespeare looks out upon his parish church. It was originally a polychrome, but after a whitewashing and subsequent repainting, the present color scheme cannot be altogether trusted, but is plausible: the hair and beard are auburn, the eyes hazel; the doublet scarlet and the gown over the doublet black.

# CHAPTER VII

## *An Early Wreath for the Monument*

### 1.

ABOUT twenty years after Shakespeare's death, the 'ever-memorable' John Hales, M.A., Oxford, Fellow of Merton, and public lecturer on Greek, afterwards Fellow of Eton and the friend of scholars and poets, was present at an ever-memorable discussion. We see him through Aubrey's eyes, 'a prettie little man, sanguine, of a cheerfull countenance, very gentile, and courteous;' and in Suckling's characterization:

> Little Hales all the time did nothing but smile,
> To see them, about nothing, keep such a coil.

On this occasion, as reported by Rowe, he left off smiling and listening long enough to launch an extraordinary event: 'In a conversation between Sir *John Suckling*, Sir William *D'Avenant*, *Endymion Porter*, Mr. *Hales of Eaton*, and *Ben Johnson*; Sir *John Suckling*, who was a profess'd admirer of *Shakespear*, had undertaken his Defence against *Ben Johnson* with some warmth; Mr. *Hales*, who had sat still for some time, hearing *Ben* frequently reproaching him with the want of Learning, and Ignorance of the Antients, told him at last, That if Mr. *Shakespear* had not read the Antients, he had likewise not stollen any thing from 'em; (a Fault the other made no Conscience of) and that if he would produce any one Topick finely treated by any of them, he would undertake to shew something upon the same Subject at least as well written by *Shakespear*.'

There are few instances in the annals of literature which crowds so many great personages into one room. Some of those present had known the subject under discussion.

### 2.

Rowe has no more to say; but fortunately another writer took up the tale where he left off.

There was a sequel, in Hales's chambers at Eton. Ben Jonson, and those who sided with him, had turned to their classics, marked the places that were to put Shakespeare to rout, and brought their evidence to the literary assizes. Others who could not be present had sent theirs in. Charles Gildon, who heard the story from Dryden, tells of the occasion and the result: 'it came to a Resolution of a trial of skill upon that Subject; the place agreed on for the Dispute was Mr. Hales's Chamber at Eaton; a great many Books were sent down by the Enemies of this Poet, and on the appointed day my Lord Falkland, Sir John Suckling, and all the Persons of Quality that had Wit and Learning, and interested themselves in the Quarrel, met there, and upon a thorough Disquisition of the point, the Judges chosen by agreement out of this Learned and Ingenious Assembly unanimously gave the Preference to Shakespear. And the Greek and Roman poets were adjudg'd to Vail at least their Glory in that of the English Hero.'

The ancient writers were read, of course, in their original tongues. There was no mention of Bacon.

Thus was justified Ben Jonson's own apostrophe to Shakespeare a decade and a half before:

> *Triumph, my* Britain, *thou hast one to show,*
> *To whom all Scenes of* Europe *homage owe.*
> *He was not of an age, but for all time!*

*William Shakespeare*
*From the 1640 Edition of the* POEMS

# NOTES

# Notes

Elizabethan and Jacobean works identified by author and title in the text are not given here. Books listed in the *Selected Bibliography* are identified by author or editor.

## BOOK ONE

**CH. I.** The Baconian methods are sometimes surprising; *e.g.*, for the authorship of *Psalm 46* (King James version) read down 46 words, then up 46 words (omitting 'Selah' at end).

**CH. II.** The chief repositories of Shakespeare documents and related materials are: the Birthplace Museum, Stratford; the Bodleian Library, Oxford; the British Museum, London; the Folger Shakespeare Library, Washington, D. C.; the Huntington Library, San Marino, Calif.; the Public Record Office, London; Somerset House, London, and the Stratford Corporation archives. Documents from which extracts are given relating to Richard Shakespeare, in the order of their appearance, are from: Rolls of Court Leet, Snitterfield, *Visus Franci Plegii*, Oct. 1, 1535; Court Leet order, May 9, 1538; View of Frank Pledge, Oct. 3, 1560. Bond for administration of Richard Shakespeare's goods in Probate Court Registry, Worcester. For Henry Shakespeare: records of the Ecclesiastical Court, Snitterfield; Court Leet, View of Frank Pledge, Oct. 12, 1574; another, Oct. 22, 1596; burial of wife, Feb. 9, 1597, from Parish Register, Snitterfield. The manuscript *Charter* of 1553 is in the archives of the Stratford Corporation. Fripp, *Shakespeare's Stratford*, 3, 19 n., thinks John Shakespeare may have succeeded to Dixon's business; but apprenticeship would have to be proved first. Arden's will was originally in the Consistory Court, Worcester, but is now reported missing. John Shakespeare's fine from Court Leet, Stratford, View of Frank Pledge; alienation of Greenhill St. tenement and Henley St. house to J. S. in View of Frank Pledge, Oct. 2, 1556; see also Savage and Fripp, *Minutes and Accounts of the Corporation of Stratford-upon-Avon and Other Records 1553-1620*, I, 57, and *ibid.*, 137-141, 144-152, for chamberlain's accounts under J. S.'s stewardship. *Min. and Acc.* gives a detailed account of J. S.'s municipal offices. Documents concerning his ancestry and early career in Stratford are printed in Halliwell-Phillipps, II, 53, 207-248; Chambers, *W. S.*, II, App. A, No. II; and Lewis,

I, *passim* (list of documents, xiii-xiv). For Act of Uniformity and related matters, see Sparrow, *A Collection of Articles, Injunctions, Canons*, etc., 1661, 169-170. 'Master' and 'Magistro' are in Corporation accounts and Court of Record entries. For Shakespeare coat of arms, see CH. XI, Bk. Three, and notes.

CH. III. See Savage, *The Parish Registers of Stratford-on-Avon*, and Corney, *Argument on the Assumed Birthday of Shakespeare*. The players' passage is from the Induction to *The Taming of the Shrew*. Payments to players, in this chapter and CH. I, Bk. Three, from Malone, *Variorum*, II, 150-152.

CH. IV. Davy's hope to see London is from 2 *Henry IV*, Act V, Sc. 3. Tableau of Henley Street tailor and blacksmith is from *King John*, Act IV, Sc. 2, which fits assumption of this play as reasonably early (see CH. IV, Bk. Two). The medley of images used in description of Stratford outskirts is mainly from the plays. For books used by Elizabethan schoolboys, see Plimpton, *The Education of Shakespeare*. William's Latin lesson occurs in *The Merry Wives of Windsor*, Act IV, Sc. 1; Chiron's lines, in *Titus Andronicus*, Act IV, Sc. 2. Foot of Fine conveying property to Edmund Lambert in 1579 is in the Pub. Rec. Off.

CH. V. The quotation which opens this chapter is from Aubrey's MS account of Shakespeare; see below, CH. VII. Probate copy of Hathaway's will in Somerset House.

CH. VI. Marriage bond in Bishop of Worcester's *Register*, XXXII, f. 43$^v$. Chambers, *W. S.*, I, 17: 'the documents concerning the marriage involve a puzzle.' But Lewis, I, 169: 'in the light of English Common Law and of Roman Canon Law in the sixteenth century, actually there is no puzzle.' A learned dissertation (169-176) attempts to prove *marriage* when *betrothed*, and puzzle remains. The dramatic reconstruction of Shakespeare's marriage is based on the service in use at the time (see Staley, *The Booke of the Common Prayer*, 1549, 325-334). Prospero's admonition is from *The Tempest*, Act IV, Sc. 1. Marlowe's renderings of Ovid are from the *Works*, 1910 (ed. Brooke).

CH. VII. Arber, *A Transcript of the Registers of the Company of Stationers of London*, 1875-94, II, 93. Davies' memorandum is from *Corpus Christi College MS.* 309, 22 (in C.C.C., Oxford, library). Rowe's account is from the *Life* prefixed to the *Works of Shakespeare*, 1709. Oath of abjuration in *Folger MS.* 1068.1, fol. 102$^r$ (Lewis, I, 323-324). Ward's *Diary* (ed. Severn,

1839) 183. *Bodl. MS. Aubrey* 6, fol. 109. Dowdall's letter, written at Butler's Marston, Warwickshire, is addressed to a 'M^r Southwell' and was once in the family papers of the Lord de Clifford, whence it passed into the possession of Halliwell-Phillipps. Nothing more is known of it or the writer.

## BOOK TWO

**CH. I.** Ascriptions of Shakespeare: by Jonson (poem in First Folio); Anthony Scoloker (Epistle in *Daiphantus,* 1604); Henry Chettle in *Kind-Harts Dreame,* 1592 (see CH. VII, Bk. Two); Aubrey, *circa* 1681; and Rowe, *Life.* The Martin Droeshout engraving on the title-page of the First Folio (illustration facing p. 3) has some points in common with the bust in Holy Trinity Church (see CH. VI, Bk. Eight). The bust and the niche that contains it were the work of Gheerart Jannsen, son of a Dutch tombmaker whose shop, in Southwark, was near the Globe theater. Both engraver and sculptor may have worked from a painting, perhaps the so-called Droeshout portrait (for an uncle of Martin) in the Shakespeare Memorial Gallery, Stratford. The bust was originally a polychrome; in 1793 Malone persuaded the vicar of Stratford to have it whitewashed. In 1861 the whitewash was removed and the present colors put on. Perhaps there were traces of the original coloring to guide the limner.

**CH. II.** Dasent, *Acts of the Privy Council,* XV, 141 (in *The Muses' Darling,* 6, with facsimile). Marlowe quotations are from *Faustus,* ll. 1301-1303; *Tamburlaine,* Act II, Sc. 1; Prologue; Act II, Sc. 5.

**CH. III.** Description of London from *Sloane MS.,* 2596. The Puritan (view of playhouses) was Stephen Gosson in *Playes Confuted,* sig. G, 6. The attack on Kyd is from Nashe's preface to Greene's *Menaphon* (McKerrow's *Nashe,* III, 300-325). Lines from *Titus Andronicus:* Act I, Sc. 1; III, 1; IV, 1; V, 3; from *Tamburlaine:* Act V, Sc. 2.

**CH. IV.** Prologue to *Jew of Malta;* also, line 342 in that play. For Marlowe's tabletalk, see *Muses' Darling,* CH. XIII and XXII. Lines from *King John:* Act V, Sc. 7, at close; also, I, 1; *ibid;* III, 4.

**CH. V.** For account of duel, see Eccles, *Christopher Marlowe in London,* 1934, 9-35; and for translation of Latin documents, *Muses' Darling,* 90-98. Henslowe (*Diary,* I, 13) records a performance of 'Harey the vj' on March 3, 1592; the take was three pounds, sixteen shillings, eight pence. The play continued popular throughout March, April, May and June.

CH. VI. For a thoroughgoing discussion of the three parts of *Henry VI*, see Chambers, *W. S.*, I, 268, 279, 289-93; II, 188, 308. Expanded speech in 2 *Henry VI*, Act I, Sc. 3; also, IV, 1; see also 3 *Henry VI*, Act I, Sc. 4.

CH. VII. Defense of Greene by Nashe, attack by Harvey (for expanded account, see *Muses' Darling*, 152-170); Nashe's quarrel with Harvey, Mc-Kerrow, V, 65-110.

## BOOK THREE

CH. I. Line from *Tit. And.*, Act I, Sc. 1. John Shakespeare stays away, in *Minutes and Accounts*, III, 170. Suit against Lambert, *Coram Rege Roll* 1311, f. 516; in H.-P., II, 11. Other suits, Court of Record entries. Recusants' list in *Minutes and Accounts*, IV, 148, 159; *Warwick Castle MS.* (Greville Papers) 2262, under date of Sept. 25, 1592.

CH. II. It is from the pious ejaculation of citizens and preachers that Nashe got the refrain for his poem (in *Summer's Last Will and Testament*):

> Brightness falls from the air,
> Queens have died young and fair,
> Dust hath closed Helen's eye,
> I am sick, I must die—
> Lord, have mercy on us.

CH. III. For more about Aspinall, see Fripp, *Sh. Strat.*, 50-51.

CH. IV. Portrait of Southampton in Welbeck Abbey, Eng. 'I see no more in you,' etc., from *As You Like It*, Act III, Sc. 5 (the play belongs to this supposed visit to Stratford and the lines may therefore be appropriate). Registration of Shakespeare's poems, from Arber, *Transcripts*, II, 630, 655. Echo from Marlowe's *Dido*, Act II, Sc. 1 (see also CH. V, section 3).

CH. V. Adam's praise, from *AYLI*, Act II, Sc. 3. I have tried to synthesize Marlovian passages afterwards used separately by Shakespeare: *Tamburlaine—Julius Caesar, Henry IV, Hamlet; Jew of Malta—The Merchant of Venice; Dido—Lucrece; Hero and Leander—As You Like It.* Lines from *Love's Labour's Lost*: Act V, Sc. 2; IV, 1; *ibid*; II, 1; III, 1; *ibid*; II, 1; IV, 3; *ibid*.

CH. VI. For other dates for the plays under discussion in this and preceding chapter, see *W. S.*, I, 305-312, 322-328, 331-338, 401-404. Lines from

*AYLI*, in Act IV, Sc. 1; from *Comedy of Errors*, Act II, Sc. 2; *Taming of the Shrew*, Act V, Sc. 2; *ibid*.

CH. VII. The complete poem is in Harrison *Willobie his Avisa*, but some of the accompanying conclusions seem unwarrantable.

CH. VIII. *Gesta Grayorum*, ed. Greg (Malone Society Reprints).

CH. IX. Court payments, Chambers, *Elizabethan Stage*, IV, the standard work.

CH. X. Von Klarwill, Fugger letters of 1592-1596, first and second series.

CH. XI. The cut at the head of this chapter is reproduced from a drawing made by Dr. S. A. Tannenbaum for his *The Shakspere Coat-of-Arms*, 1908. *College of Arms Vincent MSS.* 157, art. 23, and 157 art. 24. The Lord Chamberlain's Men toured the provinces 1596-7, playing in addition to Faversham in Rye, Dover, Bristol, Bath and Marlborough (*Eliz. Stage*, CH. XIII; *W. S.*, II, 321).

## BOOK FOUR

CH. I. & II. Subsequent to the production of the two parts of *Henry IV*, and the change of name from Oldcastle to Falstaff, the Lord Admiral's Men saw an opportunity for profitable rivalry with *The true and honorable historie, of the life of Sir John Old-castle, the good Lord Cobham:*

> It is no pampered glutton we present,
> Nor aged Councellor to youthful sin.

(Brooke, *Shakespeare Apocrypha*, xxvi-xxviii and 129). Lines from 1 *Henry IV*, Act II, Sc. 4; I, 2. Davies' *Epigrams*, because they appeared with Marlowe's *Amores*, and were burned with them, are in M.'s *Works* (*In Katam*, 630). Additional quotations, from 1 *Henry IV*, Act II, Sc. 4; 2 *Henry IV*, Act II, Sc. 4; V, 5.

CH. III. Dennis, a Cambridge man, was a dramatist and critic. The Epistle appeared in *The Comicall Gallant*, 1702, which is based on *The Merry Wives*. Rowe's account is from the *Life*, 1709. Gildon was a dramatist, sneered at in the *Dunciad*. His *Remarks* appeared in 1710. *M. W.*, Act V, Sc. 5. Writ of attachment, *Controlment Rolls*, K. B. 29/234, Michaelmas Term, 1596.

CH. IV. Much of the material in this and the preceding chapter is based on *Shakespeare versus Shallow*, another of Dr. Hotson's skilfull literary detections; *W. S.*, which antedates it by a year, came close to the solution (I, 427 *et. seq.*).

CH. V. For diplomatic contretemps possibly connected with suppression of *Isle of Dogs*, see *Eliz. Stage*, III, 455. Meeting between Jonson and Shakespeare from Rowe's *Life*.

CH. VI. *Exemplification of Fine*, B. P. *Cat*. 30, from *Wheler MSS*. Chancery suit, in H.-P., II, 14-15.

CH. VII. Report by London Commissioners, *Certificate* dated Nov. 15, 1597, for the second instalment of third subsidy granted by Parliament 1593. Second assessment, from London Commissioners' *Indenture* with petty collectors of Bishopsgate Ward for collection of first subsidy granted by Parliament 1597-8. *S. A. Misc. Doct.* 1.106. Quiney correspondence in full, in Fripp, *Master Richard Quyny*, 1924. Letter to Shakespeare in Birthplace Museum, Stratford; in facsimile, with address, *W. S.*, II, Plate XVII, and Lewis, I, between 226-227. *Cham. Acc.*, Stratford, *B. P. Cat.* 42.

## BOOK FIVE

CH. I. Meres (1565-1647) was living in London in 1597 and 1598.

CH. II. Poet's coloring explained, *ante*, Bk. Two, CH. I, note; reference to manners, from Rowe, *Life*. Lock-and-key passage based on Wordsworth's iambic ejaculation and Browning's commentary.

CH. III. The dedication is reproduced from the first edition of the *Sonnets* in the Folger Shakespeare Library, Washington, D. C., as is the title-page; photographs by Horydczak. The abortive marriage plans are memorialized in two letters from Rowland Whyte to Sir Robert Sidney (*Sydney Papers*, I, 353, 372). Under date of Oct. 8, 1595: 'My Lord [Pembroke] hymself, with my Lord *Harbart* [are] come vp to see the Queen, and (as I heare) to deale in the Matter of a Marriage with Sir *George Careys* Daughter.' On Dec. 5, Whyte wrote: 'Sir *George Carey* takes it very unkindly, that my Lord of *Pembroke* broke of the Match intended between my Lord *Herbart* and his Daughter, and told the Queen it was becawse he wold not assure him 1000[ll.] a Yeare, which comes to his Daughter, as next a Kinne to Queen *Ann Bullen*. He hath now concluded a Marriage between his Daughter and my Lord *Barkleys* Sonne and Heire.' The Lord Chamberlain, father of Sir George, was a cousin of the Queen.

CH. IV, V & VI. Both the Earl of Southampton and the Earl of Pembroke had intrigues with court ladies, undergoing disgrace and imprisonment as a result. In 1598, Southampton married Elizabeth Vernon; but Pembroke (1601) declined to marry Mary Fitton.

CH. VII. Portrait of Essex from painting in National Portrait Gallery, Lon. Extracts from dedication of *Seauen Bookes of the Iliades* from the first edition in the Folger Shakespeare Library.

CH. VIII. How wonderfully Shakespeare had mastered his medium may be seen, in little, by the first quatrain of Sonnet 73 (quoted in CH. IV, Bk. Seven). The most moving effect that can occur in English verse is the *caesura*, a pause or breath-taking; in the fourth line of this sonnet it is impossible to read on after the word 'choirs' without literally catching the breath, which transfers to the reader the full impact of the poet's emotion. Likewise wonderful is the musical combination of sounds in this line. Lee, *Life*, 1916, xii, says: 'My conclusion is adverse to the claim of the sonnets to rank as autobiographical documents.'

## BOOK SIX

CH. I. Silk button passage from *Romeo and Juliet*, Act II, Sc. 4. Bill of Complaint, Allen *v.* Burbage 44 Eliz. (in H.-P., I, 360-361). Fortune playhouse contract from original in Dulwich College.

CH. II. *Deposition* of Daniell Nicholas, Belott *v.* Mountjoy, in Pub. Rec. Off.; see also CH. IV, Bk. Eight. The documents relating to this suit were discovered by Prof. C. W. Wallace; see *Nebraska University Studies*, X, 1910.

CH. III. *Sydney Papers*, II, 175.

CH. IV. *Shakespeare's Plutarch*, ed. W. W. Skeat, 1892. Platter's description from account of his travels, ed. G. Binz, *Anglia*, XXII, 456; orig. in German. Lines from *Julius Caesar*, Act II, Sc. 1; *ibid*; *Troilus and Cressida*, Act I, Sc. 2.

CH. V. Trial of Essex and Southampton from *A Complete Collection of State Trials*, 1816, I, 1334-1360; for the two points of law, *ibid.*, 1355. *Examination* of Merrick and Phillips, from *State Papers Dom Eliz.*, CCLXXVIII, 78, 85. Lines from *Richard II*, Act V, Sc. 2.

CH. VI. *Harl. MS.* 5353, f. 29ᵛ; *Diary* printed 1868, ed. Bruce; facsimile of entry in Tannenbaum, *Problems*, p. 110. A month before, on Feb. 2, Manningham had seen a play at the Middle Temple, which he describes thus (*Diary*, p. 18): 'At our feast wee had a play called 'Twelue Night, or What You Will', much like the Comedy of Errores, or Menechmi in Plautus, but most like and neere to that in Italian called *Inganni*. A good practise in it to make the Steward beleeve his Lady widdowe was in love with him, by counterfeyting a letter as from his Lady in generall termes, telling him what shee liked best in him, and prescribing his gesture in smiling, his apparaile, &c., and then when he came to practise making him beleeve they tooke him to be mad.'

## BOOK SEVEN

CH. I. 'English Seneca' passage from Nashe's preface to *Menaphon* (see *ante*, notes, CH. III, Bk. Two). Henslowe's memorandum from *Diary*, I, 17. Lines from *Hamlet*, Act I, Sc. 2; III, 1; I, 2; from *Edward II*, 2627-2634; 753-763. Also, *Hamlet*, Act II, Sc. 1; I, 1; III, 1; V, 2.

CH. II. *Hamlet* again, Act II, Sc. 2; *ibid.*; *Dido*, Act II, Sc. 1. More *Hamlet*, Act III, Sc. 2; II, 2; III, 2; and *Ed. II*, ll. 2362-2367.

CH. III. Lines from *All's Well That Ends Well*, Act I, Sc. 1; II, 3. *Conveyance* of 107 acres from *B. P. Cat.* 31; cottage copyhold, from *Court Roll* of Rowington Manor, in *B. P. Cat.* 32.

CH. IV. King James's *Ane schort Treatise* (1584) is in Smith, I, 208-225. Sketch of James from *Relation d'Angleterre*, by Correr, Venetian ambassador 1608-11; in Rye, 228-229. Chamberlain's Men become King's, *Patent Roll*, *I Jac. I*, 2, m. 4. For account of Spanish ambassador's peace mission and reception, see Rye, 182. Cope's letter is in *H. M. C.* III, 148, from *Hatfield MSS*. Record of performance at Wilton, from *Cham. Acc.*: 'Dec. 2. John Hemyngs one of his Maiesties players . . . for the paynes and expences of himself and the rest of the company in comming from Mortelake in the countie of Surrie . . . and . . . presenting before his Maiestie one playe.' See also, *Accounts*, in *R. O. Lord Chamberlain's Books*, printed N.S.S. Trans., 1877-9. Attendance on Spanish ambassador, from Audit Office, Roll 41, Bundle 389. Phillips' will, *P. C .C.* 31 Hayes, proved May 16 1605. He also left 'To my Servaunte Christopher Beeston thirty shillings in gould'— meaning an apprentice? Beeston was the father of William Beeston to whom Aubrey went to seek biographical data about Shakespeare. For exegesis on sonnet quatrain, see note, CH. VIII, Bk. Five. Lines from *Measure for Measure* are from Act III, Sc. 1.

CH. V. Aubrey's account, from *Bodl. MS.* 6, f. 46; Wood's, from *Athenae Oxonienses*, 1692, II, 292; Hearne's, from *Remarks and Collections of Thomas Hearne* (O.H.S.), II, 228. Davenant's will proved Oct. 21, 1622, *P. C. C. Saville*, 113 (in H.-P., II, 46-48).

CH. VI. Lines from *Antony and Cleopatra*, are from Act I, Sc. 1; I, 3; I, 5; *ibid.*; II, 3; II, 5; *ibid.*; *ibid.*; V, 2; *ibid.*

## BOOK EIGHT

CH. I. Purchase of tithes in *B. P. Cat.* 33, from *Wheler MSS.* Dr. Hall's notes are now *Egerton MS.* 2065, *Curationum Historicarum et Empjrjcarum, in certis locis et notis personis expertarum et probatarum libellus*; ref. to his daughter, fol. 18$^v$. Portions of his case-books trans. by James Cooke, *Select Observations on English Bodies* (1657).

CH. II. Suit against Addenbrooke, from Court of Record, *S. A. Misc. Docts.*, V, 139, 127, 115, 116, and *Wheler MSS.*; *B. P. Cat.* 49-55. Thomas Hornby, bondsman for Addenbrooke, succeeded his father as blacksmith in Henley Street 1606. Nothing further is known of the defendant.

CH. III. Lines from *The Tempest*, Act IV, Sc. 1; *ibid.* Foot of Fine conveying 20 acres from *Finalis Concordia* in Common Pleas (*P. R. O. Pedes Finium Warwick*, Trin. 8, Jac. I, m. 15). Highway maintenance list, in *S. A. Misc. Doct.* I.4; Combe's offer to pay more, *ibid.*, X.9. *Tempest* again, Act IV, Sc. 1 and V, 1.

CH. IV. See CH. II, Bk. Six, and notes.

CH. V. Lists of plays and payments for performances from *Cham. Acc.* Lines from *Tempest*, Act IV, Sc. 1; *ibid.* Blackfriars *Conveyance* in Guildhall Library, Lon.; *Deed* in Folger Shakespeare Library. Susanna's charge in Consistory Court Register (minute of action in facsimile, H.-P., I, 242). Destruction of *Globe* in *Letters of Wotton*, II, 32. Enclosure deal in *Wheler Papers*, I, 64; *B. P. Cat.* 36; memoranda of Greene transcribed in *Shakespeare and the Enclosure of Common Fields at Welcombe* (Ingleby, 1885).

CH. VI. See CH. VII, Bk. One, and note. Ward had studied medicine before taking holy orders, but I doubt if this can bolster the credibility of a statement made so long after the event. Original of Shakespeare's will in Principal Probate Registry, Somerset House. The draft is thought to be from the pen of a scribe in the employ of Collins, also attorney for John Combe, whose will exhibits a similar disregard for punctuation, paragraphing and general neatness. I follow Chambers, *W. S.*, II, 169-174, in adding a minimum of punctuation. Holy Trinity Church from Folger Shakespeare Library print; photograph by Horydczak. Signature on third sheet is from a photograph in the possession of Dr. Tannenbaum, made directly from the will.

CH. VII. Account of Hales in *Bodl. MS. Aubrey.* 6, fol. 119$^v$. Gildon, *Some Reflections on Mr. Rymer's Short View of Tragedy*, 1694, addressed to Dryden, gives back to that poet and to the world the story he had told Gildon 'about the noble Triumph [Shakespeare] gain'd over all the Ancients by the Judgment of the ablest Critics of that time.' The Marshall engraving of Shakespeare in the 1640 edition of the *Poems* is from the first edition in the Folger Shakespeare Library; photograph by Horydczak. It appears to be a reversed copy of the First Folio engraving, stiffly drawn, but attractive.

# SELECTED BIBLIOGRAPHY

## The *Works*

*The Complete Works of William Shakespeare,* edited by W. J. Craig, London and New York, Oxford University Press, 1945.

*The Shakespeare Apocrypha,* edited by C. F. Tucker Brooke, Oxford, The Clarendon Press, 1929.

*Shakespeare's Library: A Collection of the Plays, Romances, Novels, Poems and Histories employed by Shakespeare in the composition of his works,* London, Reeves and Turner, 1875.

## The *Sources*

*The Shakespeare Documents: Facsimiles, Transliterations, Translations & Commentary,* by B. Roland Lewis, Stanford University Press, Stanford University, California: London, Humphrey Milford: Oxford University Press, 1940.

*William Shakespeare,* by Sir Edmund Chambers, Oxford University Press, 1930.

*Outlines of the Life of Shakespeare,* by J. O. Halliwell-Phillipps, London, Longmans, Green & Co., 1887.

*Shakespeare versus Shallow,* by Leslie Hotson, London, Nonesuch Press, 1931.

*Henslowe's Diary,* edited by W. W. Greg, London, A. H. Bullen, 1904-1908.

*The Elizabethan Stage,* by E. K. Chambers, Oxford, The Clarendon Press, 1923.

309

## Collateral Readers

'*Brief Lives,*' *chiefly of Contemporaries, set down by John Aubrey, between the Years 1669 & 1696*, edited by Andrew Clark, Oxford, The Clarendon Press, 1898.

*The Fugger News-Letters*, edited by Victor von Klarwill (First and Second Series), New York, G. P. Putnam's Sons, 1925-1926; London, John Lane, The Bodley Head.

*England As Seen By Foreigners in the days of Elizabeth and James the First*, by William Brenchley Rye, London, John Russell Smith, 1865.

*Elizabethan Critical Essays*, edited by G. Gregory Smith, London, Humphrey Milford: Oxford University Press, 1904.

*Willobie his Avisa*, edited by G. B. Harrison, London, John Lane: The Bodley Head, Ltd., 1926.

# Index

311

criticism of, 103-104
dedication of, 102, 185-186
publication of, 101
and *Venus and Adonis*, 103, 104
Lucy, Sir Thomas and Justice Clodpate, 40

Manningham, John, diary of, 229-230
Marlowe, Christopher, xiii, xiv, 5, 9, 14, 98, 117, 145, 148, 179, 210, 242-243
authorship of *Titus Andronicus*, 89, 96
at Cambridge, 28
career of, 51
Chapman's invocation to, 199
character of, 60
as collaborator with Shakespeare, 234
and *The Contention*, 75-77
death of, 106-110
and Edward Blount, 3
grammar school attended by, 25
and Robert Greene's *Groatsworth of wyt*, 80, 81
hatred of Catholocism, 65-66, 67-68
and *Henry VI*, Part One, 74
influence of Edward II on *Hamlet*, 235-237
London residence of, 70
and *Love's Labour's Lost*, 113
Ovid's *Amores* translated by, 37-38
patron of, 59-60
and Pembroke's Men, 159
as possible collaborator of Shakespeare, 61-64
possible meeting with Shakespeare, 59
as Shakespeare's master, 51-53
Shakespeare's tribute to in *Hamlet*, 240
and *Tamburlaine*, 63-64
and *The Troublesome Raigne of John King of England*, 65-69
and Watson-Bradley duel, 70-71
Marlowe, John, 14
Mary, Queen of Scots, 17, 18
*Massacre at Paris, The*, 108
*Measure for Measure*, preoccupation with death in, 252-253
*Merchant of Venice, The*, 3, 194
Meres, Francis, 175, 176
*Merry Wives of Windsor, The*, xiv, 4, 161
biographical material in, 152-154
first performance of, 150-152
and Queen Elizabeth, 150-152
reference to deer-stealing in, 40
*Midsummer Night's Dream, A*, publication of, 4
Montaigne, 3, 98
Montgomery, Philip, Earl of, 3, 5
Mountjoy, Christopher, Shakespeare as witness in case of, 214-215, 273-275
Mountjoy, Mary, Shakespeare as witness in case of, 214-215, 273-275
*Much Ado About Nothing*, 4, 194, 277
*Muses' Darling, The*, xiv

Nashe, Thomas, 52, 61, 72, 75, 234
and Pembroke's Men, 159

on Robert Greene's *Groatsworth of wyt*, 80, 81-82, 83
*New Letter of Notable Contents, A*, 109
New Place, bought by Shakespeare, 41, 162-164
Newington Butts, Theater at, 58
*Night of Errors, The*, 125

*Odyssey*, Chapman's translation of, 197
Oldcastle, Sir John, and Falstaff, 142, 143-144
*Othello*, 253
Ovid, 98, 145, 183
effect on Shakespeare, 37-38
and *Fasti*, 101
*Metamorphoses*, 62, 96, 99
Oxford's Men, 39

Palace of Pleasure, 244
Palmer, John, 12
*Pandosta, History of*, 243
*Passionate Pilgrim, The*, 4
*Passionate Shepherd to his love, The*, 107
Paynter, William, 244
Peele, George, 52, 60
on Marlowe's death, 109
Pembroke, Countess of, 5-6
Pembroke, William, Earl of, 5-6, 10, 186, 188, 195, 197, 250
and dedication of the *Sonnets*, 6, 180-188
and First Folio, 3, 5-6
Pembroke's Men, 75, 117
end of, 159-160
Pericles, 3
*Perimedes the Blackesmith*, 63
"Petty France," 214
Philip III, 251
Phillips, Augustine, 208
bequeaths money to Shakespeare, 252
*Pierce Penilesse*, 72, 82
Plague, 93-94, 130, 131, 185, 250
Platter, Thomas, 221-222
Plautus, 116, 125
*Pleasant Conceited Historie, A*, 117
Plutarch's *Lives*, xiv, 221, 233
Pope, Thomas, 208
Portrait, of Shakespeare, 47, 48-49
Prince Hal, characterization of, 212-214
"Prince of Purpoole," enthronement of, 123-125
Prothalamion, 200

Queen's Men, 21, 56, 65, 68, 78, 201
Quiney, Adrian, 18, 170, 283
Quiney, Judith, 41, 87, 170, 171, 278, 282-283, 289
Quiney, Richard, 169, 283
letter to Shakespeare, 170-171
Quiney, Thomas, 170, 289
weds Judith Shakespeare, 282-283

Raleigh, Sir Walter, 107, 119, 141, 227
*Remarks on the Plays of Shakespeare*, 150-152
Renaissance, 130-134